"Finally a book expla[...] [...]ematic way that Leadership is not about [...] you are and how you act. I truly recomm[...] [...]nuinely strives to unleash the power of a[...] [...]us enough to start this exciting journey by looking at thems[...] [...] the book, everything seems so obvious, but then again, this always tends to be the case with masterpieces."

– **Sandro Giuliani**, Managing Director of the Jacobs Foundation, Switzerland

"This book is packed with new thinking and yet resonates easily as if I had always known it! Since the values and ethics spotlight on the City of London after 2008, we have been looking to identify behaviours, which when championed by motivated and engaged leaders, could change culture and make capitalism more inclusive. My focus has been on capturing the benefits of diversity where leaders have expressed frustration at the slow progress. The essences and steps to Transpersonal Leadership in this book link leadership for the 'greater good' to enabling others to do the right thing, increasing performance, productivity and profitability. It is key to unleashing the power of diversity and rising to many of the challenges that society faces."

– **Dame Fiona Woolf DBE**, **DL**, Lord Mayor of London 2013–14; Partner at CMS Cameron McKenna, UK

"It's not hard to see, in business and society, how the old model of an ego driven, charismatic leader has failed. I recommend this book as required reading for anyone who wants to develop as a leader – and who wants to make a positive difference to the world."

– **Natalie Ceeney CBE,** former CEO of the Financial Ombudsman Service, National Archives and HM Courts & Tribunals Service, UK

"People who talk and write about leadership fall into two groups. Firstly, there are people who are good at doing it and often they are inarticulate, shrugging their shoulders and just saying 'well we just did it this way' and usually, they are impatient to analyse why they did it in a particular way because they are keen to get on to the next leadership challenge. At the other end of the spectrum, there are people who write, at length. The LeaderShape team has an enviable reputation at both ends of this spectrum, with deep understanding of the theory, their own particular variant of the theory of leadership, but also very many examples where they have helped individuals and organisations put the theory into practice. This book is an excellent introduction to the highly complex and often confusing field of leadership."

– **Professor Sir Muir Gray**, Director of Better Value Healthcare; Chief Knowledge Officer of the NHS; Professor of Knowledge Management, Oxford University, UK

"Leadership in the modern age is more challenging than ever before, with more uncertainty, change and disruption across many dimensions. The idea of transpersonal leadership with its heart in the notions of humility, learning, and caring is ultimately a very human centred model of leadership and has never had more relevance in helping leaders get the best out of themselves, their people and their organisations. John Knights and his team at LeaderShape have been a positive force for change, and this book provides a fantastic guide for leaders at all levels to improve themselves and their leadership focus."

– **Peter Cheese**, CEO at Chartered Institute of Personnel & Development (CIPD), UK

"This book articulates leadership in all its fascinating and rich dimensions in the most relevant, holistic, integrated and practical way that I have come across. John Knights and the LeaderShape team must be congratulated and thanked for an excellent and very valuable piece of work. Leading beyond the ego as presented and explained in the book, brings with it the fundamental focus on relationships as the field of leadership. The book presents a timely emphasis on the 'how' of becoming a more values-based leader. Lastly, science, philosophy and practical 21st Century experience is very well balanced in the argument for transpersonal leadership."

– **Dr Gerhard van Rensburg**, Chairman of Future Leaders Development; Director of Future Leaders Africa, South Africa

"Scholars, students, or practitioners of leadership will benefit from this impressive book that traverses multiple disciplines and challenges us to design values-driven pathways for leading ourselves, before leading others. An important contribution to the HOW of leadership, this book 'connects the dots' from multiple perspectives including neuroscience, servant leadership, experiential learning, and action learning. As a leadership educator for over 35 years I was challenged to reflect deeper and analyze more about my own leadership journey and effective ways to contribute to the greater whole. Through new and existing concepts and case studies, this is a fine blueprint for sustainable leadership practices."

– **Dr Ronald J. Kovach**, Vice President of Academic Affairs, Virginia International University and Past President of the National Society for Experiential Education, USA

"A great read. *Leading Beyond the Ego* is an excellent book about transpersonal leadership – a much needed concept in this day and age. The way transpersonal leadership has been defined in the book, as the overlap between Rational Intelligence (RI), Emotional Intelligence (EI), and Spiritual Intelligence (SI), is particularly valuable. The authors not only explain what it means to be a transpersonal leader, but also describe how to become one. A must read for every aspiring leader, who is looking to create an emotionally-bonded, ethical, high-performing and sustainable organization."

– **Warren Harris**, CEO at Tata Technologies, USA and India

"While the entire journey covered in the book is impressive, I found the use of a combination of intuition, instinct, insight and ethical philosophy to support rational logic particularly interesting and immensely powerful for improving judgment and decision making. The case studies are very insightful and support the concepts effectively. The concepts are straightforward to learn and can be easily put into practice. Constant practice will undoubtedly yield the desired results. *Leading Beyond the Ego* is a manual for creating sustained leadership in the challenging environment of rapid change."
– **Vishnu R. Dusad, MD**, CEO at Nucleus Software, India

"Although you may or may not agree with all of the many conceptual models and conclusions in this densely packed short volume that links emotional intelligence and neuroscience with practical approaches to leadership from a transpersonal vantage, it is sure to be thought provoking."
– **Professor Harris Friedman, PhD**, Research Professor of Psychology, University of Florida; Editor of the *International Journal of Transpersonal Leadership*

Leading Beyond the Ego: How to Become a Transpersonal Leader

Building on the concept of Transpersonal Leadership, as defined by LeaderShape Global, *Leading Beyond the Ego* offers a practical approach to becoming an authentic, ethical, caring and more effective leader.

Rooted in the experience of senior organisational leaders and mentors, readers will embark on a personal journey to innovate and enhance their leadership skills. Reflections are rooted in recent advances in neuroscience, and acknowledge the challenges faced by leaders in light of new organisational and commercial structures, technological developments, increased diversity and rapid globalisation. The reader is encouraged and supported in the process of transcending the individual ego to develop beyond emotional intelligence to a higher level of consciousness and ethical behaviour; able to build strong, collaborative relationships, and to create a caring, sustainable and performance-enhancing culture.

Learn how to lead beyond your ego!

An essential read for current and aspiring organisational leaders, HR professionals, executive coaches and mentors, *Leading Beyond the Ego* is a vital point of reference for anyone in a position of leadership.

John Knights is a Co-founder and Chairman of LeaderShape Global. He is an author, lecturer and thought leader in leadership development.

Danielle Grant is a Director of LeaderShape Global with many years' experience coaching and facilitating programmes at CEO and Director level. She is a thought leader in blended learning methodologies.

Greg Young is a Co-founder and Chief Executive of LeaderShape Global. He is inspirational in the field of leadership development and a thought leader in women in leadership.

Leading Beyond the Ego

How to Become a Transpersonal Leader

Edited by John Knights,
Danielle Grant and Greg Young

Routledge
Taylor & Francis Group
LONDON AND NEW YORK

LeaderShape
Shaping Transpersonal Leaders

First published 2018
by Routledge
2 Park Square, Milton Park, Abingdon, Oxon OX14 4RN

and by Routledge
711 Third Avenue, New York, NY 10017

Routledge is an imprint of the Taylor & Francis Group, an informa business

© 2018 selection and editorial matter, LeaderShape Global Ltd.; individual chapters, the contributors

The right of LeaderShape Global Ltd. to be identified as the author of the editorial material, and of the authors for their individual chapters, has been asserted in accordance with sections 77 and 78 of the Copyright, Designs and Patents Act 1988.

All rights reserved. No part of this book may be reprinted or reproduced or utilised in any form or by any electronic, mechanical, or other means, now known or hereafter invented, including photocopying and recording, or in any information storage or retrieval system, without permission in writing from the publishers.

Trademark notice: Product or corporate names may be trademarks or registered trademarks, and are used only for identification and explanation without intent to infringe.

British Library Cataloguing in Publication Data
A catalogue record for this book is available from the British Library

Library of Congress Cataloging in Publication Data
Names: Knights, John, 1946- editor. | Grant, Danielle, editor. | Young, Greg, 1961- editor.
Title: Leading beyond the ego : how to become a transpersonal leader / edited by John Knights, Danielle Grant & Greg Young.
Description: Abingdon, Oxon ; New York, NY : Routledge, 2018. | Includes bibliographical references and index.
Identifiers: LCCN 2017035533 (print) | LCCN 2017056812 (ebook) | ISBN 9781315178806 (ebook) | ISBN 9781138897670 (hbk) | ISBN 9781138897694 (pbk) | ISBN 9781315178806 (ebk)
Subjects: LCSH: Leadership—Psychological aspects. | Management—Psychological aspects. | Executive coaching.
Classification: LCC HD57.7 (ebook) | LCC HD57.7. L437436 2018 (print) | DDC 658.4/092—dc23
LC record available at https://lccn.loc.gov/2017035533

ISBN: 978-1-138-89767-0 (hbk)
ISBN: 978-1-138-89769-4 (pbk)
ISBN: 978-1-315-17880-6 (ebk)

Typeset in Bembo
by Keystroke, Neville Lodge, Tettenhall, Wolverhampton

Printed and bound by CPI Group (UK) Ltd, Croydon, CR0 4YY

To all the leaders we have learned from who have made this project possible.

Contents

List of figures — xv
List of tables — xvii
List of contributors — xix
Acknowledgements — xxiii

1 **The background to this book** — 1
  JOHN KNIGHTS

PART 1
The intermediate journey of the Transpersonal Leader — 13

2 **Introduction of Part 1, "The intermediate journey"** — 15
  JOHN KNIGHTS

3 **Understanding leadership** — 22
  JOHN KNIGHTS

4 **The neuroscience of leadership: default and emotions** — 36
  JOHN KNIGHTS

5 **Increasing self-awareness** — 47
  JOHN KNIGHTS

6 **Understanding emotions and how to deal with them** — 58
  JOHN KNIGHTS

7 **The power of emotional intelligence (managing emotions)** — 66
  JOHN KNIGHTS

xii Contents

8 Using different leadership styles   80
   JOHN KNIGHTS

9 Coaching style of leadership   94
   JOHN KNIGHTS

10 Creating a performance-enhancing culture   106
   JOHN KNIGHTS

11 Identifying strengths and improving development areas   125
   JOHN KNIGHTS

PART 2
The advanced journey of the Transpersonal Leader   133

12 Introduction of Part 2, "The advanced journey"   135
   JOHN KNIGHTS

13 The Eight Integrated Competencies of Leadership (8ICOL®)   143
   JOHN KNIGHTS

14 The neuroscience of consciousness and how it applies
   to leadership   152
   JOHN KNIGHTS

15 Beyond the ego: working for all stakeholders   163
   JOHN KNIGHTS

16 Improving judgement and decision-making   174
   JOHN KNIGHTS

17 The values of leadership: personal conscience and
   self-determination   186
   JOHN KNIGHTS

18 Managing diversity   200
   JENNIFER PLAISTER-TEN

19 The inner development of a Transpersonal Leader   211
   SUE COYNE

20	**Choice and for the greater good** JOHN KNIGHTS	223
21	**Continuous personal development** JOHN KNIGHTS	231

PART 3
Implementation of Transpersonal Leadership development 241

22	**Modern learning principles and methodologies** DANIELLE GRANT	243
23	**Infusing ethics in leadership learning and development** TONY WALL	260

Index 270

Figures

1.1	Transpersonal Leadership	2
1.2	REAL Transpersonal Leadership development journey to excellence	9
2.1	REAL Transpersonal Leadership development journey to excellence	16
2.2	Impact of emotional intelligence on rational intelligence	18
3.1	Levels of leadership	28
3.2	Vision to performance	31
4.1	Different kinds of neurons	39
4.2	The brain's emotional highway	41
4.3	The emotional highway: interactions of the amygdala	42
5.1	The learning cycle	53
5.2	Learning styles	53
6.1	The six basic facial expressions	59
6.2	Non-verbal communication: words are a low impact factor	62
7.1	Four EI Competencies	69
7.2	Emotional intelligence: the four competencies and nineteen capabilities	69
7.3	Development priority analysis	72
7.4	Emotional intelligence Capabilities	75
9.1	The continuum	95
9.2	Spectrum of 1:1 styles	102
9.3	Spectrum of 1:1 styles	104
10.1	Transformational and transactional culture	110
10.2	Impacts on performance	111
10.3	The four culture parameters	112
10.4	Ideal culture in the twenty-first century?	114
10.5	Relationship: culture parameters vs. leadership styles	115
10.6	Relationship between leadership and performance	118
10.7	Improved performance by behavioural change	119
10.8	Making change happen	121
11.1	REAL Transpersonal Leadership development journey to excellence	126

11.2	List of SMART actions	131
12.1	REAL Transpersonal Leadership development journey to excellence	136
12.2	Transpersonal Leadership	138
13.1	Eight Integral Competencies of Leadership (8ICOL®)	144
13.2	Hierarchy of intelligences	145
13.3	8ICOL®	148
14.1	The brain's left hemisphere	157
15.1	Ego self image	165
16.1	Five decision-making processes	175
16.2	Decision-making routes	176
17.1	Transpersonal resilience	194
18.1	The Cross-Cultural Kaleidoscope™: a systems approach	207
19.1	Inner development for Transpersonal Leaders	211
19.2	Nine motivators	215
19.3	Reflection in action	217
20.1	Example touchstone	225
20.2	Transpersonal touchstone	229
21.1	The transpersonal cycle	232
21.2	Hierarchy of intelligences	238
22.1	Blended learning processes	245
22.2	Ripples on a pond: factors that underpin successful learning	246
22.3	Stone Age man in mirror	249
22.4	An engaging exercise using real workplace content	250
22.5	A social and creative exercise	251
22.6	Benefits of ALIVE© learning	255
22.7	Levels of leadership	256

Tables

3.1	Leadership vs. Management	24
3.2	Explanation of questionnaire answers	25
3.3	Characteristics of good and bad leaders	32
5.1	Learning style preferences	54
7.1	Emotional intelligence Capability definitions	70
7.2	Emotional intelligence self-assessment	78
8.1	The six leadership styles	81
10.1	Culture parameters: positive and negative traits	113
14.1	Connecting the philosophy and neuroscience of consciousness	156
17.1	Personal conscience	188
17.2	Self-determination	191
17.3	Criteria for ethical behaviour	195
17.4	Values self-assessment	197
21.1	The six levels of awareness and full consciousness	234
21.2	Eleven transpersonal practices of a CAS	235
23.1	The United Nations' sustainable development goals	262
23.2	Possible principles towards shorter-term individual gain	263
23.3	Possible principles towards connectedness, collectiveness and beyond 'the now'	265

Contributors

John Knights – lead author and editor of contributing author chapters

John's business life changed when in 1998 he had the serendipitous opportunity to learn to coach other chief executives and started to understand the real issues around leadership. His passion and purpose is to support leaders on their journey to become excellent Transpersonal Leaders. John, chairman of LeaderShape Global, is an experienced senior executive coach and facilitator, and an expert in emotional intelligence, Transpersonal Leadership and neuro-leadership. He has been a senior executive in major international corporations, a serial entrepreneur and lecturer at Oxford University. He is the author of *The Invisible Elephant and the Pyramid Treasure: Tomorrow's Leadership – the Transpersonal Journey*, co-editor/author of *Leadership Assessment for Talent Development* and author of a white paper on *Ethical Leadership* published by Routledge. John now focuses on growing LeaderShape globally. More details at: www.leadershapeglobal.com/john-knights-1.

Danielle Grant – editor, general contributor and author of Chapter 22

Danielle's career epitomises embracing change. She held director level positions in UK, US and European blue chip and executive search businesses, including Disney. In 2004 she gained her Advanced Diploma in Executive Coaching and embarked on a journey that fulfils her passion for growing Transpersonal Leaders. Danielle, a director of LeaderShape Global, is an accomplished coach and facilitator, and an expert in the development of neuroscientifically-based leadership programmes, using leading-edge blended methodologies for which she achieved an MA with Distinction;

she focuses on developing LeaderShape's team capability and leading edge programmes globally. She is an accredited university lecturer and has led Masters' programmes in leadership and coaching. Danielle is a contributing author of *Leadership Assessment for Talent Development*. More details at http://leadershapeglobal.com/danielle-grant.

Greg Young – editor and general contributor

In a Damascene moment in Greg's first role as MD he realised that instead of measuring his day by what he did, a more effective assessment was what he caused to happen. Embracing non-directive leadership styles, building a sense of vision, values, and coaching those around him to achieve more than they felt they were capable of achieved greater results. He is a founding director and CEO of LeaderShape Global and has been a thought leader in the field of leadership development for over ten years following careers in the lifesciences and telecommunications. He is a contributor to *The Invisible Elephant and the Pyramid Treasure: Tomorrow's Leadership – the Transpersonal Journey* (2011) and *Leadership Assessment for Talent Development* (2013). Greg has authored a white paper published by Routledge on *Women in Leadership*, a theme to which he is committed. See http://leadershapeglobal.com/greg-young.

Sue Coyne – contributing author – Chapter 19

Sue is a member of the LeaderShape Global faculty. She spent 20 years as a business leader, and has been a sought-after leadership and team coach since 2003. She is a thought leader and speaker on leadership issues and complements her work with expertise in neuroscience. Sue is the author of *Stop Doing Start Leading: How to Shift from Doing the Work Yourself to Becoming a Great Leader* (2016). She is a contributor to *Leadership Team Coaching in Practice: Developing High-performing Teams* by Peter Hawkins (2014) and *Enabling Genius* (2016) by Myles Downey. See her full bio here: www.leadershapeglobal.com/sue-coyne.

Jennifer Plaister-Ten – contributing author – Chapter 18

Jenny is a member of the LeaderShape Global faculty and is dedicated to the development of global leaders and their teams. Following a stellar international career in the IT industry during which she lived and worked in the US, Asia/Pacific and Europe, she ran her own consulting practice working in over 30 countries. Jenny is now a thought leader on the impact of culture in the coaching relationship and upon global leaders. Her book, *The Cross-Cultural Kaleidoscope*, a systems approach to working among different cultural influences, was published in 2016. She is also a contributing author to *Intercultural Management* (Barmeyer and Franklin, 2016). See her full bio here: www.leadershapeglobal.com/jenny-plaister.

Tony Wall – contributing author – Chapter 23

Professor Tony Wall is an international leadership development innovator working across the UK, US and Australia, work for which he was awarded a prestigious National Teaching Fellowship Award. As Director of International Thriving at Work Research Group, University of Chester UK, he leads three Santander International Research Excellence grants, and numerous practice impact projects, each focusing on "human thriving" in multiple cultural and ecological contexts. His consultancy and advisory work extends across multiple professional bodies to facilitate international impact (e.g. the European Mentoring and Coaching Council in Brussels; the Chartered Institute of Personnel and Development and Lapidus International – the words for wellbeing association).

Acknowledgements

Thanks to the contributing authors, Sue Coyne, Jenny Plaister-Ten and Tony Wall, and all the other faculty and staff at LeaderShape Global who have participated in developing the Transpersonal Leadership journey; and most of all to our respective spouses (Bella, John and Grainne) who have stood with us on what has sometimes been a difficult journey.

1   The background to this book

John Knights

> *Everyone thinks of changing the world, but no one thinks of changing himself.*
> —Tolstoy, 1869

In this "early morning" of the information and communication age with its attendant dramatic changes, not only in technology but even more so socially, traditional leadership is just not working. The authoritarian, or at best paternal, leadership styles of the past, along with hierarchical and non-diverse organisations, are struggling to cope in this new world. Today's organisational environment is one that requires more attention to sustainability, ethical cultures and caring behaviours, while still being geared to enhancing performance.

A new, more relevant way of leading will probably take a few decades to work its way through the global system but we must start *now*, by identifying, preparing and developing leaders who can run organisations successfully in this new reality. We call them Transpersonal Leaders.

First of all, what is Transpersonal Leadership? A description of the concept of **Transpersonal Leadership** was first published in a report on tomorrow's leadership based on a leadership development journey developed by LeaderShape (Knights, 2011). The word "transpersonal" was inspired by the use of the word in "transpersonal psychology", of which one of the founders of that movement was Stanislov Grof (Bynum, 1992). An overview of the history of transpersonal psychology can be found in Grof's *Brief History of Transpersonal Psychology* (Grof, 2008). "Transpersonal" is defined as "Extending or going beyond the personal or individual, beyond the usual limits of ego and personality". We define Transpersonal Leadership in full as follows:

> **Transpersonal Leadership**
>
> **Transpersonal [definition – *Webster's Dictionary*]:** Extending or going beyond the personal or individual, beyond the usual limits of ego and personality.
>
> **Transpersonal Leaders [definition – *LeaderShape Global*]:** Operate beyond their ego, continuing personal development and learning. They are radical, ethical and authentic while emotionally intelligent and caring.
>
> They are able to:
>
> - embed authentic, ethical and emotionally intelligent behaviours into the DNA of the organisation
> - build strong, empathetic and collaborative relationships within the organisation and with all stakeholders
> - create a performance enhancing culture that is ethical, caring and sustainable.
>
> Acronym: **BE REAL**
> Beyond Ego – Radical, Ethical, Authentic Leadership

Transpersonal Leadership is built on the foundation of the three levels of intelligence shown in Figure 1.1. The combination of any two is required to provide the different aspects of performance-enhancing, ethical, caring and sustainable leadership. It is only when we combine all three intelligences – the sweet spot in the middle – that we have Transpersonal Leadership.

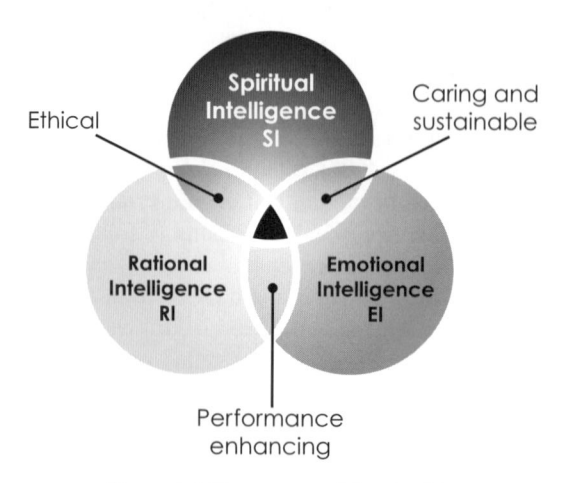

Figure 1.1 Transpersonal Leadership

This book has its roots in the experience and reflections of a number of senior organisational leaders who had successful careers but became disaffected with the corporate world or public sector or their entrepreneurial business context and decided to take a new personal course that would make a difference! This change of direction manifested itself as working with leaders across a broad spectrum of industries and sectors, supporting them in overcoming their issues and challenges and, through that, helping them to become better leaders and run more successful organisations.

What is the purpose of this book?

This book describes the journey a person needs to take if they wish to commit to becoming a Transpersonal Leader. It is very much a book about HOW "you" can become a Transpersonal Leader rather than WHAT an individual needs to do to become an excellent leader. A number of great American leadership experts such as Peter Drucker, Stephen Covey, Warren Bennis, Bill George, Jim Collins, Peter Senge, Robert Greenleaf and Daniel Goleman as well as others have established much of WHAT good leadership is, but in fact there has been surprisingly little written about precisely HOW an individual goes about becoming a better leader. This book not only addresses that factor but also several other aspects that are relatively new to leadership, including:

1. The recognition of the implications for leadership of the increasingly rapid pace of change. It is only over the past 20 years that the impact of the internet really started to influence our lives in terms of availability of information, communication and the accelerating changes in technology that is now at all of our fingertips, all the time.
2. The Millennials (defined as born between 1980 and 1993), who will be our next generation of leaders, to be followed by the Z Generation (born after 1993), have different expectations, needs and ambitions than previous generations (IBM, 2015).
3. The increasing level of globalisation and rapid changes in society, including popularism, extremism, secularism and the full range of diversity parameters are all making new demands on leadership that our traditional hierarchical world cannot respond to with any success.
4. Neuroscience: a young science that is increasingly enabling us to understand how the brain works and how we can change our natural default instincts into consciously developed behaviour.
5. The role of women and attitudes toward all forms of diversity and inclusion will impact leadership at least for the rest of this century.
6. There has been a whole movement over the last 30 years that provides a different way of learning that is much more effective than traditional "teaching", particularly for adults. It generally goes under the term of Work-Based Learning. It is also referred to as andragogy (as opposed to pedagogy), and it is today synonymous with adult learning but, in essence, means self-directed

learning. It is the opposite of teaching; it is about providing the environment, techniques and tools so that people can learn – rather than be told. We refer to this as "pull" rather than "push" and it is much more effective in developing an individual's potential. The best-known "technique" within this realm is coaching, although even that has many different approaches, and there are many other techniques that will be discussed in this book.

There are many leadership experts from around the globe who are making important contributions to leadership development. However, most of the globally known ones are American and tend to be consultants or academics. This is probably because the US spends a lot of money on research and has a huge homogenous domestic market to build brand and volume as a foundation for these experts to take themselves global. We should also not take for granted that the most famous have the most to offer. Some of these experts tend to quote "what top leaders do" as an implied suggestion that is what all developing leaders *should* do. The reality is that most "top leaders" have been better at getting to the top than actually leading successfully when they get there. We need to move beyond the hero and celebrity leader phenomenon and for organisations to identify and develop leaders that are going to be excellent when they get to the top. Finally on this point, I don't believe anyone should try to copy successful leaders but rather focus on being the best leader they can be in their context. By all means learn good habits and attributes from great leaders but to copy them might mean adopting their bad behaviours and persona too and is unlikely to be authentic and sustainable.

We believe that everyone is a leader! We all make decisions or take initiatives that have an impact or influence on others.

Example

I particularly remember the receptionist at the headquarters of a large European energy company who, while we were waiting for our appointment, enquired how much we knew about the organisation and then proceeded at our agreement to give us an objective briefing of the highlights of the company's history and current operations. The senior leader we were due to meet had no idea the receptionist was doing this but that company will remain in my sub-conscious as a very positive experience.

The journey this book takes you on can enable you to become the best leader you can be. It does not promise you will become a great leader because leadership is a blend of innate capability and learned habits, but with the right amount of practice, focus and time you will become a better leader. In all our experience, most people who have no material personality disorder issues can become a competent leader if they have the will to put in the time and effort. Unfortunately, as we shall see, personality disorders are not that uncommon among top leaders.

Who is this book for?

It is primarily written for senior leaders – not only for those currently in senior leadership positions but especially those who aspire to senior leadership and want to make a positive difference to the world.

It is also for HR professionals, including learning and development and talent specialists to enable them to develop leadership development programmes for their organisations, and for use by executive coaches and mentors in supporting those people they are working with. Finally but not least, it is for all those participants in LeaderShape Global programmes around the world as a reference manual.

How to use this book

The book is designed so you can either read it from front to back cover as a programme each person can follow and make relevant in their own context or alternatively dip into any single chapter that speaks to your own needs. More experienced and senior leaders may find it interesting to just glance through the early chapters but focus more on those later in the book (Part 2), which are more likely to include new concepts and learning.

For those who have just started on the path of leadership development and want to become the best leader they can be, we suggest you read the book from cover to cover. It takes you from the first stages of leadership development through to the most advanced aspects.

This book is not about "management" although any leader needs to do some management. If you would like some clarity on the difference between management and leadership see Chapter 3. This book assumes you will get the necessary business skills from other reputable sources such as a business degree, an MBA and/or training and work experience with your organisation. In fact this book is very much about what they don't usually teach you at business school.

Developing the transpersonal journey

The group of us who have put together this composite programme over the last 20 years come from a variety of backgrounds from engineering, science, marketing, finance, the military, etc. and from a range of private, public and not-for-profit sectors. We have all been organisational leaders in one form or another, most of us in business. We have each been on our own journey but we came together within a common desire to understand the needs of leadership in the twenty-first century and then develop a programme that can produce the complete leader for these times, and also be fit for the future.

Our approach in constructing the elements has been to use best practice developed by others where it is of a high standard and in the public domain. We have brought together work from different sources and integrated them. Where there have been gaps, we have developed our own solutions. Finally, we have wrapped around the programme many techniques from coaching to facilitation and from Action Learning to 360° assessments while blending online, remote and face-to-face learning to meet the logistical and budgetary requirements of demanding organisational clients.

Concerning my own journey, my tipping-point moment was in 1998 after having a successful international corporate career for 18 years followed by 12 years as an entrepreneur. At that time I was the CEO and largest shareholder of a small but global IT distribution company specialising in Auto-ID equipment and systems. I was also a shareholder and non-executive director of a strategy consultancy that had recently used my services to create a successful solution to help a Dutch-based client (I had lived and worked in Holland). As a result the MD of the strategy firm and I were both approached by the auditing firm BDO, who explained they were setting up a new business to provide professional development for the CEOs of their clients and asked whether we would each be interested in moderating one of these peer groups of CEOs. At the time I thought it a no-brainer as they were offering a very professional programme to learn to coach and facilitate as well as on-going learning support for the peer group moderators. I was sure I would learn from the experiences of the other CEOs, and I would get paid for doing it! I couldn't think of a better personal development programme so rearranged the management responsibilities within my company to allow me the four days a month it would require.

I initially worked with BDO until they sold the business but continued my involvement in the peer groups. By 2003 a few of us decided to give up our day jobs to establish LeaderShape (www.leadershapeglobal.com), and formed a relationship with the UK's Institute of Directors who marketed the peer group concept as the pinnacle of their director development programme. The CEOs ranged from a French woman who ran a small specialist marketing company to a Brit who ran the European operations of a giant Japanese enterprise. The peer groups met every 4–6 weeks and always included an Action Learning[1] session where one or more of the cohort members would bring an issue for the group to solve. This part of the programme was invariably the most popular and saw many real successes. My fellow moderators and I soon realised that the vast majority of issues were about people and relationships (about 70 per cent compared to 20 per cent being strategic and 10 per cent being about their own careers) especially including issues with fellow directors. Although the specific problems were being solved, the CEOs continued to bring similar types of problems to the table. It was obvious we were solving the symptoms rather than dealing with the cause.

A reflection on my own career

This resonated strongly with my own career, where I had come up against numerous issues and challenges of how to deal with people to achieve goals and objectives with each one being met and solved, or not, on a case-by-case basis. I had a successful fast-track international corporate career and received considerable traditional training in management and leadership including a customised advanced leadership programme designed by the

University of Columbia for my then Fortune 100 US employer, Combustion Engineering (since acquired by ABB). But nothing prepared me for how to behave in complicated human circumstances such as how to manage people who were much older or how to recognise and handle people who were jealous before they tried to stab me in the back. I also had to learn to deal with usually older clients from a variety of countries and how to put together a multi-national management team. I know now that if I had a higher competence in just some of the aspects of Transpersonal Leadership in my earlier career I would have been much more successful in creating win-win solutions.

We first involved behavioural psychologists to help us solve this conundrum but the response from the CEOs was not positive. To these hardnosed business people the concepts were too ephemeral and nebulous. They said they wanted practical help, not vague theories. We had to find a different solution; and then serendipity came along. I was on one of my frequent business trips to the US (from the UK) to review our US operation when I saw a book on the newsstand at New York's JFK Airport: *Primal Leadership* (Goleman et al., 2002). I was attracted by the title but excited by the sub-title, *Realizing the Power of Emotional Intelligence*. I had read about emotional intelligence and was interested in the concept but had not thought of a practical way to use it.

I started to read the book on the plane back to the UK and had finished it by the time we landed, realising that this single book had connected emotional intelligence with leadership and provided a model we could use to help our CEO clients to build their self-awareness, emotional self-management, awareness of others, and finally how to build relationships. We searched for experts in emotional intelligence, tried a few but at the time could not find anyone suitable who would be effective working in the context of leadership. Suffice to say, we decided we had to become the experts if we were going to make this happen and, with the knowledge and support of our group member CEOs, this became our informal "laboratory" for the next few years where we tested out various workshop modules and tools. In parallel to emotional intelligence was the emerging field of neuroscience, which could explain how the brain works and why, in terms of physics and chemistry, the brain reacts and performs in certain ways. At the time this approach rapidly replaced psychology as an explanation for and prediction of behaviours, although in most cases neuroscience is actually pretty consistent with psychology theory such that today they work hand in hand. The difference was these hard-nosed business people could more rapidly and easily be convinced by scientific proof than by psychological theories.

Through this process our CEOs became aware of the causes of these people issues, could work on managing their behaviours and so the issues brought to the Action Learning sets developed into a much richer conversation and solutions that were to the benefit of all. The greatest learning was in the area of empathy, where our CEOs could more clearly see and understand the perspective of others, which in turn led to much more acceptable and sustainable solutions. We focus on building empathy in Chapter 7.

The next challenge was how to take this concept beyond the individual leader into the culture and performance of the organisation. Here, emotional intelligence alone was not sufficient. We found, adapted and integrated various other published research that enabled us to connect different leadership styles with specific culture parameters and to identify the ideal organisational culture profile for the twenty-first century. The outcome was that we could identify specific granular behaviours that, when championed by leaders and adopted would change the culture of an organisation in the way desired. We also developed explicitly the contract between leader and follower where both have responsibility and accountability, thus providing everyone in an organisation with a clear understanding of mutual expectations.

We searched through the 360° assessment tools and culture surveys that were on the market in order to evaluate and monitor the leaders and the organisation cultures. We were unable to find what we needed so we developed our own unique approaches to measuring personal and cultural development and change.

We delivered our first full programme in 2005–6 to a Swedish recruitment company who had recently acquired a UK firm. More than 10 years later a number of those participants remember the programme as the best training they ever had, and one of them is now a faculty member of LeaderShape. Shortly after, we delivered a programme to the MDs of an international division of Disney. It was seen by the participants as the most valuable intervention ever provided to them in developing their awareness of leadership strengths and needs and thus created a practical actionable outcome.

As can be seen in Figure 1.2, and using the REAL acronym, the programme so far developed enabled us to take leaders from the beginning of their journey as Rational Ego-based, As-usual Leaders to the intermediate stage where leaders are Robust, Emotionally Aware Leaders. This is all explained in more detail throughout Part 1 of the book.

But we had still not yet built a programme that could develop the complete leader and we were now driven to do so as we felt what we had done so far was not enough. Any leader can use emotional intelligence in a malevolent way by using their behavioural skills to influence, persuade and hoodwink their followers. We had read a lot about values-based leadership describing "what" it is but there was very little about "how I become" more values-based as a leader and what that will achieve. As we explain later, values can only be turned into positive actions through learning and using the right behaviours.

The detail of how we developed the advanced part of the journey to develop leaders into Radical Ethically Authentic Leaders is provided in Chapter 12. However, the essence was that whereas reaching the intermediate level of the journey was about emotional intelligence, the advanced part of the journey was clearly about spiritual intelligence. Unfortunately, the word "spiritual" in the Western world has negative connotations associated with the mystical and religious, which sets up barriers. I like Cindy Wigglesworth's definition, "the ability to behave with wisdom and compassion, while maintaining inner and outer peace, regardless of the situation" (Wigglesworth, 2012). As you might

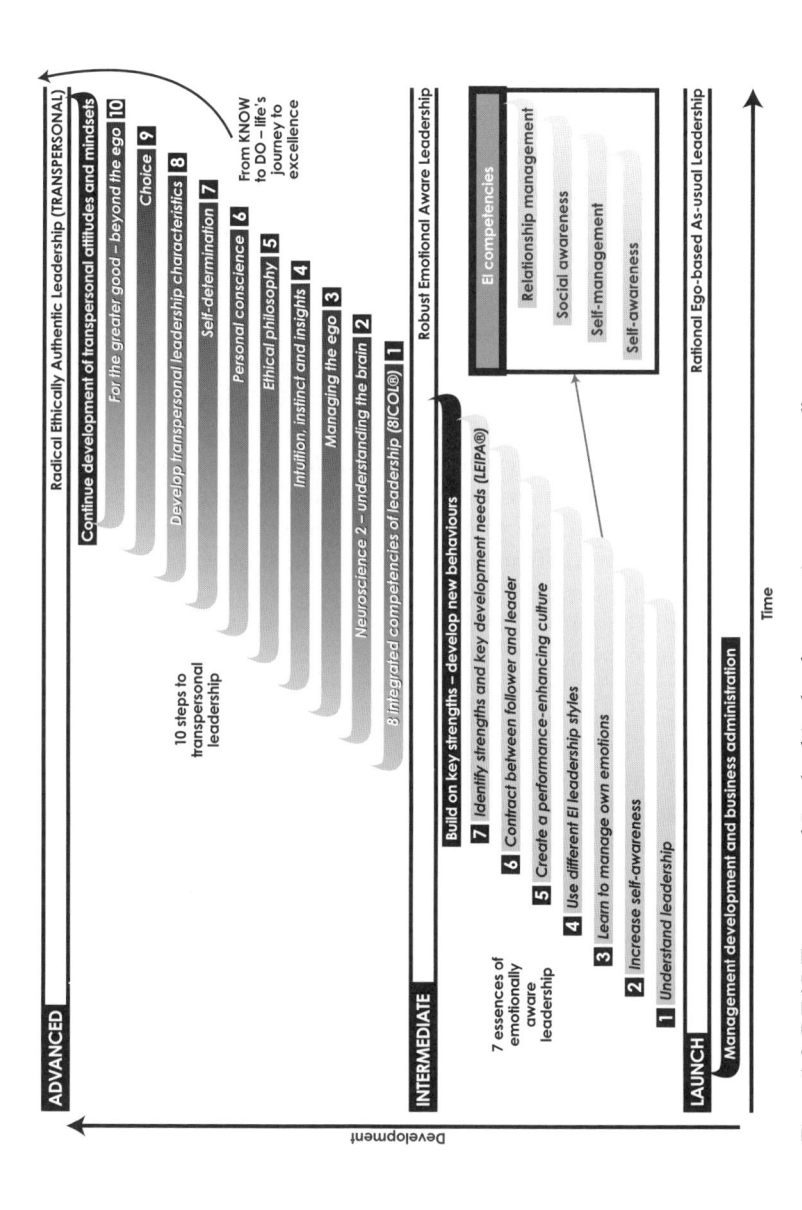

Figure 1.2 REAL Transpersonal Leadership development journey to excellence

Source: © LeaderShape 2017. All rights reserved.

expect, in much of Asia the word "spiritual" is more commonly used and rarely seen as uncomfortable. The Indian spiritual teacher Brahma Kumari Shivani explains that spiritual intelligence is the expression of innate spiritual qualities through your thoughts, actions and attitude (Varma, 2011). The Dalai Lama explains spirituality as being "concerned with those qualities of the human spirit – such as love, compassion, patience, tolerance, forgiveness, contentment, a sense of responsibility, a sense of harmony, which brings happiness to both self and others" (Craig, 2002).

So in essence it is about how to be a good person and as a leader translate that into positive actions and impact. *So how do we do that?* Well, fortunately I was introduced to *Spiritual Intelligence: The Ultimate Intelligence* by Danah Zohar and her husband Ian Marshall (Zohar & Marshall, 2000). This book explained spiritual intelligence in terms of philosophy and, more importantly, neuroscience. It explained how the brain operates differently for rational, emotional and spiritual intelligence and brought logic to a hitherto fuzzy dimension. Danah is originally a quantum physicist so one should expect no different.

This set us on the way to identify intuition, instincts, insights and ethical philosophy as key to judgement and transpersonal decision-making, to separate each value into either personal conscience and/or self-determination and to develop the Eight Integrated Competencies of Leadership (8ICOL®). From this we realised that in terms of human development as leaders we were dealing with the conflict between our instincts and our conscious behaviour. To overcome those unhelpful instincts we need to raise our level of consciousness to understand we really do have choices and that to be excellent leaders we need to operate beyond our ego.

That is what Part 2 of the book is about: how to lead beyond your ego! Again, using the REAL acronym, becoming Radical Ethical Authentic Leaders (Transpersonal Leaders) as shown in Figure 1.2.

Part 3 starts off with a chapter by my LeaderShape colleague, Danielle Grant, who explains the learning principles and methodologies we recommend for this transpersonal journey. Most of us were brought up on rote learning where the teacher or lecturer acted as "the sage on the stage". Today's advances in neuroscience show us that to motivate and embed learning there are different principles at play. Creating personal meaning and multiple hooks that enable recall and embedded behaviour, engaging reflection and practice in the real world, are all key. Priming the brain to maximise experiential learning flips traditional "homework", thereby strengthening emotional and social aspects of learning that together enable transpersonal behaviour to be integrated into a leaders' way of being.

Today's learners and organisations need to connect across geographies and time zones. They need on-demand learning where they are, rather than a requirement to always travel to a learning centre, while not losing the social and emotional aspects that are a key to embedding learning, especially that associated with behavioural change. Younger learners in particular expect to have greater control over when and where they engage with learning. A variety of remote delivery methods and choices around social group interaction and support are key to enable the continuous self-development that is crucial in the journey to Transpersonal Leadership.

The final chapter (Chapter 23) is written by Tony Wall, a co-editor in an earlier book (Wall & Knights, 2013) and LeaderShape's partner at the University of Chester when accrediting our Transpersonal Leadership programme to Master's degree level. He explains that whether or not ethics is explicitly covered in leadership learning and development activity, every intervention has the potential to reinforce or disrupt ethical values, standards and behaviours. How it is organised, how it is delivered, what it covers, what it excludes and who is involved, all contribute to the learning of being an ethical leader. It considers subtle but key considerations in designing leadership learning and development towards ethics. The chapter also highlights cutting edge research and practice of how to re-orient the content, delivery, assessment and evaluation, towards infusing greater connectedness and collectiveness in leadership learning and development.

Note

1 Action Learning – our definition in this context: small cohort meeting to tackle real problems or issues brought by one person; facilitated session where colleagues first ask questions for understanding and then provide individual opinions and possible solutions. The individual then reflects on all the input and decides on a course of action. The usual result is everyone in the cohort has a valuable take-away relevant to their own situation.

References

Bynum, E. B. (1992). A Brief Overview of Transpersonal Psychology. *The Humanistic Psychologist* 20(2–3): 301–306.
Craig, M. (2002). *The Pocket Dalai Lama by the Dalai Lama (abridged)*. Shambhala Publications Inc.
Goleman, D., Boyatzis, R. and McKee, A. (2002). *Primal Leadership: Realizing the Power of Emotional Intelligence*. Harvard Business School Press. Published in the UK as *The New Leaders*.
Grof, S. (2008). Brief History of Transpersonal Psychology. *International Journal of Transpersonal Studies* 27: 46–54.
IBM (2015). *Myths, Exaggerations and Uncomfortable Truths: The Real Story behind Millennials in the Workplace*. IBM Institute for Business Value.
Knights, J. (2011). *The Invisible Elephant and the Pyramid Treasure*. Tomorrow's Company. http://www.leadershape.biz/invisible-elephant [accessed on: 18/07/2017]
Tolstoy, L. (1869). *War and Peace*. The Russian Messenger.
Varma, A. (2011). What Is Spiritual Intelligence? *The Times of India* (March 27, 2011).
Wall, T. and Knights, J. (2013). *Leadership Assessment for Talent Development*. Kogan Page.
Wigglesworth, C. (2012). Spiritual Intelligence: Living as Your Higher Self. *Huffington Post* (October 10, 2012).
Zohar, D. and Marshall, I. (2000). *Spiritual Intelligence – The Ultimate Intelligence*. Bloomsbury.

Part 1
The intermediate journey of the Transpersonal Leader

2 Introduction of Part 1, "The intermediate journey"

John Knights

Developing as excellent leaders is a continual battle between instinct and conscious behaviour.

Overview

Part 1 of this book is fundamentally about how leaders learn to raise their awareness and implement new behaviours that will increase their own performance, and through that the organisations they serve.

As we can see from Chapter 1 (Figure 1.2), the entire "Transpersonal Leadership development journey to excellence" is made up of the programme to the intermediate level followed by the one to the advanced level. Part 1 of the book is about following the path to the intermediate level as replicated in Figure 2.1.

To do this leaders must understand what leadership is about in the twenty-first century, investigate how the brain actually works in the context of leadership, learn to increase self-awareness, and understand how emotions impact our behaviour and leadership styles impact culture.

Part 1 is the stage of the journey that brings leaders to a level where, using our REAL mnemonic, they are **Robust, Emotionally Aware Leaders (REAL-2)**. At this level, they possess a high level of emotional intelligence, and understand that sustainable performance can only be achieved by having the right kind of organisational culture. To do this leaders must fully comprehend what leadership is about in today's world. This is achieved through appreciating how the brain actually works in the context of leadership, learning to increase self-awareness, understanding how emotions impact our behaviour and the way leadership styles determine the climate and culture of the organisation. Figure 2.1 provides a summary of this part of the journey.

This is the foundation of the leadership development journey, the ultimate objective of which is of course to provide improved, sustainable organisational performance.

A reflection from my own journey may help bring this idea to life. In the late 1980s, Protecht was the first company I had set up from scratch. I raised the necessary venture capital to build a European environmental technology business. Over a

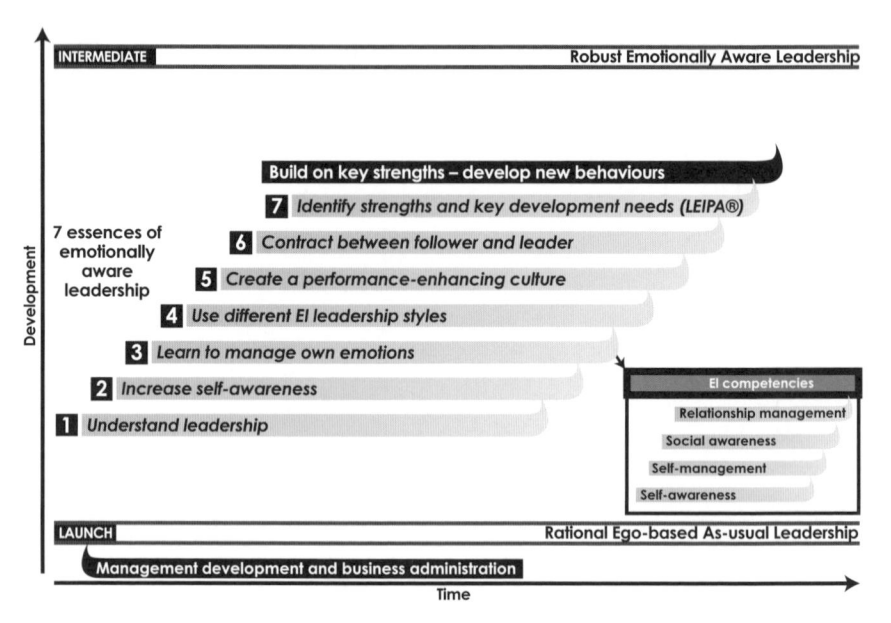

Figure 2.1 REAL Transpersonal Leadership development journey to excellence
Source: © LeaderShape 2012. All rights reserved.

period of 2 years I had acquired technology-rich businesses in the UK, Ireland, Sweden, Holland and Hungary. To make these work I realised we needed a European management team and used an industrial psychologist to help me bring the diverse team together. Part of this programme included each of us carrying out a 360° assessment, which in those days was done personally by the external psychologist. I was shocked by my results. Although there were many positive statements about my leadership, I can only remember the two main negative comments: I was perceived by people as being intimidating and also as not caring about them! I had no idea I intimidated people and I knew that I cared deeply about those in the organisation, but obviously did not show it. I understood this behaviour would have a negative impact on the performance of others in the long term. Tragically, the psychologist concerned died a few days later in a car accident and, lacking immediate follow up, it was another 10 years before I really learned how to change these behaviours. It was fundamentally about developing and communicating empathy and becoming more "emotionally aware".

Step-by-step

At the very start of the journey, a leader functions as a **Rational, Ego-based, As-usual Leader (REAL-1)**.

What do we mean by this? Throughout our education (school, university, work-place and probably at home too) most of us are taught, told or persuaded to think logically and analytically; it is certainly what we are praised and measured on. Our answers, responses and decisions should be thought out rationally and objectively. We are rarely (if ever) encouraged to think intuitively, emotionally or spiritually. By the time individuals are in a position of responsibility and take on a leadership role most of us will have had any non-rational thinking "knocked" out of us.

When we start our role as leaders we usually have relevant job skills and know how to use them. However, we often assume that other individuals think and act like us, although, in reality, we all have different preferences. Every individual will have varying levels of innate intuitive thinking and emotional awareness, but most often we will not be fully aware of our capabilities and therefore will not be managing these attributes to maximise levels of self-management, relationships and performance. That takes care of **Rational**.

In our early careers, both from a human maturity perspective and one of economics and sustainability, it is natural and usual to focus more on our personal needs. We want to get ahead with our careers, find the right partner, earn more money, get a nice car, buy a house, take care of our children, etc. We want to establish ourselves, build our persona. It is primarily about "me". Fundamentally we seek power, reward, prestige or recognition, or any combination of these. Usually, one or more of these needs will be the prime motivator for the leadership decisions we make. We are **Ego-based**. There is nothing wrong or immoral in any of this and it is the nature of things, but as an employee and, especially as we develop as a leader, we should instead be making decisions in the best interests of the organisation we work for and for the stakeholders of that organisation. Many of the corporate disasters during and since the financial crisis of 2008 were the result of the top leaders, unfortunately, never moving beyond being ego driven.

Finally, let me explain what we mean by **As-usual Leadership**. For the vast majority of us, our default leadership style, the "As-usual" style, is to know everything and tell people what to do. That is how most people who have not learned otherwise think leadership is. Many of those who have learned otherwise will nevertheless maintain this style as they feel it gives them power. Even those who, most of the time, make the effort not to lead like this will revert to it when stressed or hijacked by their emotions. Just think of any situation when you were "hijacked" in the last 24 hours. Wasn't your tendency just to want to do it your way without discussion? That is how our brain works genetically in an attempt to reduce uncertainty (since that is experienced as an evolutionary existential threat). As we will see in the following chapters this style is most often counter-productive, in the long term at least, especially in today's VUCA[1] world. So we will learn how to overcome these natural tendencies. However, there are many leaders in organisations around the world who operate "As-usual" most or all of the time.

Developing as excellent leaders is a continual battle between instinct and conscious behaviour. In this part of the book, the core purpose is to learn how conscious behaviour can win the battle against instinct, through managing

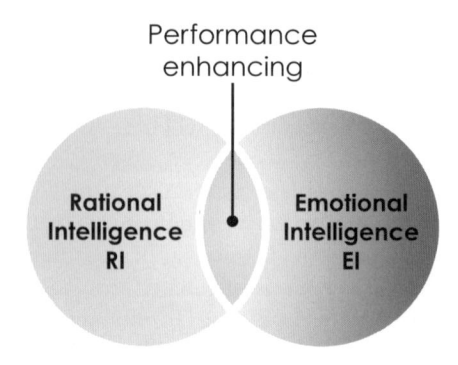

Figure 2.2 Impact of emotional intelligence on rational intelligence

one's emotions. More experienced leaders who are effective and competent may not need to join the journey at the launch point, but it will still be worth them reflecting carefully on how the world has changed since they were at the start of their leadership journey. It may remind them how many of their younger followers have been brought up in a different world, which has changed the social, logistical and technical structure of life.

The essence of this part of the journey is to build on the rational intelligence of the leader to enhance performance through adding emotional intelligence as shown in Figure 2.2. Chapter by chapter we will build on the development through the seven essences of, or steps to, emotionally aware leadership as shown in Figure 2.1.

The first step (Chapters 3 and 4) clarifies what leadership is, how it differs from management and how leadership needs to change to be successful in a VUCA world. In order for this book to be understandable we need to define what "we" mean by leadership and management and explain our default instincts about what "good" or "strong" leadership is. "As-usual" leadership was an acceptable and reasonably efficient style up to 25 years ago as it conformed to societal norms. However, it is no longer fit for purpose in this age of exponential social and technological change.

We all have our instinctive views about inspirational leadership, but the reality is often surprising. A real understanding will give more people the confidence to be inspirational themselves. We will use some aspects of neuroscience that have a direct impact on how we lead. In particular we focus on how much of our default behaviour is, on the one hand, based on how our brain developed to survive the stone age and, on the other, the environment needed to improve performance and productivity, as well as create superior learning. It will also explain how neuroscience helps us understand emotional intelligence and why and how it is possible to improve our behaviours to better manage our emotions.

The second step (Chapter 5) discusses how we can increase our self-awareness, which is one of the key building blocks to helping our development as humans, especially as leaders. This self-awareness must be on several levels: our awareness, how we react to and deal with emotions; understanding our strengths and weaknesses; knowing how we use and react to our five senses; how we react in different situations and what our drivers are; how others react to us and why; and how this is a lifelong exercise.

The third step (Chapters 6 and 7), managing emotions and emotional intelligence, is one of the real core areas of learning and development that we all need and is a key building block to increasing performance. We discuss in detail the importance of emotional intelligence (EI) as a part of leadership and how it can be developed. Having become aware of how our emotions impact our behaviour, we must now learn how to manage those emotions. We need to know which emotions and specific behaviours have the greatest impact and so how to prioritise. This requires rewiring our brains and understanding exactly how we can do that. It is not just about managing our own emotions, but, as leaders, how we can impact more positively on the emotions of the people around us. We cover in detail how to improve our capability in the four Competencies of EI: Self-Awareness, Self-Management, Social Awareness and Relationship Management.

The fourth step in the journey is about how to use different leadership styles (Chapters 8 and 9). It is a critical step because it is about how to apply emotional intelligence by using different styles in different circumstances and knowing when to adopt each style. Most of us have one preferred style, or at best two, which we tend to use all the time but, to be effective in all circumstances, we need to become competent in six styles.[2] This means honing four or five new styles, which in turn means developing specific granular behaviours not necessarily natural to us. All our research and experience, and that of others has confirmed that of the six styles, the coaching style is the least used by leaders, even though it is the second most impactful (after the visionary style). The good news though is that it is the easiest to learn because there are many simple, proven techniques that can be used to develop and implement this style. A key role of leaders and which is often missing, is to help develop the people they are responsible for. The coaching style is the best style to use to help people learn in the workplace and develop to fulfil their potential.

In the fifth and sixth steps (Chapter 10), we learn how to create a performance-enhancing culture and establish a mutually beneficial contract between leader and follower. These aspects are necessary to convert good leadership skills and styles into organisational effectiveness. Readers learn how a leader starts off creating the right kind of culture by first creating the right environment (climate) through their own consistent behaviour. Changing culture is longer term and requires the engagement of most of the people in the organisation. We use a model that has four parameters of culture (Power, Structure, Achievement and Support) and each parameter is specifically related to one or two of the six leadership styles. So by identifying the "actual" and "ideal" cultures for an organisation using these parameters (we have a well-developed tool – LeaderShape Online Culture Shaper [LOCS] to do just that) we can identify both the leadership styles the leaders need to use and granular behaviours the organisation needs to focus on in order to move towards the ideal. An important aspect of developing the right culture is the explicit contract between individual leaders and each person reporting to them, which has a psychological dimension as well as a practical one.

The seventh and final step in Part 1 (Chapter 11) is about identifying strengths and improving development areas. This chapter explains the use of a specific tool (LEIPA®)[3] developed by LeaderShape that enables leaders to identify their habitual granular behaviours and leadership styles that form the inherent strengths of their leadership competence and how to build on that. It also identifies those styles and capabilities that need developing or improving and explains how, usually, improving just two or three granular behaviours can have a major impact on a leader's competence and performance. This chapter offers a template for a detailed action plan. Finally, it also provides new and valuable analysis of LEIPA® data on the behaviour and development needs of leaders.

Working diligently through these seven steps of development will bring those on the journey to the intermediate REAL level of a Robust, Emotionally Aware Leader. Let's explain what this means as, in our experience, few leaders who have not followed the programme can tick all the boxes that indicate they have achieved this level.

Robust refers to an individual having reached a level of inner self-confidence where they are not afraid to say what they think, are willing to take risks when they feel it is right and ensure messages are communicated unambiguously. They can take criticism without taking it personally, make hard decisions and are transparent in their dealings with people. This absolutely does not mean being dogmatic or stubborn but ensuring clarity for better understanding at both a rational and emotional level.

While this type of robustness is a real necessity, without being **Emotionally Aware** this leader could be a nightmare in their relationships with people – and they are not that unusual in the work place. The **Robust** leader also needs to be conscious of and sensitive to people's feelings and, in particular, how their behaviour affects the mindset and performance of others. The **Emotionally Aware** leader deals in both facts and perceptions, avoids bias and eliminates discrimination. Perhaps, above all, they demonstrate a real interest and understanding of the people they deal with, which, in turn, will improve the performance and confidence of the people they lead.

Bringing these elements together creates a leader that people will want to follow.

As we shall see later when we get to Part 2 of the book, the emotional awareness and intelligence we cover in Part 1 provide a crucial platform to enable individuals to develop into Transpersonal Leaders. Without emotional intelligence and an understanding of how this creates performance enhancing cultures, the building of values and a greater level of consciousness that we learn about in Part 2 will never produce any meaningful positive impact towards creating performance-enhancing sustainable organisations.

Notes

1 "Volatile, Uncertain, Complex and Ambiguous." Originally used by the American military to describe extreme conditions in Afghanistan and Iraq but more recently as the state of the world in general.
2 We use Goleman's six styles: Visionary, Coaching, Affiliative, Democratic, Pace-Setting and Commanding as they correlate best with EI competencies and behaviours (Goleman et al., 2002).
3 Leadership and Emotional Intelligence Performance Accelerator. Using best practice in a 360° format, LEIPA® identifies and compares the individual's habitual leadership styles to those which will have the greatest positive impact (www.leadershapeglobal.com/Leipa).

References

Goleman, D., McKee, A. and Boyatzis, R. (2002). *Primal Leadership: Realizing the Power of Emotional Intelligence*. Harvard Business School Press. Published in the UK as *The New Leaders*.

3 Understanding leadership

John Knights

> *The role of the leader is to generate followers, bring them to a place they would not ordinarily go, and to inspire new leaders.*
> —Greg Young, CEO LeaderShape Global

Overview

There is a great deal of misunderstanding about what leadership is, how it differs from management and how leadership must change to be successful as we move deeper into the twenty-first century. In order for this book to be understandable we need to define what "we" mean by leadership and management. We discuss the different parameters of leadership and how our default instinct about what "good" or "strong" leadership is, which still had relevance 20 years ago, may be no longer fit for purpose. Finally, we bring inspirational leadership into focus to bring to the surface what it is, how it might be quite different to what you expected and how you can start to become a more inspirational leader. This understanding of leadership is a critical foundation to become a Transpersonal Leader.

Definitions

The challenge with non-rigorous subjects such as leadership is that there are many definitions of what various words actually mean. We have been coming across this problem for many years, so to make things clear we will provide our definition whenever we feel there can be ambiguity. You may not agree with our definitions but at least you will understand them.

The following is an extract from my White Paper on Ethical Leadership, published by Routledge in May 2016 (Knights, 2016) that explains how we define "leadership".

> *Leadership is usually a process which involves influencing others and happens within the context of a group. Leadership involves goal attainment and these goals are shared by leaders and their followers. The very act of defining leadership as a process suggests that leadership is not a characteristic or trait with which only a few certain*

people are endowed at birth. Rowe and Guerrero (2013) define leadership as a process which is a transactional event that happens between leaders and their followers and can happen anywhere in the hierarchy of the organisation. Our experience suggests that leading one's self is an important first step in the journey in which an individual "just" needs to face and overcome fear to act (Barrett, 2010).

In summary, **Leadership is the process of influencing others to achieve goals** *(Van Buren).*

Greg Young's quote at the start of this chapter is about how excellent leaders interpret this more general definition. Explaining it in a little more detail:

1. Generate followers because without followers you are not leading anyone other than yourself.
2. Bring those followers to a place they would not ordinarily go, which involves moving to where the followers are and metaphorically putting one's arm around them to provide encouragement and guidance, not standing in the new place whistling for them to come when they do not know the way.
3. Inspire new leaders. We know that almost all leaders have been inspired to be a leader themselves by someone in their lives. It could have been a parent, teacher, colleague, anyone!

By comparison, the definition of management is quite complex and more ambiguous. Of course many, including academic institutions, describe management as if it were "leadership". Even the Oxford Dictionary describes it loosely as "The process of dealing with or controlling things or people". For our purposes we need a much tighter definition of "management" so we are clear when we use each of the words.

The following describes in summary what *we* mean by management: "**Management** is about implementing the strategy of the organization and coordinating the efforts of the people to accomplish objectives by using available human, financial and other resources efficiently and effectively." **Fundamentally "management" is about process, structures and measurement.**

Leadership vs. management

Table 3.1 provides a comparison between leadership and management for the path from idea to performance. Everyone in an organisation will be required to perform a combination of leadership and management to accomplish their role effectively. Usually the more senior the role, the greater the balance should be towards leadership.

Unfortunately, this is not always the case. Many leaders got to where they are through being promoted because of their management skills. This balance regarding seniority and role becomes fuzzier as organisations become flatter, less hierarchical and more organic in structure. More and more there is a need and opportunity for everyone to be a leader.

Table 3.1 Leadership vs. Management

	Leadership	*Management*
Creating the agenda	**Establishing direction** Developing a shared vision of the future, often for the long term. Providing the strategic thinking behind the planning, initiatives and changes needed to achieve the vision.	**Planning** Developing the strategic plan, establishing detailed steps, budgets and timetables for achieving needed results. Allocating the resources necessary to make that happen.
Developing a community for achieving the agenda	**Aligning people** Involving, engaging with and building trust with and between the people in the organisation and beyond, to its stakeholders. Ensure the vision and strategy are understood, owned by and committed to by all.	**Organising and staffing** Establishing some structure for accomplishing plan requirements, staffing that structure with individuals, allocating responsibility and authority for carrying out the plan, providing policies and procedures to help guide people, and creating methods or systems to monitor implementation.
Implementation	**Motivating and inspiring** Energising people to overcome barriers, be they political, bureaucratic, resource or technical using win-win strategies wherever possible.	**Controlling and problem solving** Monitoring results vs. plan in a meaningful way, identifying variances, and then planning and organising to solve issues arising.
Outcomes	Produces sustainable improvement and performance, often transformational which is beneficial to the organisation and all its stakeholders.	Produces some level of consistency and certainty, and has the potential of consistently producing key results expected by various stakeholders.

If you would like to test how good you are at identifying the difference between leadership and management you can take the FREE questionnaire, *Is It Leadership or Management?* (available online: http://bit.ly/2dapURl). On completion you will receive a detailed report giving an explanation of your score and any specific questions you answered incorrectly.

IF YOU ARE GOING TO DO THE QUESTIONNAIRE, WE SUGGEST YOU COMPLETE IT BEFORE READING FURTHER AS YOU WILL GAIN MORE LEARNING THIS WAY.

Table 3.2 provides a list of the statements and answers of whether each one refers to leadership or management. There is also a brief explanation why, although with some questions there are grey areas depending on the interpretation of each phrase.

Table 3.2 Explanation of questionnaire answers

L = Leadership, M = Management	
Administers Clearly this is Management as it is about process, not people.	1 M
Appeals more to reason than to emotion Reason is a logical/analytical phenomenon and therefore associated with process and thus Management.	2 M
Appeals to "official" approach The "official" approach relates to rules and regulations – thus related to structure, procedures and process.	3 M
Appeals to both emotion and reason This is a more holistic approach. Appealing to emotion is a Leadership matter.	4 L
Appeals to common cause Common cause is about involving everyone and being of benefit to the organisation and its people. It is a people issue and therefore Leadership.	5 L
Applies incentive To provide an incentive suggests a "carrot" is being dangled. This also implies that the carrot is received in return for specific performance. This is not about engaging with and involving people so they *want* to achieve. It is rules and regulations and therefore Management. Having said that, it is acknowledged that the answer is not black and white and discussion is encouraged.	6 M
Asks "how, when?" This is clearly about rules, procedures and process and therefore Management.	7 M
Asks "what, why?" There are no perfect single logical answers to these questions. You cannot refer to rules and procedures. It is about opinion, judgement and feeling and therefore Leadership.	8 L
Contains risk (i.e. "keeps it under control") Anything to do with control is about rules, regulations, procedures, structure etc. and is therefore Management.	9 M
Does the right thing This is an open holistic concept that involves caring about people. It is Leadership.	10 L
Does things right Again it is following rules and procedures. It's Management.	11 M
Emphasises core values, shared good and philosophy This can't be handled by process. It's Leadership.	12 L
Emphasises structure, tactics and systems Structure and tactics are process. Management.	13 M
Engages people and aligns them to the new direction This requires emotional engagement and is also about vision, so it's Leadership.	14 L
Exercises positional authority Using the structure of the organisation for authority is Management.	15 M
First things first Clearly procedural and therefore Management.	16 M

(continued)

26 John Knights

Table 3.2 Explanation of questionnaire answers *(continued)*

Focuses on effectiveness Effectiveness is more than efficiency. Effectiveness involves values and emotions and state of mind and is therefore about Leadership.	17 L
Focuses on the future, the long term and the horizon Visioning and direction is Leadership.	18 L
Focuses on the present, the short term and the bottom line Following procedures and rules to achieve short-term results is Management.	19 M
Innovates Innovation is about the mind and the environment people are in, not a process. Leadership.	20 L
Inspires Appealing to emotions and values is clearly Leadership.	21 L
Optimises within narrower constraints Regulations means Management.	22 M
Relies on trust Requires the right kind of relationships with people and is therefore Leadership.	23 L
Relishes change Reaching a vision requires change. Prefers change to following processes and regulations. Leadership.	24 L
Seeks order Process = Management.	25 M
Sets vision and direction Clearly Leadership.	26 L
Skirts rules and policies, or has them changed Change catalyst requires Leadership. See 24 above.	27 L
Step by step This is a procedure, a process. Therefore Management.	28 M
Structures the team and organises it Again it is Process. Management.	29 M
Takes risks Risks require emotional and intuitive judgement. There is no process that makes risk fool proof. Therefore it is Leadership.	30 L
Targets efficiency Efficiency = Process = Management.	31 M
Uses control Control = Process/Rules = Management.	32 M
Uses personal Influence Influence requires relationships with people and is therefore Leadership.	33 L
With the end in mind This is the goal at the end of the vision and direction. It's Leadership.	34 L

Acknowledgements: some questions adapted from "7 Habits of Highly Effective People"(Covey, 2004) And "The Tools of Leadership" (Landsberg, 2003),

This questionnaire has been available online for 7 years and taken by many people from around the world. It is free for anyone to complete but we assume that the overwhelming majority of those whom partake are interested in leadership. There are just two statements people choose incorrectly more than 50 per cent of the time.

The first is "Q6, Applies incentive", Management, for which there is a huge amount of evidence that incentive or rewards do not work (Kohn, 1993). Only 20 per cent of employers in North America say merit pay is effective at driving higher levels of individual performance (Willis Towers Watson, 2016). The second is "Q17, Focuses on effectiveness", Leadership, suggesting that those taking the questionnaire may not see "effectiveness" as a more holistic characteristic that includes emotions and values.

At the other end of the spectrum "Q21, Inspires", Leadership, was answered incorrectly only 3 per cent of the time. It is of course a very important aspect of "Leadership", which we discuss in more detail later in this chapter.

If you completed the questionnaire it may be useful to reflect on your scores and what you learned in the process.

Levels of capability of a leader

Leadership is complex and has many dimensions. One dimension is to look at the various levels of capability a leader needs in order to operate at the highest level. We can see in Figure 3.1 that the first level is business and organisational skills, which, as we have discussed, is actually management.

These are the skills required to carry out, amongst others, the activities described in the right hand "Management" column of Table 3.1. Despite being "management" these skills are nevertheless a threshold requirement for leaders; that is a leader needs these skills to even be on the ladder of leadership growth even though they don't contribute directly to competence in leadership. I often suggest to final year MBA students that an MBA provides them with a ladder and a toolbox but it does not help them climb the leadership ladder.

The second level is strategic thinking (note this is different than strategic planning, which we would include within Business and Organisational Skills). Whereas strategic planning has a thought process that is analytical, convergent and conventional, strategic thinking is synthetic, divergent and creative (Heracleous, 1998). The purpose of strategic thinking is to discover new, imaginative strategies that can rewrite the rules of the game and to envision futures significantly different from the present. Strategic planning on the other hand is about organising and implementing the strategies developed through strategic thinking. If a leadership team can't think strategically then they would be unable to develop a vision or set a direction.

Although shown as the third level of leadership, vision and direction is closely entwined with strategic thinking. One of the difficulties with vision is it is another of those words with many definitions and interpretations and often confused and interchanged with mission. Indeed I have been in meetings where

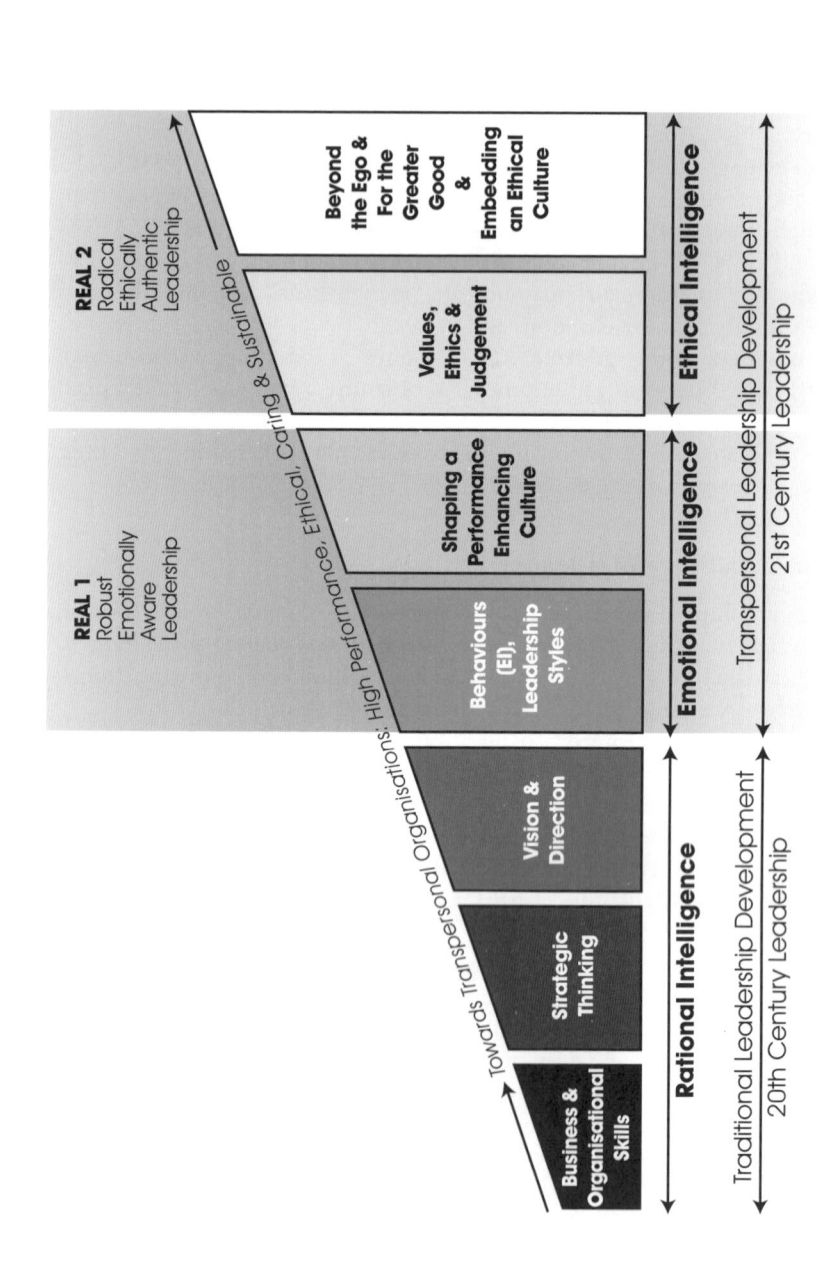

Figure 3.1 Levels of leadership
Source: © LeaderShape 2015.

more time is spent discussing the meaning of the word than actually developing the vision and mission. To address this we developed a model called "A Rose by Any Other Name". In this model we avoid the words vision and mission altogether and instead developed a few statements that talk to different groups of people, as follows:

1. A short externally focused memorable statement of what we do.
2. An externally focused statement of how we want the world to perceive us.
3. An internally focused statement of the reason for the existence of the organisation.
4. An internally focused statement of how we work.
5. What are the goals we want to achieve?

Once this is achieved it becomes much easier to define and understand one's vision and mission. One of our clients, the *Ridgeway Partnership (Oxfordshire Learning Disability NHS Trust)*, who went through this process, produced a mission and vision statement and placed it on their website:

Case study – Ridgeway Partnership

Mission

Our mission describes the purpose of the organisation:
   Ridgeway Partnership exists to create healthier, fulfilling lives for people with complex disabilities through the design and delivery of tailor-made services.
   This means that we:

- deliver services for people with learning disabilities and other complex needs
- acquire and transform services
- design and reconfigure services
- offer training, advisory services and consultancy.

Vision

Our vision will describe our aspirations, what the organisation wishes to achieve, over the next 5 to 10 years. The board has decided that it would like to develop our vision in partnership with people who use our services, staff and other stakeholders, as part of our membership strategy. Meanwhile, to provide direction and structure, we will use the following aims of our vision to be:

- a high quality, innovative, specialist provider
- a competitive and growing business

> - a constructive and mutually beneficial partner
> - an influential leader with a national reputation for knowledge and expertise
> - an outstanding and empowering employer.

Perhaps the most important lesson in this process was the realisation that to be visionary, the top leader or even the leadership team do not need to have all (or even any) of the creative ideas for the vision. This is one of the secrets of a visionary leader, as we shall discuss more in Chapter 8. We were thrilled when the Ridgeway board decided that their vision statement should refer to including all stakeholders in the development of their vision.

One of the things leaders need to bear in mind if they value the input of their people is to adopt an "excellence through partnership and inclusion" strategy so that each individual has the right to:

- a fulfilling life
- be treated with dignity and respect
- make choices and decisions about their own lives
- be valued by others
- be actively involved in their local and wider communities.

This better enables the organisation's vision to be compatible with the aspirations and beliefs of each individual. This in turn builds their buy-in and ownership and through this a greater commitment to meet goals.

Although business skills, strategy and vision are important, they are what we refer to as twentieth-century leadership. Strategic leadership and the implementation to get results has been the "leadership" focus of business schools, universities and leadership consultancies for decades. Although it was never sufficient to produce excellent leadership, it was adequate until about 20 years ago, when all the rapid change we have discussed earlier started to gain traction. That required new dimensions in leadership and is what this book is all about. The twenty-first-century dimensions of leadership (as shown in Figure 3.1) include: behaviours and leadership styles; shaping a performance-enhancing culture; values, ethics and judgement; operating beyond the ego for the greater good and embedding an ethical culture. All these areas will be covered in details throughout the book and are what enables leaders to become Transpersonal Leaders.

Vision to performance

Another perspective on leadership can be seen in Figure 3.2, where we show the path from vision to performance. The usual main focus is down the left hand side of the diagram through objectives, strategy and execution with often

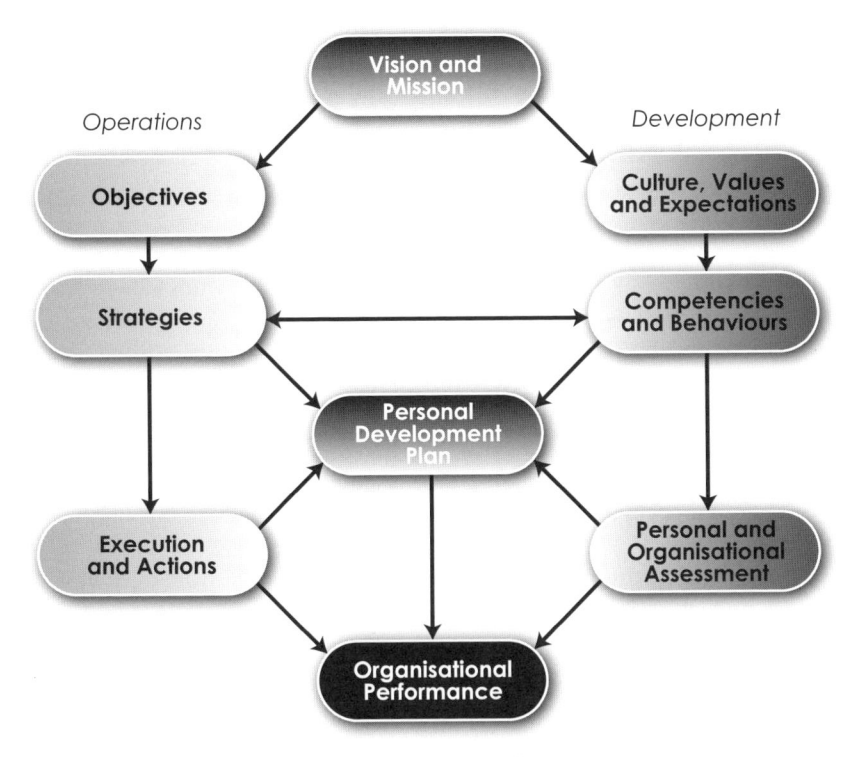

Figure 3.2 Vision to performance
Source: © LeaderShape 2015.

only token or tactical acknowledgement of the "development" right hand side of the chart. We believe strongly that there needs to be a good balance between operations and development and they need to be integrated rather than siloed.

First of all, strategies need be considered in parallel with competencies and behaviours. Then the operational and development aspects need to be integrated at the personal level such that personal objectives should include goals and commitments to behavioural development as much as those to fulfil strategies. This brings together the cognitive and emotional parts of the brain. An organisation can have the best thought out strategy but if individuals' behaviour is not aligned with it, the strategy will usually fail; a simple example is where discourteous customer service stops sales targets being met. More on this in the coming chapters, especially Chapters 4 and 11.

What is "good" leadership?

Although most people fundamentally have good values and a real sense of what is right and wrong, organisations still tend to overlook the importance of these traits when identifying future leaders. Instead they favour traditional leadership characteristics of self-confidence, assertiveness, influence and achievement, which, without the good values to temper them, may regress to high-ego, aggression, manipulation and ruthlessness, and an obsession for total control. It is therefore not surprising that 1 in 25 CEOs are considered sociopathic (Knights, 2016). Even those with good basic values have most often been taught to "leave values and ethics at the front door when you come to work".

Another challenge is that many potentially good ethical leaders (as well as unethical ones) are unable to motivate and engage staff to reach their potential in order to raise the sustainable productivity of the organisation. These leaders often generate stress and fear, releasing cortisol, which directly results in a reduction of creative thinking and openness to new ideas (Shiv, 2012). However, we also know clearly from neuroscience research that positive behaviours can be learned and negative behaviours unlearned in the same way we learn to drive a car and change from driving an automatic to a manual gear shift or vice versa. The methodologies and experience are available to enable real behavioural change (Wall & Knights, 2013) as we shall see throughout the chapters of this book.

In our leadership programmes we always ask the participants to discuss the characteristics of good and bad leadership by thinking of the best and worst leaders they have worked under. The list in Table 3.3 has been generated from the views of the middle management team of a large pension fund. It is very typical of the feedback we receive from around the world. We have not attempted to put any order to this list and every organisation we work with will produce a slightly different list, but only slightly!

Table 3.3 Characteristics of good and bad leaders

Best leaders	Worst leaders
Involvement of people	Bullying
Engaging	Short attention span
Transparent	Fear (ruled by fear)
Listened	Aggressive
Encouraging	Cold
Supportive	Pretence
Approachable	Chaos
Inspirational	Threatened
Consistent	Lack of trust
Trustworthy	Not trustworthy
Shares information and experiences	Blame culture
Visionary	Poor communicator
	No vision
	Loud and abrupt
	Self-oriented

What is important to note is that we find very few characteristics about a leader's knowledge or business skills in the list. It is all about their behaviours and their values.

Inspirational leadership

Being inspirational is seen as an important aspect of leadership yet it is often misunderstood. Our default Stone Age brain tends to think of an inspirational leader as being the hero type or a celebrity with lots of charisma who (we perceive) can do anything. As we shall continue to learn in this book, this kind of leader only appeals to a connection through our ego and is rarely sustainable.

> *There were once two bricklayers, one of whom went about his work with competence but without enthusiasm, looking forward only to completing his work and going home to supper. The other bricklayer worked with delight and took pleasure in his achievements at the end of each day. When each was asked what he was doing, the first man said, "I am laying bricks". The second man said, "I am building a cathedral".*

In this probably apocryphal story we ask, "So who is the more inspirational and what makes him so?"

Note Greg Young's words above: "the role of a leader ... Is to inspire new leaders." Many people would like to be an inspirational leader but know they can never be that charismatic, hero leader. The good news is that leaders that are really inspirational don't usually conform to that stereotype at all. The encouraging part is that any leader can be inspirational if they follow through with some simple ideas and learn a few specific behaviours.

The stereotype of the inspirational leader as someone extrovert and charismatic tends to be the exception rather than the rule... many are quiet, almost introverted (Farrington, 2012). But what do they have that makes them different? They have a novel outlook, that "turn-on" capability and the ability to engage with those they lead. Their novel outlook can be summarised as thinking laterally; taking risks; bending rules; being highly accessible; liking pressure; strongly visionary; rating attitude; being customer obsessed. They are also principled and reflective. And how do they "turn-on" people and get engagement? They listen, involve, trust, appreciate, care for and have fun.

The bad news is that while only 27 per cent of bosses believe they inspire their employees, a paltry 4 per cent of employees actually feel inspired (Boston Research Group, 2011).

The answers to what you can do to become an inspirational leader will be discussed throughout the book but perhaps especially in Chapters 6, 7 and 8. In emotional intelligence terms, of which there is much more in Chapter 7, inspirational leadership behaviour is described by the following four statements:

- effectively communicates and arouses enthusiasm for a shared vision and mission
- steps forward to lead as needed, regardless of position

- leads by example and sets standards
- makes considered decisions based on both logic and intuition.

> ### Questions and actions for personal development
>
> Here are a few questions you might want to think about. Spending some time answering them will enable your personal development and make each subsequent chapter in the book (each level in the journey to Transpersonal Leadership) more meaningful.
>
> 1. How would you define leadership?
> 2. What are your reflections on how you scored on the "Leadership vs. Management" questionnaire?
> 3. What is the balance between leadership and management in the way you work?
> 4. What is the difference between strategic thinking and strategic planning?
> 5. Where do you think you are today on the different levels of leadership capability (ref. Figure 3.1)?
> 6. What were the characteristics of the best and worst leaders you have worked for?
> 7. What would people say are the best and worst characteristics of your leadership? How would you like to change that?
> 8. What is one thing you could do differently to become more inspirational?
>
> ACTION: what are you going to do to implement questions 6 and 7, when would you like to achieve it by and how will you know when you have achieved it?

References

Barrett, R. (2010). *The New Leadership Paradigm*. Self-published at www.valuescentre.com [accessed on 18/07/2017].

Boston Research Group (2011). *National Governance, Culture and Leadership Assessment*. http://www.economist.com/node/21530171 [accessed on: 18/07/2017].

Covey, S. (2004). *The 7 Habits of Highly Effective People*. Simon & Schuster UK.

Farrington, J. (2012). *Is Your Leader Inspirational?* Sales Pro Blog. www.salesprorecruitment.co.uk/blog/is-your-leader-inspirational/ [accessed on: 18/07/2017].

Heracleous, L. (1998). Strategic Planning or Strategic Thinking? *Long Range Planning* 31(3): 481–487. Elsevier Science.

Knights, J. (2016). *Ethical Leadership: Becoming an Ethical Leader*. Routledge. http://bit.ly/1Uh6vHL [accessed on: 18/07/2017].

Kohn, A. (1993). Why Incentives Cannot Work. *Harvard Business Review*. https://hbr.org/1993/09/why-incentive-plans-cannot-work [accessed on: 18/07/2017].

Landsberg, M. (2003). *The Tools of Leadership: Vision. Inspiration. Momentum.* Profile Books.
LeaderShape (2017). *Is It Leadership or Management?*, http://bit.ly/2dapURl [accessed on: 24/07/2017].
Shiv, B (2012). What Is the Path to Increased Innovation? *Insights by Stanford Business.*
Van Buren, J. A. (No date). *Ethical Leadership.* Noonmark Nonprofit Services. www.uvm.edu/sites/default/files/ethical_leadership_factsheet.pdf [accessed on: 18/07/2017].
Wall, T. and Knights, J. (2013). *Leadership Assessment for Talent Development.* Kogan Page.
Willis Towers Watson (2016). *Pay for Performance – Time to Challenge Conventional Thinking.* www.willistowerswatson.com/en/insights/2016/02/pay-for-performance-time-to-challenge-conventional-thinking [accessed on: 18/07/2017].

4 The neuroscience of leadership

Default and emotions

John Knights

People can raise their awareness, learn more effectively, behave more appropriately and hence be higher performers and better leaders.

Overview

We have discovered that many leaders, especially those with an analytical orientation, have difficulty accepting psychological theories or more esoteric ideas, especially when they challenge their default beliefs and behaviours. We are very fortunate that in this century, neuroscience has provided us with evidence-based research that provides a more certain underpinning of the value of taking a new approach to leadership development. This makes things more tangible and easily analysed and thus more readily accepted. Interestingly, the findings of neuroscience often confirm the previous theories and ideas.

This chapter will therefore focus on some basic information about aspects of neuroscience that have a direct impact on how we lead, especially concerning awareness and behaviours. It will help us understand "why" we behave the way we do. The "how" we use this neuroscience knowledge to improve our leadership competence will be explained in Chapters 5–10.

One area of focus will be how much of our default behaviour is a result of how our brain was developed to survive in the Stone Age and how it must adapt to the modern world for us to be a successful leader. Then we will discuss the mechanics of how the brain can be reconfigured proactively so we have more control over our behaviours.

Next we explain how our brain identifies, processes and manages emotions and why being told what to do is less effective than obtaining insights in maximising performance and potential. Finally, we will learn the key lessons from this for leaders.

"Neuroscience of leadership (part 2)" can be found in Chapter 14 where we will focus more on the aspects of the brain that relate to consciousness, spiritual intelligence, values and ethics.

The value of neuroscience in leadership

There are many prominent experts who warn about the hype of neuroscience (Gazzaniga, 2006) and there are many others who believe it is ground breaking for the science of leadership and personal performance (Rock, 2009). We must remember that in its current form it is a new science – we have only been able to map the brain in real time since 2000 – and new discoveries are being made all the time. The neuroscience findings referred to in this book strongly support the most recently developed methods of effective learning (see Chapter 22), which is counter to the "talk and chalk" approach that is still happening to a large degree in our schools, universities and business schools. There are those who will hype neuroscience for their own personal benefits, and in some cases maybe dangerously so. My view is that the neuroscience presented here provides useful information towards building a total picture about how people can raise their awareness, learn more effectively, behave more appropriately and hence be higher performers and better leaders.

Our brain is from the Stone Age – but it's still amazing

One of the most important facts in the connection between neuroscience and leadership is that when we are born our brains are virtually the same in function as Stone Age man. Although recent DNA evidence is contradicting what most experts thought just a few years ago that the genetic human brain has not changed significantly since the first Homo sapiens arrived on the plains of East Africa ca. 200,000 years ago (McAuliffe, 2009), there is no suggestion that the functions of the brain have changed. It was only after the Ice Age, ca. 12,000 years ago that the Stone Age ended, replaced by the dawn of the first Agricultural Revolution when humans started to cultivate crops, breed animals and create permanent settlements. By this time it is believed Homo sapiens were the only remaining human species (Harari, 2014). Twelve thousand years is a very short time in evolutionary terms and represents just 400–600 generations, hardly enough time for the brain to change significantly although nutrition has had an impact on the intellect and behaviour (Benton, 2011).

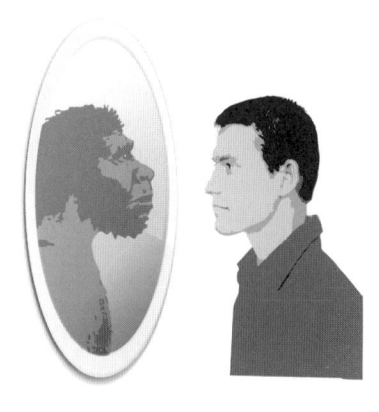

In some ways it is strange to contemplate that the brains of babies born into today's world are so similar to those delivered during the Stone Age.

However, the beauty of this Stone Age brain of ours is that many of the neural connections are reconfigurable, dependent on its environment. So the neural cell network of an adult today is very different to one in the Stone Age. This is because these neural networks have been changed by and adapted to the environment and society in which the brain's "owner" has been brought up.

In this context, there is both good and bad news. The bad news is that within the hardwired genetic make-up of our brain there is a natural default to behave like someone living in the Stone Age. The better news is that certain parts of our brain are reconfigurable. This neuro-plasticity (as it is often termed) is reactive to the environment and circumstances we live in (which can be good or bad) BUT most importantly, we can use it to be proactive in developing our conscious behaviour and thought management.

The essence of becoming a Transpersonal Leader is born in awareness. We must consciously and proactively enable the reconfiguration of our brain in the way WE want in order to improve our emotional and spiritual intelligence, and ultimately our sustainable, ethical and caring performance.

Let us first look at how our genetic default would like us to behave. Our brain was designed for survival in a world of danger and uncertainty so we are programmed to:

- be in control
- amplify the negative
- keep doing more of the same
- prepare for the worst
- exhibit powerful emotions.

This programming is highly suitable for a life-threatening situation and general survival, but not for what we usually encounter in today's modern society.

Our brain adjusting to the modern world

While the human brain has developed genetically at a very slow pace, society has developed comparatively rapidly through the agricultural, scientific and industrial ages and into the current information age. It is this latest age we are at the beginning of, which is providing the most rapid external change and the greatest potential for behavioural conflict.

Genetically, the brain works through the inter-relationships between energy, memory and neural wiring, which defaults the brain to resist change while at the same time wanting to be creative.

The only reason we cannot merely survive but also prosper in today's world is that our brain is able to change how it operates, either reactively or proactively. Reactively, our neurons make new connections in order to adapt to external influences. We can see this already in small children who will, for example, copy their parents or maybe pick up bad habits from other children when they start school. It is therefore a mixture of luck and circumstance how our brain is likely to reconfigure in this unconscious state. This is the state of the follower.

As a leader we must be proactive and use our consciousness, our free will and our determination to force ourselves to change how we want to behave to become a Transpersonal Leader and more generally succeed in our society (Rock & Schwartz, 2007). The more we can achieve this, the more successful we are likely to be.

However, at the same time, and perhaps bizarrely, humans are also "pro-creative" in that we have a natural tendency to want to shape further change, including social change (Zohar & Marshall, 2000). How does all this happen?

How the brain works

Brain cells and connections

All neurons[1] have the same basic components but they may vary in appearance and structure (there are four basic types – see Figure 4.1). The average human brain has about 100 billion neurons, each of which may be connected to up to 10,000 other neurons, passing signals to each other via as many as 1,000 trillion synaptic connections. This would be equivalent by some estimates to a computer

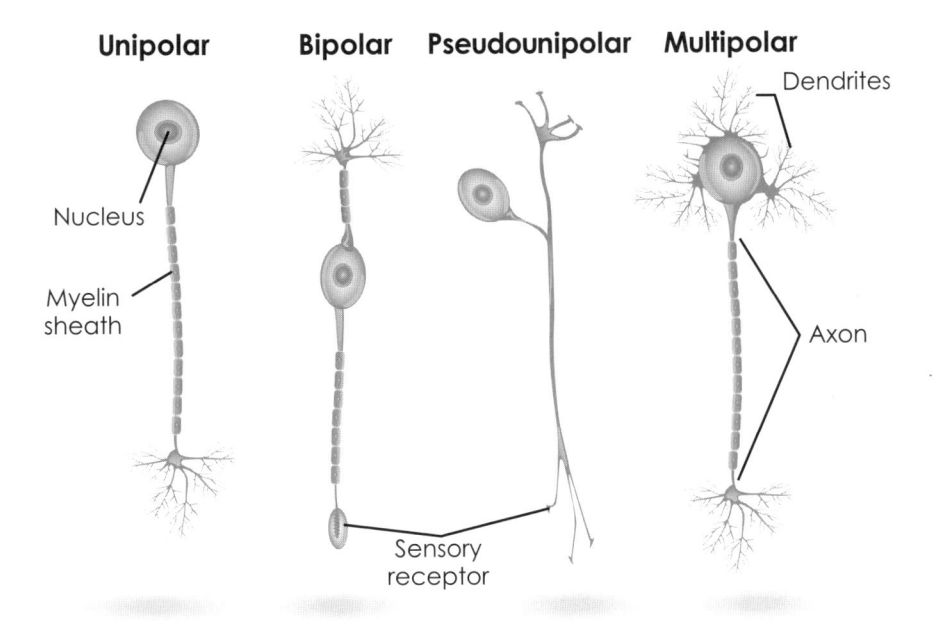

Figure 4.1 Different kinds of neurons

with a 1 million megabit per second processor (Human-Memory.net). Estimates of the human brain's memory capacity vary wildly from 1 to 1,000 terabytes (for comparison, the 19 million volumes in the US Library of Congress represents about 10 terabytes of data). It has been discovered in recent years that there are also many more neurons in the heart and gut but we will discuss that in Chapter 14.

We grow new neural connections (i.e. connections between neurones) throughout our life, or at least we have the capacity to do so. It is these neural connections that determine how we act and behave, and if we want to change how we behave through forming new habits, we need to make new neural connections. Neural systems (i.e. many neural interconnections) that are little used either shrink, disappear or are taken over for other purposes (Bruer, 1999). It is the neural connections and systems that give us our intelligence.

Babies are born only with the neural connections to regulate breathing, heart beat and body temperature etc., which are all sub-conscious and remain with us all our lives. These are often referred to as physical intelligence. When they are born, babies cannot recognise faces or objects, and they are unable to form concepts or utter coherent sounds. These evolve over time and through experience. By about 18–22 years of age the human being is fully wired, equipped to cope with life. By this time their IQ is fixed and their emotional intelligence fully developable. However, it is suggested by experts that the full potential development of spiritual intelligence has to wait until the forties for most of us, perhaps to rely on sufficient experiences of life.

There are three kinds of neural connections (Zohar & Marshall, 2000).

Serial connections (like a string of Christmas tree lights) provide our IQ, instinct and learned habits. These are more or less hard-wired and very difficult to rewire; think about phobias, such as fear of spiders (instinct) or breaking addictions such as smoking (habit).

Associative connections are where bundles – maybe billions – of brain cells connect with each other creating new intra-serial wiring; this provides for our emotional intelligence and conceptual thinking. The more we practise a particular action or behaviour the stronger the connections become, until eventually they become a habit and act more like serial wiring (think learning to drive or swim!). This is often referred to as the plasticity of the brain or neural rewiring.

Synchronous neural oscillations is where wave motions form across all the parts of a brain that relate to a particular event. These oscillations are thought to enable unitive and holistic thinking, ranging from the relative simplicity of understanding the totality of a coffee mug (form, use, smell, feel, etc.) up to the high order of things such as the meaning of life. There is more about these kinds of connection in Chapter 14.

Finally, continued focus and attention, and even visualising or practising mentally, keeps neural circuits open and stabilises the new neural connections (created by insights) thus becoming memorable and a new habit. This is how behavioural change occurs.

The emotional highway

Although the brain is incredibly complex, and the various parts of the brain are all interconnected, in this chapter I want to concentrate on the connection between four parts of the brain: the prefrontal cortex and the amygdala, supported by the thalamus and hippocampus (see Figure 4.2). These are the most significant connections in the brain when it comes to emotions, emotional self-control and emotional intelligence. First, we need to have a general understanding of what each of these parts of the brain do (Robertson, 2016; TheBrain.McGill.ca, 2016).

The **amygdala** is the centre for emotions, emotional behaviour and motivations. There are two almond-shaped and sized amygdala, one on either side of the middle of the brain, made up of nerve tissue. Its historical role has been concerned with the perception of fear and preparing for emergency events. In fact, it is where we perceive and process all emotions. The amygdala together with the hippocampus help to store memories of events and emotions so that an individual can recognise similar events in the future. For example, if you have ever suffered a dog bite, then the amygdalae may help in processing that event and increase your fear or alertness around dogs. The size of the amygdala is positively correlated with increased aggression and physical behaviour and is usually larger in men.

The **prefrontal cortex** (PFC) is the part of the brain located behind the forehead at the front of the frontal lobe. It is responsible for a variety of complex activities, including thinking skills, planning, analytical processing and rational

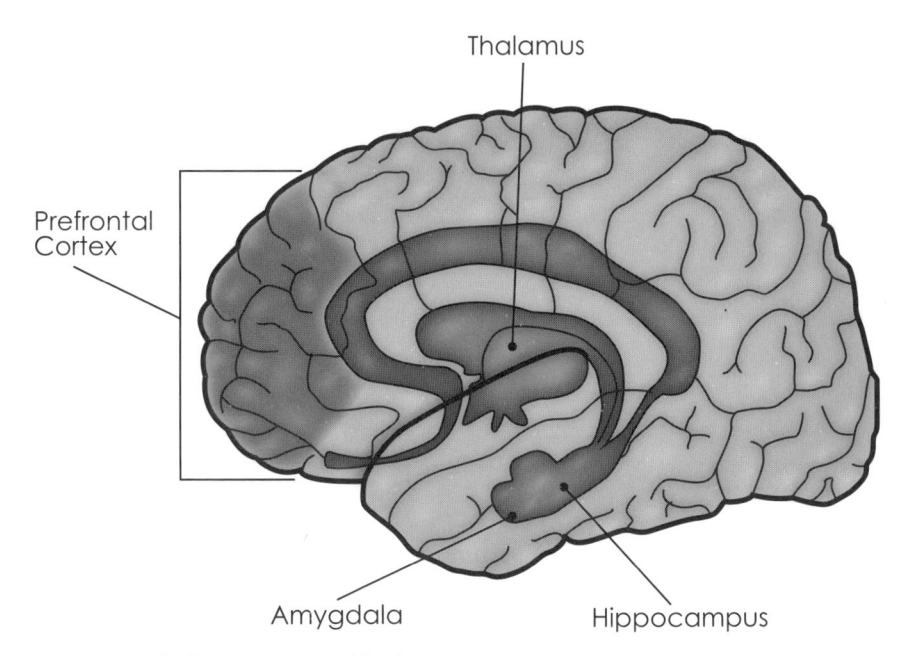

Figure 4.2 The brain's emotional highway

decision making. It greatly contributes to personality development and is also in charge of helping with behaviour modification. Its historical origin is debated as to whether it evolved with mammals or whether it has a more prehistoric origin from birds or reptiles. What is known, however, is that while the size of the human brain has increased threefold over the last 5 million years the prefrontal cortex has expanded by a factor of six.

Another related part of the brain, the **thalamus**, captures all the information from our senses (except smell, which is processed through the olfactory parts of the brain that involves the amygdala) and sends it to the PFC to process. It is also believed to be responsible for our consciousness. The latest thinking is that the thalamus also sends urgent information directly to the amygdala bypassing the PFC and as it is a shorter and quicker route can explain the rapid reaction of our natural alarm system.

Finally, the **hippocampus** is the part of the brain that is associated with memory, especially long-term memory.

What is most important is how these parts of the brain interact (see Figure 4.3).

The thalamus receives a sensory stimulus that may be visual, audio, touch or taste. The information is then sent to the amygdala in one of three ways. The short, quick, direct route creates an impression of the situation and generates an emotional response. At the same time the information is sent to the prefrontal cortex and is processed to form a more considered view as to what the response should be. Also, at the same time, the information is forwarded from the prefrontal cortex to the hippocampus to assess if anything in the memory (experience) would add further information for the amygdala to determine the emotional response. All these pathways are activated and completed in a fraction of a second (Birn et al., no date; Gold et al., 2015; Salzman & Fusi, 2010) as can be seen from the following example.

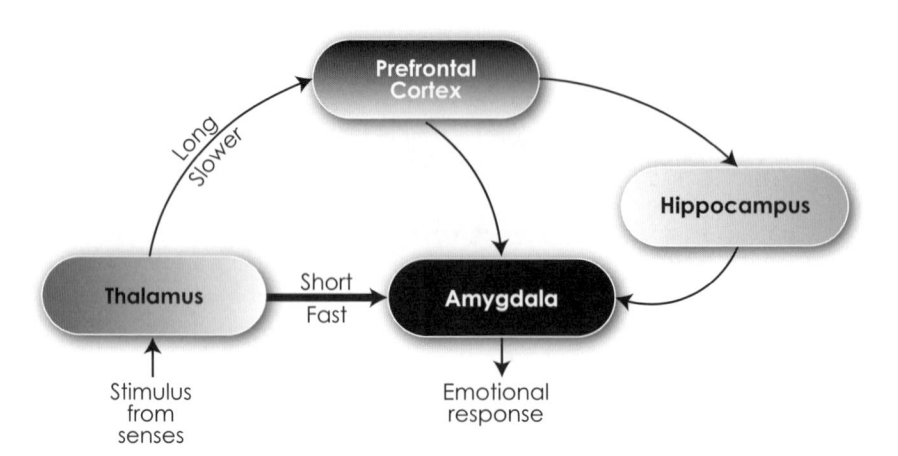

Figure 4.3 The emotional highway: interactions of the amygdala

Source: © LeaderShape 2016.

Example of how it works

Imagine you are a Stone Age hunter just returning to your family cave after an exhausting unsuccessful chase of a deer when suddenly something jumps on you from behind. This "attack" sets in motion, via the short route, the physiological reactions of fear that are so useful for mobilising you to face the danger. But this same sensation, after passing through the thalamus, will also be relayed to your cortex. A few fractions of a second later the cortex, thanks to its discriminatory faculty, questions whether what you felt was really a dangerous animal. It offers the logical perspective that maybe it's not that likely, given you are so near to your cave with the fire in the entrance and therefore your cortex suggests caution to the amygdala's response. At the same, time via the hippocampus, you are reminded that your daughter loves to jump on your back when you are at home. And you think, "I almost stabbed my own daughter". After a while your heart stops racing and you hug your daughter.

What is important for everyday life and particularly for a leader is that this process works for every sensory stimulus we receive. As we shall see in later chapters (especially Chapter 7), being able to control and manage our emotions is one of the keys to unlocking the door to excellent leadership. This is the process we need to learn to manage and to make sure that, except in a crisis or extreme danger, the short route does not control the process. Here is a leadership situation that actually occurred.

A simple leadership example

Valerie was sitting in her office when one of the directors, Ken, who reports to her, comes into the room and throws an envelope on her desk and screams, "I have had enough, this is my notice". Via the short route Valerie's reaction was to be angry for the way he had barged in and she wanted to tell him to leave the building immediately and never return. The prefrontal cortex however, was able to think that there might be something more important lying behind this action to cause it and, via the hippocampus, she was reminded that Ken had had a close family bereavement only a couple of weeks before and also was known to flare up when stressed. So, very quickly, Valerie gathered her emotions, went around her desk and asked Ken to sit down and explain why he was so upset. It turned out that not only was Ken grieving but that Valerie was the only person in the company who had known of the death of his brother (at Ken's request). When a co-director jibed him about taking a few days off at a time when they were very busy with working out some strategic decisions, Ken had snapped. After hearing this, Valerie persuaded Ken to take a few more days off and that she be allowed to explain to the staff why he was away. Ken returned to work after a week or so and was greeted with great sympathy including an apology from his co-director and an enhanced feeling of loyalty to and respect for Valerie.

Brain efficiency

The brain is enormously costly to the rest of the body, in terms of oxygen and nutrient consumption. It can demand up to 20 per cent of the body's energy – more than any other organ – despite making up only 2 per cent of the human body by weight (Swaminathan, 2008; Truex et al., 1983). The brain is at a high energy usage level when being told what to do and resists this, so that it can be on alert for any danger (Rock & Schwartz, 2006). We all know how we start to lose concentration after a short time when we are being told to do something. Working things out for ourselves or having insights also uses high levels of energy but the difference here is that adrenaline-like chemicals are released that sustain the energy levels. These activities feel more positive and are more likely to be sustained and successful.

We now know that continued focus and attention keeps neural circuits open and stabilises the new neural connections (created by insights). They become increasingly memorable and eventually a new habit. This is how sustainable behavioural change occurs. Finally, we know that happy people have more insights especially when in a calm frame of mind and, when in a happy environment, people think about future possibilities rather than past performance (Seligman, 2002).

What does all this mean for leadership?

The importance of this neuroscience is that it provides us with the information to enable us to improve our personal performance and leadership skills.

We all know the old idiom "knowledge is power" (Bacon, 1597). This is no longer true in the Information Age. Knowledge is no longer the domain of the top leaders of organisations as it was in the past. Knowledge is increasingly available to everyone. Also, whereas in 1985 an executive could retain 75 per cent of the information they needed to do their job in their head, by 2005 it had reduced to less than 10 per cent (Kelley, 2008). At the current rate of increase in availability of information, the percentage is likely to soon be below 1 per cent. This is despite the immense overall capacity of our brain described earlier in the chapter. So our brain default of "know everything and tell people what to do", which we all tend to return to when we are stressed, even if we have learned more progressive behaviours, is just not effective in this new world! We need to learn new leadership styles and new behaviours. Here are just a few of the things leaders need to do differently in light of the implications of the neuroscience we have discussed in this chapter:

1. Leaders must support individuals and provide them with the right environment to reach their own solutions through insights. See Chapter 10 for more details about how to create the right environment and culture and Chapter 16 for more on insights for decision-making.
2. Leaders telling people what to do does not provide sustainable effective change. See Chapter 10.
3. To learn new behaviours, leaders must provide the opportunity and environment for their people to focus on and spend the necessary time learning them in order to sustain change. See Chapter 9.

4. As the essence of leadership is change, it is equally important that the leader uses this approach for personal change as well as for enabling the change of others. The whole essence of this book is about personal development but in particular see Chapters 11, 19 and 21.
5. Happy people are more effective and are more likely to sustain any behavioural change. See Chapter 10.

The conclusion is that rather than "know everything and tell people what to do", in today's world, perhaps the most important thing a leader can do is provide the right environment so that the people in the organisation can learn and perform effectively.

Questions and actions for personal development

Below are some questions to help you to review this chapter, reflect on what you have learned and decide what you might do differently. An understanding of this subject will act as another foundation to your development as a Transpersonal Leader.

1. Why is it useful to understand neuroscience as part of one's leadership development?
2. What is the relevance, to leadership development, of the development of the human brain through and since the Stone Age?
3. What are the most important things to you that you have learned about how the brain works?
4. What have you learned about your own leadership while reading this chapter?
5. How do you think this knowledge will help you on your journey towards becoming a Transpersonal Leader?

ACTION: What one thing are you going to do differently, when would you like to achieve it by and how will you know when you have achieved it?

Note

1 Brain cells are also called neurons, neurones and neural cells.

References

Bacon, Sir F. (1597). *Religious Meditations, Of Heresies*.
Benton, D. (2011). *Lifetime Nutritional Influences on Cognition, Behaviour and Psychiatric Illness*. Woodhead Publishing.

Birn, R., Burghy, C. and Essex, M. (No date). *The Amygdala–Prefrontal Cortex Connection is Crucial.* University of Wisconsin-Madison. www.raisingofamerica.org/amygdala-prefrontal-cortex-connection-crucial. [accessed on: 12/2016].

Bruer, J. (1999). Neural Connections: Some You Use, Some You Lose. *Phi Delta Kappan* 81(4): 264–277.

Gazzaniga, M. S. (2006). *Breakthrough Ideas for 2006: 19. The Brain as Boondoggle.* Harvard Business Review (February 2006).

Gold, A. L., Morey, R. A. and McCarthy, G. (2015). Amygdala–Prefrontal Cortex Functional Connectivity During Threat-Induced Anxiety and Goal Distraction. *Biol Psychiatry* 77(4): 394–403. www.ncbi.nlm.nih.gov/pmc/articles/PMC4349396/ [accessed on: 18/07/2017].

Harari, Y. V. (2014). *Sapiens: A Brief History of Mankind.* Harvill Secker.

Human-Memory.net (No date). *Neurons & Synapsis.* www.human-memory.net/brain_neurons.html . [accessed on: 12/2016].

Kelley, R. (2008). *Longitudinal Study with Knowledge Workers.* Carnegie-Mellon University.

McAuliffe, K. (2009). They Don't Make Homo Sapiens Like They Used To. *Discovery Magazine,* March 2009. http://discovermagazine.com/2009/mar/09-they-dont-make-homo-sapiens-like-they-used-to [accessed on: 18/07/2017].

Robertson, S. (2016). What Does the Thalamus Do? *News Medical Life Sciences.* www.news-medical.net/health/What-does-the-Thalamus-do.aspx [accessed on: 18/07/2017].

Rock, D. (2009). *Your Brain at Work.* Harper Collins Publishers.

Rock, D. and Schwartz, J. (2006). A Brain-Based Approach to Coaching. *International Journal of Coaching in Organizations* 4(2): 32–43.

Rock, D. and Schwartz, J. (2007). Neuroscience of Leadership. *Strategy & Business.*

Salzman, C. D. and Fusi, S. (2010). Emotion, Cognition, and Mental State Representation in Amygdala and Prefrontal Cortex. *Annu. Rev. Neurosci* 33:173–202. www.neurotheory.columbia.edu/pdfs/SalzmanFusi2010.pdf [accessed on: 18/07/2017].

Seligman, M. (2002). *Authentic Happiness: Using the New Positive Psychology to Realize Your Potential for Lasting Fulfillment.* Simon & Schuster.

Swaminathan, N. (2008). Why Does the Brain Need So Much Power? *Scientific American,* a Division of Nature America, Inc. (Feb, 2008).

Truex, R. C., Carpenter, M. B. and Sutin, J. (1983). *Human Neuroanatomy – 8th Revised Edition.* Lippincott Williams and Wilkins.

The Brain.McGill.ca. (No date). *The Amygdala and Its Allies.* http://thebrain.mcgill.ca/flash/a/a_04/a_04_cr/a_04_cr_peu/a_04_cr_peu.html#2 [accessed on: 12/2016].

Zohar, D. and Marshall, I. (2000). *Spiritual Intelligence: The Ultimate Intelligence.* Bloomsbury.

5 Increasing self-awareness

John Knights

Self-awareness is always a precursor to self-knowledge and thus also a sub-section of a continuous learning journey.

Overview

Continually increasing our self-awareness is one of the key building blocks in supporting our development as humans, and especially as leaders. This growth in self-awareness needs to be across a broad spectrum of areas. We don't operate in isolation, which means we must be aware of more than just who we are. We must be conscious of our surroundings, the world we live in, the context of the roles we have (personal and business) and, perhaps most importantly, have an awareness of how our actions and behaviours impact on ourselves and other people. In other words, we are part of a complex and intricate interconnected system.

We have already raised awareness in earlier chapters about our role as a leader and how our brain works; self-awareness will continue to grow as we work our way through the Transpersonal Leadership journey. In this chapter we focus more on who we are in terms of our primarily genetic or unconscious preferences and how we might manage them to be more effective.

On a personal level this self-awareness needs to be across several parameters:

- appreciating our personality preferences
- understanding how we each learn
- knowing how we use and react to our five senses
- identifying how we react to and deal with emotions
- recognising how we behave in different situations and from different drivers.

How others react to us and why in that way will be dealt with in later chapters. Increasing self-awareness is a life-long exercise and one that is certainly high on the agenda throughout the journey to becoming a Transpersonal Leader.

What is self-awareness?

As we have discussed elsewhere, it is often helpful to define what we mean by certain words or phrases. Self-awareness has many definitions depending on the context.

Our definition is very simple: "**awareness of our own personality and character.**" This is different from self-knowledge, which in our view is more about understanding *why* you are who you are and what your purpose and motivations are. According to the ancient Greeks, self-knowledge is the highest form of knowledge. From a slightly earlier period, the great Chinese philosopher Confucius is quoted to have said, "To know oneself is simultaneously to perfect oneself". So self-knowledge is very much aligned with the journey of the Transpersonal Leader. Self-awareness is always a precursor to self-knowledge and thus also a sub-section of a continuous learning journey.

Self-awareness in leadership

In this chapter we want to focus on a few specific areas that are the preliminaries to becoming a more emotionally intelligent leader and towards understanding how leaders influence the desired organisational cultures. It is only through this kind of self-awareness that we can move away from our default Stone Age self and develop the behaviours that enable us to better manage our personality.

Self-awareness has always been an important tenet of great leadership and is the first rung on the ladder of the journey. It seems clear that the need for it has increased rapidly as modern leaders look to better engage with the people around them and maximise the potential as well as the output of those they are responsible for. The following are the key areas we need to address:

- our personality preferences
- how we learn
- the role played by each of our five senses.

There are a multitude of tests and exercises to measure all these variances and in this chapter we shall mention some of those we are familiar with. The problem is that often these tests are used to tell you what you are like and no more. They are valuable in building up a picture of who you are "now" but more importantly they bring an opportunity to develop yourself further. Rather than being stuck in the box with a label as "this is who I am" it is an opportunity to increase the size of the box or even break down the sides of the box to let the "potential you" emerge. Increasing self-awareness enables you to take on challenges more effectively and is a sure way to increasing your inner self-confidence when approached in the right manner.

Personality preferences

There is a real value in understanding our personality preferences and how these influence the way we work. Do we think our way to solutions or feel our way? Do we like to leave things open and fluid or make judgements and decisions quickly? Do we think rationally when making decisions or intuitively, or both? Do we come to our decisions by talking to others or reflecting internally?

The most well-known and commercially successful personality self-assessment tools are based on the Jungian theory of psychological types (Jung, 1971) – see separate box for details – which categorises people in terms of their primary modes of psychological functioning. The most well-known internationally is the Myers Briggs Type Indicator. There are, however, a number of alternative tools (e.g. Insights and the Jungian Type Index – JTI) some of which are said to be more user-friendly.

The science behind Jung's theory

It is based on the assumption that there are different functions and attitudes of consciousness. The **functions** of consciousness refer to the different ways in which the conscious mind can apprehend reality. According to Jung, these are provided in two pairs of opposites, Sensation and Intuition and Thinking and Feeling. The **attitudes** refer to the basic direction of a person's conscious interests and energies. They may either be inward focused or outwards to other people. These are defined as the two attitude types of Introversion and Extraversion. For both functions and attitude, whichever of these is dominant in an individual, will tend to result in the opposite attitude being repressed and this "opposite" will characterise the functioning of the unconscious, which may only show itself in stressed situations.

Jung's definitions of these words are not necessarily what you would find in the dictionary and also may be different from how we define these words in other contexts later in the book. It is therefore important to understand Jung's definitions of these functions and attitudes and their relationships with each, which are explained in many texts (e.g. Daniels, 2014).

Non-rational functions

Sensation perceives objects as they are – realistically and concretely. It fails to consider context, implications, meanings or alternative interpretations, but instead attempts to represent factually and in detail the information that is available to the senses. It is not about being "sensitive", rather about what can be seen, and touched.

Sensation's opposite, **Intuition** ignores or skims over the details and focuses instead upon the general context or atmosphere. Intuition never directly reflects reality but actively, creatively, insightfully and imaginatively adds meaning by reading things into the situation that are not immediately apparent to a purely objective observer. It is not just "gut feeling".

Rational functions

Thinking is based upon the intellectual comprehension of things and, in particular, of their conceptual interrelationships. It is a rational, systematic process that seeks to understand reality through analysis and logical inference.

Thinking's opposite, **Feeling** involves judging the value of things or having an opinion about them on the basis of our likes and dislikes. Experiences are therefore evaluated in terms of good and bad, pleasant or unpleasant, acceptable or unacceptable. It is not about "emotions".

Introversion and Extroversion

People who are more Extrovert (in Jung's definition) get energy from people and experiences and they focus their energy and attention outwards. They tend to be action oriented. Those who are Introvert get energy from reflections and thoughts and tend to focus their energy and attention inwards. They tend to be reflective. These attitudes are not about social confidence or social skills.

The Myers Briggs Type Indicator adds another dimension to measure personality: Judging and Perceiving. Unhelpfully, they don't relate to our usual understanding of these words. People who are judging in this context prefer a planned and organised lifestyle; they enjoy coming to closure and being decisive; they like to avoid last minute rushes; tend to make plans and follow them through to completion. Perceiving individuals prefer to live in a spontaneous and adaptable way; enjoy keeping their options open; feel energised by last minute pressures; adapt to changing priorities and respond to them resourcefully.

We would certainly recommend that everyone takes a personality assessment tool based on Jung's theory but we also offer a word of caution. The danger is that you will receive a report and be typecast as an extreme on each of the parameters and a computer programme will provide a list of recommended actions of which some will be obvious and others might be inaccurate or irrelevant in your context. In the original Myers Briggs Indicator there are only 16 personality types of which each of us is stamped as one of them. Myers Briggs has developed a Step II, which divides each of the four dimensions into five sub-parameters, making nuancing much more possible.

The best advice we can provide here is to ensure that your Jungian personality test report is fed back to you by someone who is both accredited in the specific tool and also a qualified coach. Our experience is that it is more important that your coach understands the tool being used than any particular tool being superior to another. It is important to understand where you stand on each of the personality dimensions and then to identify what actions you can take to moderate your preferences to maximise both your own performance and that of your team.

For example, if you are found to be more extrovert, then it could be of great advantage to learn how to reflect more and likewise if you are an introvert, to challenge yourself by discussing your ideas with colleagues at an early stage rather than only sharing your ideas once you have come to a conclusion.

Example

I recently worked with a high level team in a government quango in the financial sector when delivering a Transpersonal Leadership programme. At an early stage in the programme it was realised from completing the Myers Brigg Step II test that all six individuals liked leaving decisions until the last moment. While everyone was comfortable with the decision-making process of the team – they were in harmony – nearly all the deadlines were either being missed or the outcomes fell short. This awareness enabled them to more consciously learn to operate in a more planned way.

Jung's theory of psychological types is by no means the only basis for personality self-awareness tests and we would advise anyone to regularly search for and take tests that are relevant to their needs. But as with any test, we would recommend you use your increasing self-awareness and common sense to analyse any advice that is given to you from a computerised analysis. Three of the most popular personality tests are 16PF, DISC and Hogan Personality Index. Such tests are used for a range of applications from recruitment to psychiatrics, as well as for personal development.

How do we learn?

> *Learning may be defined as the process of making a new or revised interpretation of the meaning of an experience, which guides subsequent understanding, appreciation and action.*
> —Jack Mezirow [1923–2014], American sociologist and adult education expert

How do YOU learn best? Is it through reading, just doing and experiencing things, by reflecting on what you have done, when you plan, or by trying out different alternatives?

As we learned in Chapter 4, although our memories reside in certain parts of our brain, our neural wiring is changing all the time. In order to learn and remember we are making up new connections through a physical-chemical process. So most memories don't stay the same for very long – they change!

The brain pays more attention when it is surprised with something novel, so we should try to learn in new ways with different stimuli. Since most of our learning is not conscious we need to feed our brain with the stimuli it will respond to. One of the best ways to really learn something is to teach it to others; or sing it, or paint a picture or create an advert using the learning. For some people moving to different places or settings helps them to learn. In other words the richer the stimulus around the learning, the better the recall.

Also, *when* do we learn best? Most people have better long-term memory capacity in the evenings (which is presumably why we teach children in the morning) and we learn more effectively in intervals with breaks (say 90 minutes stretches with 30 minutes rest in between) (Edlund, 2011). We also learn better when we get sufficient sleep and exercise.

Ultimately, our level of learning depends on our motivation, which in turn depends on our belief in its value, our enthusiasm, our curiosity, our courage and our resilience. As a leader you not only have to be a keen learner yourself but you need the people around you to be effective learners too. You can achieve this by explaining what you think the value is, by being enthusiastic, making it interesting and igniting their curiosity, and by providing an environment that is safe to sustain energy and be courageous.

It is critical that we appreciate how we learn best, because only learning can drive personal development. Each of us has different approaches to learning, influenced by our culture, education, personal learning experiences and, of course, our genes. Some learning experiences are easier, more constructive and more enjoyable than others. We learn more when we enjoy the experiences, so it is worth identifying which learning opportunities suit us best.

On the other hand, sticking to the experiences we enjoy limits our opportunity to learn. Therefore identifying and learning to enjoy new ways of learning will maximise the opportunity to reach our potential.

One of the most useful models for leaders to understand is the learning cycle and their preferred learning styles. This was first developed by Kolb (Kolb, 1983) and more recently updated (Kolb & Kolb, 2005). A number of people have developed and simplified Kolb's theories for practical use and a number of questionnaires have been developed; the best known commercially, at least in the UK, is the Honey and Mumford Learning Styles Questionnaire developed in the 1980s (Honey & Mumford, 2000). Several versions of related questionnaires are available online, some free of charge.

Considering this "Learning Cycle" in more detail (Figure 5.1), the most effective learning takes place when we complete all four stages. The cycle is continuous so can start anywhere. Let us start with Experience/Action. This is where we actually do something and the experience it provides is where we get our learning. It can be reactive or proactive.

The next stage is where we reflect and review the event. It is a non-judgemental look back at what actually happened. This is a vital stage but often missed by the action-orientated leader. When actions have been important one valuable technique is to complete a Reflection Note (this is explained in Chapter 9). The third stage in our cycle is where we draw conclusions. From the thoughts and notes made at the reflection stage we identify the lessons learned. From this we can move on to the final stage and plan for the next

Figure 5.1 The learning cycle

action, the new experience. In the planning phase we test the lessons learned from previous conclusions and get prepared to relate them to similar situations in the future. Now we are ready to start a new cycle.

The question we need to ask ourselves now is which stage we find easier, or more difficult. Each stage represents a learning style (Figure 5.2). The four learning styles (or preferences) are **Activist**, **Reflector**, **Theorist** and

Figure 5.2 Learning styles

54 *John Knights*

Table 5.1 Learning style preferences

Activist
ACTION, EXPERIENCE
Tends to be open-minded and driven by enthusiasm for anything new, though bored with longer-term consolidation
Strengths: Optimistic about anything new, therefore unlikely to resist change
Weakness: Rush into action without sufficient preparation

Reflector
ANALYSE, REFLECTION
Tends to thorough collection of data, postponing definitive conclusions
Strengths: Good at listening to others and assimilating information
Weakness: Slow to make up their minds and reach a decision

Theorist
RESEARCH, STUDY, CONCLUDE
Tends to adapt and integrate observations into complex but logically sound theories, shying away from ambiguity
Strengths: Good at asking probing questions
Weakness: Low tolerance for uncertainty, disorder and ambiguity

Pragmatist
PLAN, TRY-OUT
Tends to be impatient with ruminating and open ended discussions but wants to try ideas to see if they work in practice
Strengths: Keen to test things out in practice
Weakness: Tendency to reject anything without an obvious application

---

Pragmatist (see Table 5.1 for details). Which do you prefer? Which do you think you need to develop?

Over the years you have probably developed learning "habits" that help you benefit more from some experiences than others. As you may be unaware of this, a questionnaire will help you pinpoint your learning preferences so that you are in a better position to select learning experiences that suit your style. It will also help you to identify which learning styles you need to consider developing further if you wish to maximise your overall potential. There are various versions of Kolb Learning Styles questionnaire available online. Search "Kolb based questionnaire" to find alternatives to select.

Having completed a learning styles questionnaire that is based on Kolb's theory, we recommend you do the following:

1. Choose the two learning styles where you score lowest.
2. Choose two questions from each of these two styles where you disagreed with the statement but you would most like to work on to be able to turn to "agreed".

This will provide you with an action plan to improve your learning habits. A trained coach can help you find many more ways to use this data to improve how you learn, but there are just a few more things to bear in mind:

1. Try to identify the learning styles of those you are working with.
2. If you have a similar learning style to others it will mean you can build a rapport easily but at the risk that some learning opportunities may be missed.
3. If you have a disparity of styles with others it may take longer to establish a relationship but learning opportunities will be increased.

Finally, in our experience, there are complementary and conflicting pairs of learning styles. Complementary styles are Reflector/Theorist and Pragmatist/Activist, whereas Action/Reflector and Theoretical/Pragmatic are conflicting. If we consider the Action/Reflector, which is quite common, they are likely to make a quick decision and then after reflection change their mind, which can, of course, be very infuriating for other parties involved. Someone who is both theoretical and pragmatic (less common) might be conflicted because of wanting to try things out to see if they work while being a perfectionist and needing to prove everything rationally.

There are many other insights that can be gained working with an experienced coach that are beyond the scope of this chapter.

Kolb's learning cycle is only one of many dimensions of learning styles. A good summary of the range of learning styles methodologies can be found at the Brain Boxx website.

Our five(?) senses

Think of your favourite place and describe it aloud to yourself or a colleague – in maximum one minute.

Now reflect on how you described it and which senses were in play and how frequently. That will give you a quick idea of which of your senses dominate and which are less active.

We are born with our senses. Sight (vision), hearing (audio), taste, touch (feel) and smell.

Most of us are lucky enough to have all of them for most, if not all, of our lives but we often take them for granted and don't realise which of our senses are most dominant and which are the weakest. This spectrum helps shape who we are.

Consider these two descriptions:

> *I am sitting on the balcony of my summerhouse in Sweden, which is about 50 metres from the lake. The summerhouse is yellow with white window and door trimmings and stands in an acre of grass surrounded by tall birch and pine trees. We are 3 miles from the nearest tarmacked road and rarely see anyone else when we are here.*

The lake is a bright glittering blue and I can see a pair of Eurasian cranes standing in the shallows. It is beautiful.

I am relaxing on the balcony of our summerhouse listening to the distinctive cry of the cranes over the gentle sound of the birch waving in the breeze while sipping sweet homemade lemonade. This place has a very special smell of luscious growth in the pure forest air close to the lake. When I am here I feel a part of nature but also where I belong, as I watch the dragonflies darting around and listen to the honey bees taking pollen from the wild flowers.

These are the descriptions from two people of the same place at the same time. Both are very descriptive but very different. You can immediately tell which senses dominate, and you will be thinking (or sensing!) what kind of person made each of the statements. When we combine the two descriptions we get a much more complete picture. The more we are aware of and in touch with all our five senses, the more alive we are, the more interesting we are, the more complete we are.

The idea of five senses dates back to Aristotle. Today's neuroscientists would say we have many more senses including temperature, pain, balance, vibration, etc. not to mention the "sixth sense"! We will not go into more detail here but if interested a good source to start is the Brainfacts website (available at www.brainfacts.org/sensing-thinking-behaving/senses-and-perception/).

All the other areas of self-awareness

In this chapter we have just mentioned a few of the most important aspects of self-awareness that won't be addressed anywhere else in the book. But there is also a whole myriad of other aspects of self-awareness, not least those associated with our emotions (the next chapter) and those connected to our values (Chapters 13 and 17). Are we competitive? Are we optimistic? Do we like change? Which emotions are we most likely to react to? Which of our behaviours inhibit the performance of others? What is the perception of others about us? What are our values? Do we have a philosophy about our ethics? And what about our awareness of others?

Questions and actions for personal development

Here are some questions to help you understand and develop your self-awareness. As discussed, we recommend completing self-assessment questionnaires to help in this process. We also suggest you work on the following questions:

1. What does self-awareness mean to you?
2. What do you think are your dominant personality preferences?
3. Which personality preferences would you like to change (either increase or reduce)?
4. How do you learn best?
5. What would you like to improve about how you learn?
6. Which of your five senses are most and least dominant, how does this impact you and would you like to change anything?
7. What do you think are the best ways overall for you to increase your self-awareness?

ACTION: what are you going to do to implement questions 3, 5, and 7, when would you like to achieve it by and how will you know when you have achieved it?

References

Brain Boxx (No date). *Leadership Styles: The Debate.* BrainBoxx. www.brainboxx.co.uk/a2_learnstyles/pages/LStyles_debate.htm [accessed: November 2016].

Daniels, M. (1992. 3rd revised edition published 2014). *Self-Discovery the Jungian Way: The Watchword Technique.* Routledge. Also see www.watchwordtest.com/types.aspx [accessed on: 18/07/2017].

Edlund, M. (2011). *The Power of Rest: Why Sleep Alone Is Not Enough. A 30-Day Plan to Reset Your Body.* HarperOne.

Honey, P. and Mumford, A. (2000). *The Learning Styles Helper's Guide Paperback.* Peter Honey Publications. Questionnaire available at: www.talentlens.co.uk/develop/peter-honey-learning-style-series [accessed on: 18/07/2017].

Jung, C. G. (1971). *Psychological Types, Collected Works of C.G. Jung, Volume 6.* Princeton University Press.

Kolb, D. (1983). *Experiential Learning: Experience as the Source of Learning and Development.* Prentice Hall.

Kolb, D. and Kolb, A. (2005). *The Kolb Learning Style Inventory – Version 3.1 2005 Technical Specifications.* Hays Group.

Society for Neuroscience (2017), Brainfacts.org. www.brainfacts.org/sensing-thinking-behaving/senses-and-perception/ [accessed on: 24/07/2017].

6 Understanding emotions and how to deal with them

John Knights

> *Let's not forget that the little emotions are the great captains of our lives and we obey them without realizing it.*
> —Vincent Van Gogh [1853–90], a Dutch post-impressionist painter, among the most famous figures in the history of Western art, 1889

Overview

Having become aware of how our brain experiences and deals with emotions (Chapter 4) and how self-awareness is so important (Chapter 5), we must now learn what emotions are, how they impact our behaviours, and most importantly how we can manage them. As a leader we need to understand which emotions can impact most on our leadership competence.

What are emotions?

Emotions are amazing things. As discussed in Chapter 4 and Figure 4.3, they are mainly created as a result of charged neuro-hormones being released by the thalamus after receiving direct or indirect information from our natural senses (except smell, which is processed through the olfactory bulb to the amygdala).

The most important point about emotions is they are initiated outside our conscious control. They just happen! There is nothing we can do to stop that. Each emotion contains information, energy and influence. They grab our attention and they want to direct us. They can trigger feelings, behaviours and actions. In essence they are motivational drivers that want to guide our action in the short, medium and long term. The word "emotion" comes from the Latin "emovere" (to excite).

We often use the word "feeling" in place of "emotion" but in fact there is a difference.[1] Feelings are the feedback of the success or failure of our strategies to deal with the emotion (Ghadiri & Habermacher, 2013) and our behaviours are the result of feelings, as we shall see later in this chapter.

There are over 600 words in the English language (Moneta, 2013) to describe the subtleties of the basic emotions. We use 42 facial muscles to express them

(Ekman, 1978) and evidence over the last 50 years has demonstrated that facial expressions connected to our basic emotions are universal, regardless of race and tribe and whether sighted or blind (Matsumoto & Hwang, 2011). So emotions are an animal rather than a cultural phenomenon. However, the demonstration of emotions can be expressed, "broadcasted" and received differently in different cultures, as described in more detail in the White Paper *Leading Across Cultures: Developing Leaders for Global Organisations* (Plaister-Ten, 2017), in Chapter 18, and by Zebrowitz et al. (2010).

So how many basic emotions are there? The most well-known expert on emotions (Ekman, 1972) identified six basic emotions that were tied to distinct facial expressions (see Figure 6.1):

- anger
- disgust
- fear
- happiness (joy)
- sadness
- surprise

Later, Ekman and others developed a number of other templates for combinations of emotions (Handel, 2011). In 2011 Matsumoto and Hwang (2011) presented evidence that a seventh emotion, "contempt", had a distinct facial expression. Or perhaps it is a combination of anger, sadness and disgust?

Figure 6.1 The six basic facial expressions

In looking at the various models (including those from Eastern cultures), we prefer to stick to the original six for our purposes, as some emotions included in other models definitely cross into the area we would define as values (see Chapters 13 and 17). What is very important to note though is, whatever the number, there are more negative emotions than positive ones so we need to learn how to respond to them in a positive and productive way.

Fear is the most important and destructive emotion for a leader to understand. In today's world it is usually not about being attacked or killed as it would have been perceived by our ancestors. In today's world, fear is more insidious – it stops us wanting to change! We fear what we might have to let go of, who we might become, what others will think about us and how we will be judged or criticised. It is the main emotion that stops us wanting to change ourselves or stick to our principles. Overcoming this fear is an important key to becoming a better leader.

> *Fear will prevent us from setting any intent that is likely to take us out of our comfort zone.*
>
> —Altazar Rossiter – author of *Developing Spiritual Intelligence*, 2006

Suggestion: *when we identify fear as the emotion, we need to deal with it. A simple but effective question to ask ourselves is, "what is the worst thing that could happen?" Often the answer is that at worst someone won't like or rate us. By putting this instinctive fear into perspective, its power is significantly reduced into something we can manage.*

The second most important negative emotion most of us experience frequently is anger, which can range from little annoyances to major events. How we manage our anger can seriously impact on our own performance, but most importantly as a leader, our anger can have a major impact on the performance of the people around us.

A real "anger" example

Jo is angry because a client has just delayed a project by one week, which means she will have to re-assess who is available for the revised schedule. So when she notices Ted taking a personal call (unbeknown to Jo, his young daughter has just been taken from school to hospital with a suspected broken wrist), Jo blows up and tells Ted that he is wasting company time and will have to stay on late to make up for it. Jo soon calms down when she realises there is a solution to the client delay but Ted is left upset for days by his boss's insensitive reaction and in fact, this is the catalyst to make him decide to look for another job.

There are a number of aspects of emotions (Ghadiri & Habermacher, 2013) that it is important to be aware of:

- DRIVE: defines the motivation behind the emotion
- AROUSAL: explains how active our emotions are (provides current information and status)
- VALENCE: provides the range of positive and negative (e.g.: fear vs. happiness)
- RESPONSIVENESS: identifies the speed of influence and impact
- EXPRESSION: conveys how it is shown (or not)
- PERSPECTIVE: enables it to be seen over time (managing emotions)
- ACTIVATION: the action – how do we respond (how impulsive are we?)

"Drive" is the most important aspect if we are to understand and deal with the cause of negative emotions. Dealing with the other aspects is useful but is only treating the symptoms.

A note on extroversion vs. introversion, which we have discussed in Chapters 3 and 4: considering all these aspects of emotions the only difference is introverts tend not to express their emotions outwardly, but that does not mean that introverts are less inherently emotional.

Why do emotions still exist?

It is a good question! "Why after billions of years of evolution do emotions exist and what evolutionary advantage do they confer?" As we have discovered in the "Emotional highway" section of Chapter 4 the original purpose of emotions was to enable survival, but what is their purpose today?

Emotions are generated in the amygdala, which is the limbic part of the brain that first emerged in early mammals so as far as we know emotions are a mammalian construct. We know from recent research and what Pythagoreans believed long ago that many animal species display a broad range of emotions (Bekoff, 2000). As such, emotions are and have always been a non-verbal form of communication, which predates language and continue to be very important for our wellbeing and progress for the following reasons:

1. Fifty-five per cent of the communication between humans today is non-verbal (Mehrabian, 1972) with 38 per cent being tonal and only 7 per cent words (Figure 6.2). For example, someone speaks the words "I do not have a problem with you!" but at the same time the person avoids eye-contact, looks anxious, has a closed body language, etc. This body language is caused by emotions and it is emotions that are created in the person noticing that body language. Expression of how one is feeling can be picked up by another empathic being and interpreted, including other mammals (e.g. a female gorilla, smaller in stature and therefore vulnerable in the presence of an angry more physically powerful male).
2. Parents can only understand the needs of a new-born baby through non-verbal communication.

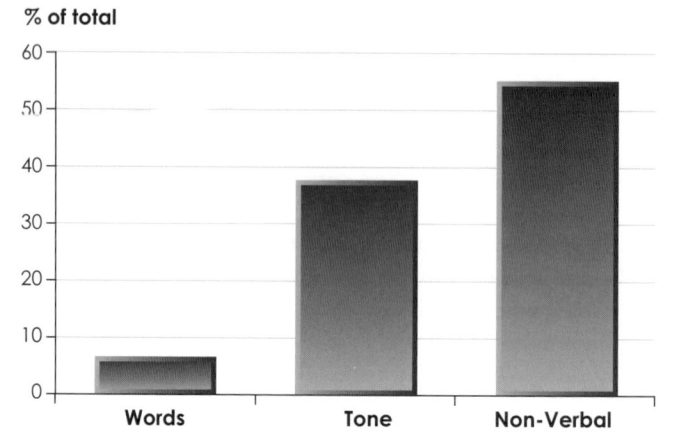

Figure 6.2 Non-verbal communication: words are a low impact factor

Source: Albert Mehrabian: Professor Emeritus of Psychology, UCLA.

How can we manage our emotions?

The essence of managing our emotions effectively is to make sure they don't hijack us so that we don't behave in a way that in hindsight we would have preferred not to. We all do it, but let's see how we can minimise it. First of all we need to understand the time line for managing our emotions. One perspective (Bolte Taylor, 2009) is that our emotions last 90 seconds from the initial trigger to total dissipation of the chemicals from the blood stream so, if our emotions are lasting longer, it is because we are subconsciously holding these circuits open. If we are aware of this then we can learn to let them pass. We should not confuse emotions with the longer-term feelings and moods these engender, such as grief.

You might also have heard that it takes 6 seconds to manage an emotion from the moment you sense it: "Each 'burst' of these chemicals, from the time they're produced, to the time they're completely broken down and absorbed, last 4–7 seconds" (Six Seconds, 2004). Many of us were told by our elders at some time to count to ten when angry, before reacting. It is all part of the same thing. We have a limited time to become aware of our emotions (some say 2 seconds) and then 4 seconds to decide what to do before we get hijacked and our emotions decide for us.

We now know that emotions are felt in response to a situation (real or imagined), which prepares us to take action. To manage our emotions effectively we need to go through the following process:

1. What am I beginning to feel?
2. What do I feel compelled to do?
3. What do I need to be aware of?
4. What important goal of mine is involved or at stake?

5. What is the key issue?
6. What response shall I choose?

How I respond will determine whether I keep on track to achieve my goal or whether I finish up frustrated. This approach would produce a very different outcome to the "anger" example above, as described as follows.

Revised "anger" example

Jo realises she is beginning to feel angry and would just love to shout at someone about anything but knows that when she has done that before it has cause unnecessary unhappiness and in one case resulted in a good worker moving to a competitor. So she needs to channel her anger positively. The goal in this case is to keep the client happy but also to makes sure her team continues to be engaged and hence productive. When she notices Ted making a private call she waits until he has finished and calmly asks to speak to him in a private office space where she asks him to explain why he was making a personal call. Of course, when she hears the reason, she fully understands and leaves him to do what he needs to for his daughter – and offers any help that he might need. Focusing on the very short term, this kind of approach may seem "inefficient" but over the longer term this kind of action will increase engagement, trust, and teamwork – and ultimately productivity.

To help you bring this process to life carry out the following exercise:

Exercise

Think of a time within the last 24 hours where you have had a negative emotion and something happened in a way you wish in hindsight had gone differently. It happens all the time so you will probably have had several! Discussing something with your teenage child? Driving to work? An interaction with a colleague?

- What actually happened?
- How could it have been handled to get a better outcome?
- What would the better outcome have been?

One of the most common strategies we use to manage emotions is to try to hide them or ignore them. It does not work! While you may feel you are controlling your emotions it will be impacting your behaviour or your mood and people will notice; most likely they will imagine it is because of them and that will distract them from their work, their engagement and their productivity.

It is vital that we acknowledge our emotions, understand them and even embrace them. Then we can treat them as our friend and ally and use the information they provide in a positive way to determine our behaviours. To achieve this we need to be emotionally intelligent! See the next chapter, Chapter 7.

> **Questions and actions for personal development**
>
> Understanding and managing our emotions are at the behavioural core along the journey to becoming a Transpersonal Leader. We highly recommend you take the time to work on these exercises to build your awareness of your own emotional intelligence and thus provide a platform for the continuing journey
>
> 1. What are emotions?
> 2. Carry out the exercise (if you have not already done so) about a personal experience described in the section of this chapter, "How can we manage our emotions?"
> 3. How do you normally manage your emotions and what areas need improving?

Note

1 Some languages (such as Finnish) have the same word for emotion and feeling.

References

Bekoff, M. (2000). Animal Emotions: Exploring Passionate Natures: Current Interdisciplinary Research Provides Compelling Evidence that Many Animals Experience such Emotions as Joy, Fear, Love, Despair, and Grief – We Are Not Alone. *BioScience* 50(10): 861–870.

Bolte Taylor, J. (2009). *A Brain Scientist's Personal Journey*. Hodder & Stoughton.

Ekman, P. (1972). *Emotion in the Human Face: Guidelines for Research and an Integration of Findings*. Pergamon.

Ekman, P. (1978). Facial Signs: Facts, Fantasies, and Possibilities. In Sebeok, T. (Ed.), *Sight, Sound, and Sense* (pp. 124–156). Indiana University Press.

Ghadiri, A. and Habermacher, A. (2013). *Neuroleadership: A Journey Through the Brain for Business Leaders (Management for Professionals)*. Springer.

Handel, S. (2011). Classification of Emotions. *The Emotion Machine*. www.theemotionmachine.com/classification-of-emotions/ [accessed on: 18/07/2017].

Matsumoto, D. and Hwang, H. S. (2011). *Reading Facial Expressions of Emotion*. American Psychological Association. www.apa.org/science/about/psa/2011/05/facial-expressions.aspx [accessed on: 18/07/2017].

Mehrabian, A. (1972). *Silent Messages: Implicit Communication of Emotions and Attitudes*. Wadsworth.

Moneta, G. (2013). *Positive Psychology: A Critical Introduction Paperback*. Palgrave Macmillan.

Plaister-Ten, J. (2017). *Leading Across Cultures: Developing Leaders for Global Organisations.* Routledge. http://bit.ly/2fxjNY5 [accessed on: 18/07/2017].
Rossiter, A. (2006). *Developing Spiritual Intelligence – The Power of You.* O Books.
Six Seconds (2004). Why "Six Seconds" – About Our Intriguing Name. *Sixseconds.org.* www.6seconds.org/2004/02/05/why-six-seconds-about-our-intriguing-name/ [accessed on: 18/07/2017].
Van Gogh, V. (1889). *Letter to Theo Van Gogh.* 14 or 15 July.
Zebrowitz, L., Kikuchi, M. and Fellous, J-M. (2010). Facial Resemblance to Emotions: Group Differences, Impression Effects, and Race Stereotypes. *Journal of Personality and Social Psychology* 98(2): 175–189.

7 The power of emotional intelligence (managing emotions)

John Knights

> *Emotional intelligence allows us to think more creatively and to use our emotions as a tool to help solve problems. It gives us the ability to allow our emotions to inform our intellect and power our achievements.*

Overview

After over 25 years, emotional intelligence (EI) is finally becoming mainstream. Not only have many books been written on the subject but we now quite regularly hear the term on the radio, on TV and in films. This is great news because EI is so important in learning to manage our emotions and thus improve our own self-management and relationship building. The problem is that most people when asked – even those who have read a book on the subject – find it difficult to explain what EI is.

In simple terms, it is about managing the development of emotions in yourself and others. If you can identify emotions (yours or others) and then decide how to respond to them in a way that will have the most positive outcome possible in the circumstances and move towards your broader goals, then you are well on your way to becoming emotionally intelligent. It is about channelling our emotions in a positive direction.

Although in my view EI should be a mainstream subject in schools alongside writing, reading and maths, in this book we focus on the importance of emotional intelligence to leadership. We delve into what EI is, the various models that have been developed and why we have chosen a specific one. We introduce the Four EI Competencies, the 19 EI Capabilities and the concept of 72 granular behaviours. We identify the common development needs of leaders and possible gender differences. This chapter is an important lead in to Chapter 8, which connects EI Competencies and Capabilities to specific leadership styles. A self-assessment questionnaire (answers are interpreted in Chapter 8) and a mobile app will allow you to identify your own priority development areas.

What is emotional intelligence?

EI was defined by Salovey and Mayer in 1990 as "the subset of social intelligence that involves the ability to monitor one's own and others' feelings and emotions, to discriminate among them and to use this information to guide one's thinking and actions" (Salovey & Mayer, 1990). It was the first formal theory of emotional intelligence.

EI has emerged over the last 25 years, in parallel with greater knowledge about how the brain works – neuroscience – into an established science. It enables individuals to better manage their personalities, behaviours and innate skills towards maximising personal performance and enabling the improved performance of others. These are important life skills for us all but within organisations they have increasing impact the more senior the leader.

Research projects in many organisations have proved that emotionally intelligent people perform better and are more successful (EI Consortium, 1996). The use of advanced MRI scanning has demonstrated EI as a science (a subset of psychology) that explains how we as individuals deal with emotions and the impact this has on performance.

Daniel Goleman, who popularised EI, defined it simply as being "about learning to manage your personality". Emotional intelligence allows us to think more creatively and to use our emotions as a tool to help solve problems. It gives us the ability to allow our emotions to inform our intellect and power our achievements. His research showed that "success at work is 80% dependent on Emotional Intelligence – only 20% on IQ" (Goleman, 1996).

The choice and development of emotional intelligence models

Having determined in 2002 that emotional intelligence was a key part of leadership development (see Chapter 1) we investigated several different models that were developing at that time. We found that the Goleman/Boyatzis model (Goleman et al., 2002) was the one most suited to our needs for four main reasons.

1. The model sticks to pure behaviours whereas other models included (in our view) values such as "trust" and business skills such as "communication". All very important but potentially confusing when dealing with EI.
2. The model connects directly to six leadership styles (see Chapter 8), which gives leaders an excellent framework for choosing which style to use in which circumstance and which EI behaviours they relate to.
3. We thought the use of EQ as an acronym for Emotional Intelligence, as used in some models, was misleading, and being referred to as Emotional Quotient (as a comparison to IQ – Intelligence Quotient) suggests measurement and hence judgement. As we will explain more in Chapter 11, we prefer to "observe" behaviour and compare it to a "desired" behaviour in

a non-judgemental way. In this way behaviour is seen contextually rather than as a norm against meaningless (and often obscurely derived) global "standards".
4. The fourth reason was that the model could be easily integrated and aligned with the models and research we had developed and adapted to enable the creation of a performance enhancing culture (see Chapter 10).

As a result, this model was the foundation from which we have developed a more extensive platform that integrates emotional intelligence, leadership styles and culture development and through this enables the accelerated development of individual leaders, leadership teams and entire organisations.

The basic tools that allow us to develop individuals, teams and entire organisations are LEIPA® (Leadership and Emotional Intelligence Performance Accelerator) (see: www.leadershapeglobal.com/Leipa) and LOCS (LeaderShape Organisational Culture Shaper (see: www.leadershapeglobal.com/culture-shaper). The use of these tools is described in more detail in Chapter 11 and 10 respectively but suffice to say here that both work by observing granular behaviours and comparing actual observed with desired behaviour.

The remainder of this chapter describes in some detail the theory and practical application of emotional intelligence we follow in our programmes, which is also the theory behind the LEIPA® performance tool.

The Four EI Competencies and 19 EI Capabilities

EI is broken down into the four Competencies shown in Figure 7.1. They are generally best learned in the following order: 1) Self-Awareness; 2) Self-Management; 3) Social Awareness; 4) Relationship Management. However, depending on an individual's relative ability in each Competency the learning might be non-linear and iterative.

Although we discuss Self-Awareness as a subject in some detail in Chapter 5, in this context Self-Awareness just contains the EI Capabilities[1] of Emotional Self-Awareness, Accurate Self-Assessment and Self-Confidence (see Figure 7.2). In fact each of the Competencies is made up of several EI Capabilities as detailed in Figure 7.2.

Each EI Capability is described in Table 7.1. This is a very powerful framework for developing our own emotional intelligence. By breaking down each Capability into four specific behavioural statements as is done in LEIPA®, we can assess where our specific strengths and development areas lie, and at that granular level, it is simpler to find strategies to work on. For example, if you realise you need to improve your empathy it is a very complex construct to get one's head around. However, if you can break that down to the first step, which is "learning to listen attentively" or the second, "giving feedback that you understand someone's feelings", then suddenly these are behaviours we can understand precisely and so find strategies to work on to improve. More details of how to do this is explained in Chapter 12.

Self-awareness

Social awareness

Self-management

Relationship management

Figure 7.1 Four EI Competencies

Self

Others

Self-awareness
- Emotional self-awareness
- Accurate self-assessment
- Self-confidence

Social awareness
- Empathy
- Service orientation
- Organisational awareness

Recognition

Self-management
- Emotional self-control
- Transparency
- Adaptability
- Achievement orientation
- Initiative
- Optimism

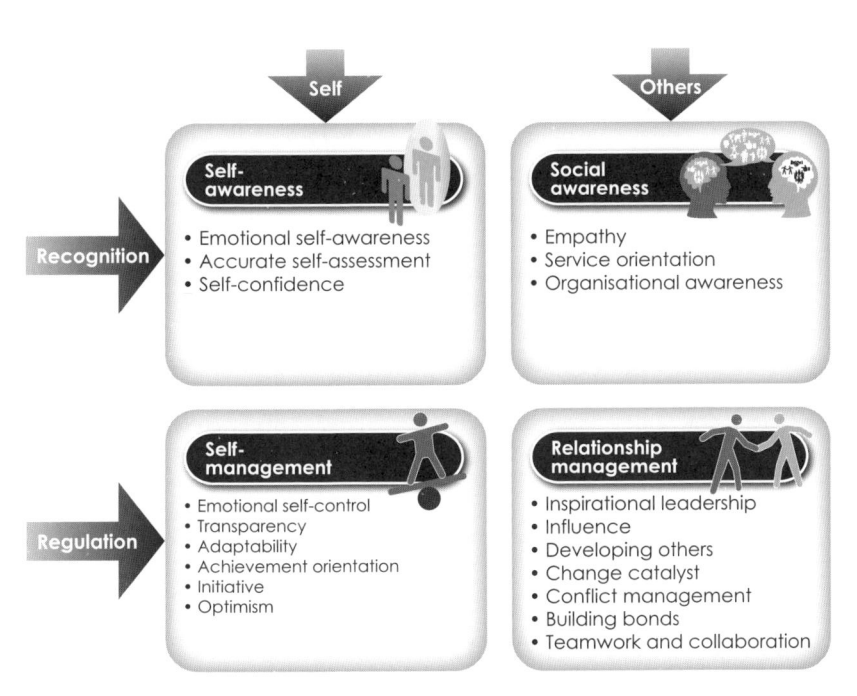

Relationship management
- Inspirational leadership
- Influence
- Developing others
- Change catalyst
- Conflict management
- Building bonds
- Teamwork and collaboration

Regulation

Figure 7.2 Emotional intelligence: the four competencies and nineteen capabilities

Table 7.1 Emotional intelligence Capability definitions

EI Competency / Capability	Definition
SELF-AWARENESS	**Being aware of oneself**
Emotional Self-Awareness	To know which emotions you are feeling and why, realise the link between feelings and what you think, say and do, to recognise how feelings affect performance and take time to understand your feelings
Accurate Self-Assessment	Aware of strengths and weaknesses, appreciate the value of reflection post-experience, open to candid feedback without being defensive and able to show a sense of perspective about oneself
Self-Confidence	Presents with assurance and presence, stick your neck out for unpopular views you believe in, able to be decisive despite uncertainty and pressure, confident in own ability
SELF-MANAGEMENT	**Being able to manage one's emotions**
Emotional Self-Control	Behaves with composure when stressed, does not act or take decisions impulsively, manages emotions effectively
Transparency	Do what you say you will do, acknowledges mistakes, acts according to own values and believes in honesty whatever the situation
Adaptability	Adapt based on new ideas, able to adjust ways of working; handles, uncertainty, ambiguity and the unexpected well
Achievement Orientation	Measurable and challenging goals, flexible in approach, takes appropriate risks to achieve those goals and takes responsibility for the results
Initiative	Seeks new information, starts new ideas, use several perspectives to generate and assess ideas, prevent potential problems through anticipation in advance
Optimism	Positive state of mind, can create the future, setbacks are used for learning and sees the bottle half full
SOCIAL AWARENESS	**Being aware of others and the environment around you**
Empathy	Listens carefully, shows awareness of other feelings, identifies the reasons behind and demonstrates understanding of others' viewpoint
Service Orientation	Meets market need with product offering, concerned to serve others, shows understanding of client needs and expectations and accurate awareness of client satisfaction levels
Organisational Awareness	Understands how things get done, politically perceptive, can circumnavigate office politics and work within the culture of the organisation
RELATIONSHIP MANAGEMENT	**Being able to lead or manage different relationships**
Inspirational Leadership	Stimulates enthusiasm for shared vision, steps forward to lead as required, is a role model and sets standards, uses logic and intuition to make decisions

EI Competency / Capability	Definition
Influence	Skilled at persuading and appealing to others' self-interest, able to build support and consensus, able to get support from influential parties
Developing Others	Recognises the achievements and good performance of others, offers feedback to help others develop, identifies opportunities for others to develop and involves people in decisions that will affect them
Change Catalyst	Identifies and champions need for change, removes barriers, challenges status quo, enlists others, demonstrates the change expected
Conflict Managements	Handles people with diplomacy, spots and discloses potential conflict early, encourages open debate and looks for win–win results
Building Bonds	Proactively meets new people to develop relationships, consistently expands networks and utilises relationships to achieve shared goals
Teamwork and Collaboration	Balances tasks and relationships, looks for opportunities for collaboration, actively encourages all team members and supports final decision of team even if don't agree

Adapted from Goleman et al. (2002)

The most common strengths and development needs

Our research since 2005, analysing the emotional intelligence of hundreds of senior leaders and their development needs through the use of LEIPA®, has provided some extremely interesting results. The original analysis can be found in Chapters 3 and 4 of *Leadership Assessment for Talent Development* (Wall & Knights, 2013). In particular, data analysis of leaders in India, published by Routledge in a White Paper about leadership in India (Bakshi, 2017) confirmed these findings. Since then the analysis of many more leaders has verified the original results. The main findings are summarised as follows.

From the full range of EI Competencies shown in Figure 7.3, the five most common EI Capabilities that are strengths or areas of development among leaders are:

STRENGTHS:

1. Organisational Awareness
2. Transparency
3. Service Orientation
4. Emotional Self-Control
5. Optimism

NEEDING DEVELOPMENT:

1. Empathy
2. Developing Others
3. Conflict Management
4. Change Catalyst
5. Inspirational Leadership

The experience of feeding back to leaders their own results and then coaching them to help them decide the actions they are going to take personally, has provided us with many insights.

72 John Knights

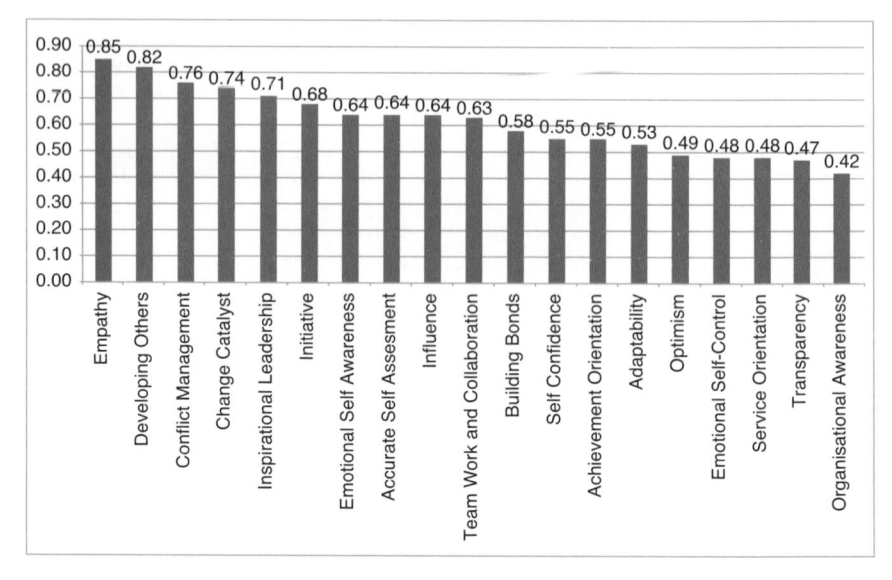

Figure 7.3 Development priority analysis. Measures difference between observed and desired. The higher the number, the greater the development need.

Bar chart values (left to right):
- Empathy: 0.85
- Developing Others: 0.82
- Conflict Management: 0.76
- Change Catalyst: 0.74
- Inspirational Leadership: 0.71
- Initiative: 0.68
- Emotional Self Awareness: 0.64
- Accurate Self Assessment: 0.64
- Influence: 0.64
- Team Work and Collaboration: 0.63
- Building Bonds: 0.58
- Self Confidence: 0.55
- Achievement Orientation: 0.55
- Adaptability: 0.53
- Optimism: 0.49
- Emotional Self-Control: 0.48
- Service Orientation: 0.48
- Transparency: 0.47
- Organisational Awareness: 0.42

Strengths

It is not surprising that individuals who have been successful in being promoted to high positions are *Organisationally Aware*. It was initially more surprising to us that *Transparency* was so high in terms of strengths until we realised that most of the participants in this study were undertaking personal development voluntarily and therefore more likely to be open to their shortcomings. Although *Service Orientation* was a key strength, the focus of most leaders was on customers more than employees.

Emotional Self-Control being a key strength is a double-edged sword. The fact that others saw our leaders controlling their emotions often means that they are good at ignoring or hiding their emotions rather than actively managing them in a positive way. The downside of this is that by hiding emotions leaders are inhibiting their ability to be empathetic or to manage conflict, thus creating a weakness in other areas.

Optimism is the final key strength. A leader must be genuinely optimistic about the opportunities and prospects of the organisation in order to get commitment, buy-in and engagement from followers. Even when times are dire, good leaders maintain hope until an ultimate negative decision is made (e.g. closing the company) and then they need to turn their energy to being empathetic; which brings us neatly to the areas most commonly needing development.

Development needs

Empathy is by far the EI Capability that is most commonly in need of development – 62 per cent of all leaders – regardless of sex, country or sector. Often men just do not "get" empathy unless they are taken on a journey of discovery and women often confuse it with sympathy, the difference being that sympathy is about sharing emotions whereas empathy is more about understanding the reasons for those emotions. Empathy is also not about agreeing but being genuinely willing to listen to the other's perspective and being open to changing one's mind, retaining real understanding and objectivity, rather than using the premise of "understanding" as a tool of persuasion of one's own view.

Developing Others is the second most common area for improvement. The problem here is that most leaders just do not realise that one of their key tasks is to develop the people around them, especially those reporting directly to them. As we shall see in Chapters 8 and 9, this is best done using the coaching style of leadership. Leaders have the opportunity to help people develop virtually every time they communicate with them by providing the right environment, as was described in Chapter 4.

A simple example: *What do most of us do when someone comes and asks us for a decision or for advice? We give them the answer. What do they learn from this? That it is easier to ask the boss than find out for themselves!*

In a development role the leader should not answer the question but instead pose one such as, "what would you have done if I was not here?" or, "what is your opinion", "how do you think I should answer this?", etc. This kind of open question provides both challenge and support at the same time, providing a platform for learning. Over time, your reports will learn to try to work out answers for themselves and come with suggestions rather than questions, and eventually maybe take more decisions without referring to you at all. Think how much more time that would give you to do the things that are important rather than merely urgent!

Conflict Management is another common area where many leaders are not very effective. There are usually two basic problems. The first is that issues are not aired early enough. We tend to put things off until they become more serious and when things do get serious, we are likely to get emotional about them and so often our emotions hijack us. The second is that we want to give our opinion and thus talk first and, frequently, too much! Far better is to put the issue on the table early and allow others to comment from their perspective. Make sure everyone's perspective is understood before trying to move to a resolution. Only that way can you work towards a win-win solution that everyone will accept.

Perhaps surprisingly, *Change Catalyst* is the fourth most common development area. We instinctively expect leaders to be the drivers of change but often they are the ones preferring the status quo; why change something that got them to the top? Change can be seen as a risk and raises fears that it could change their personal status and security. One has to be brave to be a Change Catalyst and be willing to accept opposition from others with influence or authority. Not surprisingly given the above, Change Catalyst has also been identified as the number one blind spot for leaders, a "blind spot" being where they see the need for development much less than the people around them.

Fifth is *Inspirational Leadership*. According to the Boston Research Group (BRG, 2011) CEOs in corporate America are six times more likely than the average worker to believe they work in a company where people are inspired. Inspirational Leadership was covered in some detail in Chapter 3 but the key barriers we come across are that leaders did not involve their people in developing the vision or their behaviour and values did not match the words they used.

Not in the top five, but next in the order of development needs is *Initiative* and also worth discussing. This is an EI Capability that is often misunderstood. We often come across leaders who are great natural initiators but have challenges to carry through or complete those initiatives. They often solve the problem by surrounding themselves with completer-finishers but this is a very linear solution that requires ALL the initiative from the leader even in areas where they may not have the expertise. There are many other leaders who are not so good at initiative and expect it to come from those around them. They feel their role is to challenge and critique any initiative, which often finishes up with followers being turned off from showing any. Then there are leaders of all types that complain that the people around them show no initiative. Often this is because the leader has not let them know that initiative is welcome or what they regard as showing initiative is, or even made it feel, safe to try something different.

The basic problem is that our instinct is to assume that everyone has initiative and it is just a question of whether someone is too lazy or scared to demonstrate it. The reality is that some adults do show initiative more naturally, either because of their genes or their upbringing or a mixture of both. But we should not assume everyone has initiative and it is something that can be learned. It starts with providing a safe, blame free environment where people are encouraged to take initiatives that are a little outside their comfort zone, where mistakes will not have too much impact and can be learned from. Coaching either from a trained senior colleague or an external professional coach can be very helpful in this area for all concerned.

The gender difference

The other striking result from our analysis is that women leaders perform better than men in 15 out of 19 EI Capabilities. The results have been described and discussed in great detail in the White Paper, *Women, Naturally Better Leaders for the 21st Century,* published by Routledge in May 2016 (Young, 2016), but the controversial findings are worth summarising here.

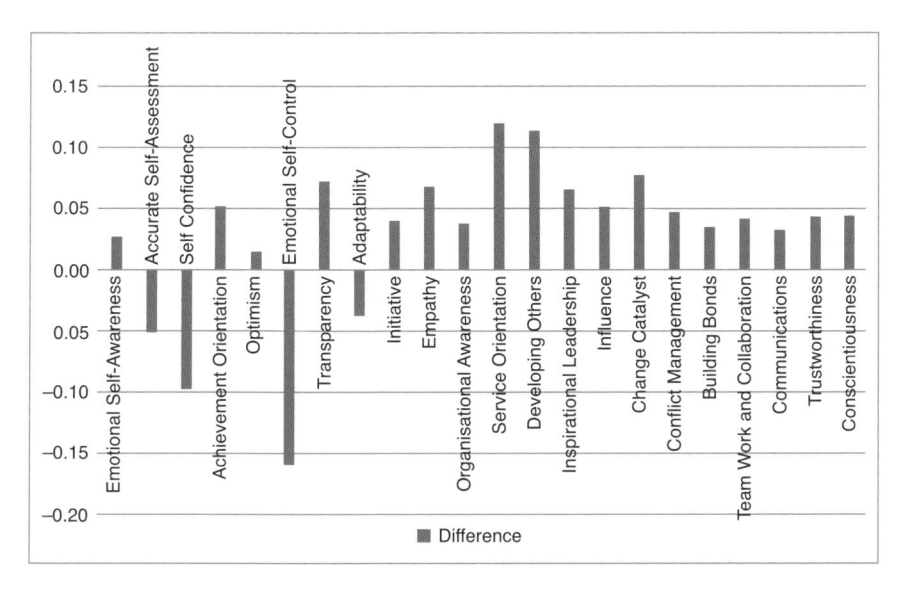

Figure 7.4 Emotional intelligence Capabilities. Shows differences between women and men. Positive difference = women stronger.

Figure 7.4 shows those EI Capabilities where women score more positively than men (above the zero line) and those few where men score better than women (below the zero line). The two with the greatest positive difference in favour of women are *Service Orientation* and *Developing Others* followed by *Change Catalyst* and *Transparency*. The first two are not surprising if we think about it. Our experience of years of working with women leaders confirms that women on average are more caring than men and are therefore naturally more interested in the satisfaction and fulfilment of other people. The second two were a little more unexpected as it shows a greater willingness to take risks either in making decisions or being more open to disclosing oneself. On further detailed analysis we found that women more naturally engage others when pursuing change and regarding *Transparency* tend to be more honest.

The area where men are perceived to be most noticeably stronger than women is *Emotional Self-Control*. Men are seen to behave more calmly under stress and manage their emotions better, although this perception may actually be due to men being better at hiding emotions and feelings rather than managing them more effectively. The fact that women score better in *Emotional Self-Awareness* would support this.

The other area where women lag behind men is in *Self-Confidence*. The one statement where women score most negatively is "Confident in own ability". Also from our experience working with women leaders we find this is actually often the key barrier to success and even promotion, especially with younger, highly competent women. Our view on this is observational but based on many coaching assignments. These women care, sometimes too much, about what others think about them. The underlying cause is often a desire to be liked that results in an attempt to be perfect and initiates the emotion of fear, a throwback to the Stone Age where not being liked could end in being cast out of the family/tribe or even death. In today's world this desire to be liked at all costs can stop a woman speaking out or taking a risk to go for a job she is not 100 per cent capable of doing. An often cited Hewlett Packard internal report claims "Men apply for a job when they meet only 60% of the qualifications, but women apply only if they meet 100% of them" (Hannon, 2014).

One of the best confidence builders for a competent woman is to take a behavioural 360° assessment (such as LEIPA®), which will inevitably provide feedback that the individual is much better than she thinks herself. This real boost and change of perception, combined with coaching, has often resulted in a new self-confident and positive outlook with our female clients being promoted and succeeding beyond their expectations.

It should be noted that self-confidence in this context is not about believing oneself to be the best or demonstrating a dominant persona as one might expect from an alpha male. It is more about being comfortable with who you are as a human being, about liking yourself, and being able to show vulnerability while always looking to develop oneself further. This puts a different perspective on what self-confidence really means – even for men!

Of course any or all of these comments about women's emotional intelligence could apply to individual men too – as could our comments about men equally apply to certain women. The analysis is, by its nature, based on averages and there is a significant overlap between the behaviours of men and women.

However, what this data tells us more than anything is that women, on average, are more emotionally intelligent than men. And while society may not yet be organised to give women a fair crack at senior positions of leadership, there is no longer a valid argument that women are less capable as leaders than men.

Questions and actions for personal development

Continually developing our emotional intelligence is critical to becoming a Transpersonal Leader. Answering these questions will help you to identify your key strengths and those areas you might want to develop or improve.

1. What is emotional intelligence?
2. From Table. 7.1 identify the three EI Capabilities that you believe are your greatest strengths and the three you most need to develop. Note and keep your answers for discussion in Chapter 8.
3. Download and complete the *LeaderShaper* app available from Apple Store or Google Play – just search for "LeaderShaper". This will allow you to do a FREE self-assessment of your emotional intelligence and receive specific advice on how to improve those behaviours you believe need developing. You will see how the 19 EI Capabilities breaks down into 72 granular statements.
4. Complete the questionnaire in Table 7.2 (see overleaf) and then add the sub-totals and totals in preparation for Chapter 8, where you will receive the code to unlock the meaning of your answers.

Table 7.2 Emotional intelligence self-assessment

EMOTIONAL INTELLIGENCE SELF-ASSESSMENT

How often do you carry out/achieve the behaviours described below?

1	Never or Almost Never	1	**Instructions:** Against each statement below score yourself from 1 to 5 according to the chart to the left. Only you will see these scores so try to be objective. Complete the sub-totals and totals for each section as marked.
2	Occasionally	2	
3	Quite Often	3	
4	Usually	4	
5	Always	5	

X

A

1	Know which emotions I am feeling and why	
2	Realise the links between feelings and what I think, say and do	
3	Recognise how feelings affect performance	
4	Take time to understand my own feelings	Sub-Total

B

5	Listen attentively to what people say	
6	Demonstrate an awareness of how others are feeling	
7	Accurately identify the underlying causes of other person's perspective	
8	Express an understanding of other person's perspective	Sub-Total

C

9	Give personal recognition to the accomplishments and achievements of others	
10	Offer useful feedback and help others to identify their personal needs for further growth	
11	Identify opportunities and stimulate individuals to develop to their full potential	
12	Involve individuals in the process of making decisions that will affect them	Sub-Total
		Total A – C

Y

D

13	Present myself with self-assurance and have "presence"	
14	Go out on a limb for what is right including voicing unpopular views	
15	Decisive, able to make sound decisions despite uncertainties and pressures	
16	Confident in my own abilities	Sub-Total

E

17	Effectively communicate and arouse enthusiasm for a shared vision and mission	
18	Step forward to lead as needed, regardless of position	
19	Lead by example and sets standards	
20	Make considered decisions based on both logic and intuition	Sub-Total

F

21	Recognise the need for change and proactively removes barriers	
22	Challenge the status quo to acknowledge the need for change	
23	Champion change and enlist others in its pursuit	
24	Demonstrate by my actions the change expected of others	Sub-Total

G

25	Always do what I says I will do	
26	Ready to acknowledge own mistakes or error of judgement	
27	Actions reflect personal values	
28	Believe honesty is always the best policy whatever the consequences	Sub-Total
		Total D – G

© LeaderShape 2009 – 2017 – this document is the intellectual property of LeaderShape Ltd

Note

1 "Capability" is the name given to a subset of a "Competency".

References

Bakshi, P. (2017). *Leadership in India: A Need to Keep Pace with India's Growth Story?* Routledge.

BRG (2011). *The HOW Report*. Boston Research Group.

EI Consortium (1996). *Consortium for Research on Emotional Intelligence in Organizations*. www.eiconsortium.org/ [accessed on: 18/07/2017].

Goleman, D. (1996). *Emotional Intelligence: Why It Can Matter More Than IQ*. Bloomsbury.

Goleman, D., Boyatzis, R. and McKee, A. (2002). *Primal Leadership: Realizing the Power of Emotional Intelligence*. Harvard Business School Press. Published in the UK as *The New Leaders*.

Hannon, K. (2014). Are Women Too Timid When They Job Search? *Forbes.com*. http://bit.ly/2hVApdv [accessed on: 18/07/2017].

Salovey, P. and Mayer, J. D. (1990). Emotional Intelligence. *Imagination, Cognition, and Personality* 9: 185–211.

Wall, T. and Knights, J. (2013). *Leadership Assessment for Talent Development*. Kogan Page.

Young, G. (2016). *Women, Naturally Better Leaders for the 21st Century*. Routledge. http://bit.ly/2aTBzj5 [accessed on:18/07/2017].

8 Using different leadership styles

John Knights

Most of us have one preferred style, or at best two, which we tend to use all the time. But to be effective in all circumstances we need to have a level of competence in all six styles.

Overview

Now we are more aware about the importance and power of emotional intelligence and have started to work on our development areas, we need to learn how to use emotional intelligence in a leadership role. This chapter provides details of six leadership styles that specifically relate to emotional intelligence. The six styles are described in detail with information about when to use each style, which other styles they work well with, the potential weaknesses or each style, the impact they have, the key EI Capabilities that are associated with each style and other observations about each style.

Most of us have one preferred style, or at best two, which we tend to use all the time. But to be effective in all circumstances we need to have a level of competence in all six styles, which means honing four to five new styles, and that requires increasing our comfort in specific granular behaviours that may not be natural for us.

The six leadership styles

There are numerous academic models for selecting and grouping leadership styles, most of which have a useful purpose. These tend to vary from five to nine diverse styles with the different models often using quite dissimilar words to describe almost the same thing, or sometimes using the same descriptive word that means something different. We found that using the Goleman/Boyatzis model (Goleman et al., 2002) based on EI Capabilities and adapted for our purposes, based on our years of experience with leaders in organisations, has met our needs very well. It also affords us the framework to link leadership styles with our parameters for culture (Chapter 10).

The six leadership styles are summarised in Table 8.1. The impact they have on the climate of an organisation ranges from very positive to usually very negative.

Table 8.1 The six leadership styles

Style	Impact	Description
Visionary	+++	Leads people towards a shared vison
Coaching	++	Enables leaders to build capability in individuals
Affiliative	+	Provides cohesiveness and harmony to a team, group or organisation
Democratic	+	Builds engagement, commitment and buy-in
Pace-Setting	– –	Sets high standards by expecting followers to "do as I do"
Commanding	– – –	Demands immediate compliance to leader's agenda and decisions

To understand these styles in greater depth read the content of Box 8.1–8.6.

Box 8.1 Visionary style

Description: Leads people towards a shared vision that everyone has bought into and owns. Best achieved by taking the best ideas from around the team or organisation and moulding them together through team work in order to get commitment.

When to use: At the start of a new venture, when change is required or where direction has been unclear.

Potential weakness: Leader may think the origination of all ideas and decisions must be their own.

Key matching style: Supported by *Democratic* – to give everyone a voice and be involved – to attain sustainable achievement.

Impact: The most strongly positive style when implemented well.

Key EI Capabilities/Competency:

1. Inspirational Leadership (Relationship Management)
2. Self-Confidence (Self-Awareness)
3. Change Catalyst (Relationship Management)
4. Transparency (Self Management)

See Chapter 7, Table 7.1 for description of EI Capabilities

Note: Occasionally a leader comes along who has excellent ideas and has the charisma to carry everyone with them without using the supporting Democratic style – but this is a very rare exception to the rule. Not recommended for most of us mere mortals!

Box 8.2   Coaching style

Explained in more detail in Chapter 9

Description: Enables leaders to build capability in individuals that are consistent with organisation's goals by helping them solve issues and challenges through listening and asking open questions.

When to use: To help individuals develop. It is a good default style to help individuals become more independent and engaged, and take greater responsibility as a result of building competence. The time spent coaching should be seen as an investment by the leader.

Potential weakness: If not explained, followers can feel it is an abdication of leadership. Alternatively, leaders without training can make the mistake of giving opinions and answers too early in the dialogue and thus undermining the process.

Key matching style: Coaching tends to support other styles, especially *Pace-Setting*.

Impact: Very positive, but needs leader to be trained in order to implement effectively. Usually used too infrequently.

Key EI Capabilities/Competency:

1. Developing Others (Relationship Management)
2. Empathy (Social-Awareness)
3. Emotional Self-Awareness (Self Awareness)

See Chapter 7, Table 7.1 for description of EI Capabilities

Note: It is a very rare organisational leader who has been assertive enough to get to the top of an organisation *and* is also a natural in the Coaching style. Coaching is counter-intuitive for most people and needs to be proactively learned. As we learned in Chapter 7, Empathy is the EI Capability most often needing development in leaders, irrespective of gender or culture.

Box 8.3   Affiliative style

Description: Provides cohesiveness and harmony to a team, group or organisation by bringing people together, focusing on the emotional needs of individuals and building emotional bonds.

When to use: Sensible to use on a regular basis to strengthen relationships and build teams, which will help avoid or heal emotionally distressing situations and provide mutual support in stressful times.

Potential weakness: Bonding "events" can be used as a substitute for genuine care in the organisation and conflict might be avoided rather than managed. Does not, by itself, provide performance.

Key matching style: Is a good support to all other styles as it does not produce performance outcomes on its own. It is the only style that can be used to support the *Commanding* style.

Impact: Positive, especially when used as part of an overall culture enhancing strategy to build caring into the organisation.

Key EI Capabilities/Competency:

1. Empathy (Self-Awareness)
2. Conflict management (Relationship Management)
3. Building bonds (Relationship Management)

See Chapter 7, Table 7.1 for description of EI Capabilities

Note: Leaders who themselves are not naturally gregarious or are introverted may be uncomfortable initiating this style. The good news is it is often something that can be delegated to naturally affiliative members to manage and organise but it is important that the leader is seen to support such initiatives and to participate. Often reluctant leaders get the most personal value using this style!

Box 8.4 Democratic style

Description: Builds engagement, commitment and buy-in by getting input and ideas from team members but also potentially from the broader community, and then explaining the reason for final decisions. It is not about one person, one vote or consensus though that can often be the outcome.

When to use: Especially with high-knowledge colleagues to get commitment, with employees who will be involved in implementing the decision, and also more broadly with major initiatives where new ideas and engagement are needed. In general to give people a voice and help them feel they have been listened to irrespective of whether opinions have been followed.

Potential weakness: If not managed well, can lead to procrastination and a lack of decision-making.

Key matching style: Democratic style is the key supporting style for *Visionary* style.

Impact: Positive, especially when used with expert colleagues and in supporting the Visionary style.

Key EI Capabilities /Competency:

1. Self-Confidence (Self-Awareness)
2. Transparency (Self Management)
3. Inspirational Leadership (Relationship Management)
4. Change Catalyst (Relationship Management)

See Chapter 7, Table 7.1 for description of EI Capabilities

Note: This is an underused style that usually increases the chances of success. Too many leaders think they have, or should have, all the ideas and are best placed to make the decision. Obtaining knowledgeable input from co-workers, other employees or the wider community, and then involving them in the decision-making process, especially those involved in implementing any decision, can maximise the information on which a decision is made and get people committed to a successful outcome. It is not about abdicating decisions to a majority vote.

Box 8.5   Pace-Setting style

Description: Sets high standards by expecting followers to "do as I do" and by setting stretching targets to produce excellence.

When to use: When quick high-quality results are needed from well-prepared, high-performing teams.

Potential weakness: Can cause burn out and stress if used as prime style for long periods, especially with inexperienced, less competent or unmotivated people.

Key matching style: *Coaching* – this is key to help build capability and capacity in individuals while enabling them to set their own goals and targets consistent with the needs of the organisation.

Impact: Often highly negative, because so frequently used in isolation and without the backup of supporting styles.

Key EI Capabilities/Competency:

1. Achievement Orientation (Self Management)
2. Initiative (Self Management)

Negative effect if missing:

1. Emotional Self-Awareness (Self-Awareness)
2. Emotional Self-Control (Self Management)
3. Empathy (Social Awareness)
4. Teamwork and Collaboration (Relationship Management)

See Chapter 7, Table 7.1 for description of EI Capabilities

Note: This is observed as the most common style across organisations – and in our view far too frequently. This style tends to be low on guidance but high on the use of management processes which tend not to take into account human emotions and preferences.

> **Box 8.6 Commanding style**
>
> **Description:** Demands immediate compliance to leader's own agenda and decisions.
>
> **When to use:** In a crisis or as a last resort in critical situations where decisions have to be made quickly and the supporting team has insufficient or no appropriate competence. It may have to be used in extreme cases with employees where no other style has worked.
>
> **Potential weakness:** If used in non-crisis situations can cause demotivation and dis-engagement. Can even be ineffective in a crisis if mutual trust and respect have not been built in advance.
>
> **Key matching style:** *Affiliative* – it is important that a good team spirit and bonds have been built in advance so that when the Commanding style is used people can trust it is being done for an approriate purpose.
>
> **Impact:** Usually, highly negative because naturally commanding leaders have most often not built the trust and respect and do not demonstrate self-awareness, empathy or self-control.
>
> **Key EI Capabilities/Competency:**
>
> 1. Achievement (Self Management)
> 2. Initiative (Self Management)
> 3. Influence (Relationship Management)
>
> Negative effect if missing:
>
> 5. Emotional Self-Awareness (Self-Awareness)
> 6. Emotional Self-Control (Self Management)
> 7. Empathy (Social Awareness)
>
> *See Chapter 7, Table 7.1 for description of EI Capabilities*
>
> **Note:** Outside a crisis, this style tends to be used by sociopaths (unable to empathise) and by leaders when they lose their emotional self-control and revert to genetic/Stone Age default (see Chapter 3).

The leadership style descriptions and other characteristics described are based on the experience of LeaderShape's faculty observing and coaching leaders over the last 15-plus years and understanding how these styles operate in practice in the work place.

Leadership styles in action

It is our experience in India, Africa and Latin America as well as Europe and North America that all *really good* leaders use all six styles during the course of their work, regardless of position, function or business sector. We have also discovered that most untrained leaders have one default style that they use when stressed (almost invariably, *Commanding*) and a preferred style they use for most situations. Most leaders have *Pace-Setting* as their preferred style because it is consistent with the implementation of the management processes they have learned at a business school or other management training, and with the culture of most organisations. This is generally sub-conscious learned behaviour from our away-from-home environment from when we started school. As a result most organisations are fundamentally Pace-Setting.

The problem is that both Commanding and Pace-Setting styles generally have a negative impact on the climate, culture and long-term performance of an organisation because they are treating people as units of production. This deflates intrinsic motivation and any sense of engagement. Productivity can be much higher by developing the capacity, resilience, capability and relationship building skills of each individual so they can achieve more, be more empowered, work together with others more effectively and feel part of something worthwhile.

We have already explained that the Commanding style is appropriate in a crisis and no more so than in the military, police and other emergency services. The potential downside, however, is that this style often continues to be used even when there is no crisis situation, which reduces overall effectiveness and commitment. The supporting styles are particularly important to implement when there is no crisis situation to build the trust and fellowship that enables success when action, compliance and obedience are required.

This does not mean that no Pace-Setting organisations are effective, even though they usually have a higher turnover of staff, greater levels of illness and stress and disaffected employees. What it means is that these organisations could be even more effective if they used a broader range of leadership styles. The more effective Pace-Setting organisations also usually have leaders who are Visionary and use that style but where we find the gaps almost without exception are in the supportive styles of *Coaching*, *Affiliative* and *Democratic*.

Where organisations make an effort to include supportive styles it is often delegated to the HR department or for the organising of "events" to bring people together and make them feel better. There have been so many times when I have heard someone say, "yes, we had a great day doing so and so as a team but it will be just back to normal tomorrow because everyone will still behave the same".

So let's focus on how we can improve the sustainable performance and productivity of the majority of organisations, the Pace-Setters, by increasing the range of leadership styles used throughout the organisation. The first most important style to ensure is present is the *Visionary* style. Without the Visionary style there will be no long-term future of the organisation. We have often found when brought into an organisation to help with the behavioural leadership, and having carried out a diagnostic, that the organisation does not have a coherent vision, mission and/or strategy. In such cases we work with the organisation on the rational elements of their business in parallel with the behavioural and cultural (see Figure 3.2).

The next most important style to introduce in a Pace-Setting culture is the *Coaching* style. For details of how to become a Coaching-style leader go to the next chapter, Chapter 9. What this achieves is a realisation that helping people to find their own solutions that are consistent with the organisation's needs and increasing their personal capacity will over time reduce one's own time that needs to be spent in monitoring and giving instructions, and in its place provide time for the visionary, strategic and supportive roles that are so vital. As the Coaching style becomes more embedded and in turn develops into a coaching culture, the need for having strict processes to achieve goals becomes less important as individuals and teams find better ways based on simpler guidelines. The Coaching style provides the EI Capabilities of Emotional Self-Awareness and Empathy to support the action oriented Pace-Setting EI Capabilities of Achievement Orientation and Initiative.

Case study 1 – true and anonymised

Shalini worked for an international recruitment firm as a senior manager responsible for three teams, each with several consultants who were either responsible for identifying the right candidate for a position or managing a client portfolio, or both, for both temporary and permanent staff. She worked tirelessly working with each individual to show them exactly how to do their job and setting weekly targets of how many calls they should make, etc. Although she was very intelligent, had good values and worked very hard, her team's results were disappointing. She had a high turnover of staff and was not particularly liked by her direct reports.

While participating in an EI leadership programme she had the opportunity to learn about coaching and to practise it both in a safe environment with peers and take these new skills forward in the work place. The change was dramatic, and it was the same for her colleagues in similar roles on the same programme. As soon as they started coaching their people, helping them to work out their own solutions and through that to learn rather than be taught, the staff turnover reduced from 48 per cent to 23 per cent (very low for a recruitment firm) in under a year. Additionally, the time it took for new consultants to come up to full speed and be profitable in the business reduced by a third, resulting in the gross profit produced by each consultant increasing by between 5 per cent and 10 per cent.

We have explained that the Visionary style is the most impactful but it works best if supported by the *Democratic* style. Unfortunately, it is often supported by the Commanding style. In the latter case, the leader has all the ideas (or claims them even if originated by others) and then tells their people to follow instructions. This will cause staff, especially the talented ones (who want to be involved in creating the solutions rather than just following instructions), to very quickly become disaffected and disenchanted.

We have come across a few leaders who understand the democratic style from an intellectual perspective but emotionally just use it to persuade people that his/her own way is best. This is the worst of all worlds because people see it immediately as being manipulative and there is a complete breakdown of trust.

Case study 2 – true and anonymised

Malcolm was the Director of Distribution Operations in the UK and Head of Distribution for Europe for a major global toy retailer. He had been identified as a future top leader of the organisation and as such had been on various leadership programmes held at the company's US-based university and sent on a high level leadership programme to a famous US business school. Although this was helping him build a valuable network it was not producing the effect that was required to promote him to higher levels.

So the organisation appointed a LeaderShape coach/mentor to provide a leadership coaching programme.

The objectives set between the coach, the organisational sponsor and Malcolm were as follows:

- to have a better awareness of how to use different leadership styles in different circumstances
- to make the transition from being a very good manager to a very good leader
- to take a more strategic view of life and business
- to understand better the strategic implications of decisions.

Malcolm and the organisational sponsor identified his key strengths and challenges as follows:

Strengths: communications, achievement focus, keeps high standards, commitment and loyalty.
Challenges: see bigger picture, financial acumen, needs more patience, believing a "half-empty" perspective was realistic, time management.

The leadership coaching programme included learning the equivalent of the content of Chapters 3 to 8 of this book over time and then discussing the implication of this learning in the context of Malcolm's role and future ambitions. Part of the programme was to complete a LEIPA ® 360° (LeaderShape, 2017) process, which revealed that, according to his raters, his strengths were Organisational Awareness, Service Orientation and Achievement Orientation, all in line with the strengths identified above. It also detected a couple of development areas reflecting his identified challenges, namely Optimism and Emotional Self-Control but ALSO two others, Emotional Self-Awareness and Empathy. It was these two latter behavioural development areas that turned out to be key.

His conclusion was, "What is clear to me is that in order for me to create 'resonance' I very much need to work on some of my softer skills – namely Empathy, Emotional Self-Control and Emotional Self-Awareness. While my peers see only the business-related side of me and require different things to change, the people whose feedback I most value are my direct reports with whom I interact on a daily basis and are best placed to provide the most accurate and realistic feedback. If I can change, their feedback and support will be invaluable going forward. In addition, I am going to follow the same approach at home and within my circle of friends. I work a lot closer on a day-to-day basis with my direct reports who are able to provide the more valuable feedback. My peers work 100 miles away and are interested more in the business decisions rather than the personality. They want different things out of our relationship than my direct reports. As does my boss."

As a result of these insights he set the following action plan:

1. Empathy – demonstrate more clearly to people I interact with that I am interested in them. Work on techniques that demonstrate this. Actively seek opportunities to do this.
2. Emotional Self Control – ask for feedback on when emotions came through from team so I can become more aware of this and then how to curb.
3. Emotional Self-Awareness – become more considerate to other people but also consider my own feelings more and how these come across. Create time for self!
4. Developing others – spend more dedicated time with direct reports and stick to it! Hold their regular reviews, be more supportive and understanding.

This led to him developing a coaching style to support his learned Pace-Setting preference and Commanding default when hijacked by his emotions. In addition to all this he also identified from the LEIPA® that he needed to accept more risk if he was to achieve his ambitions and put this into action initially at board meetings by offering opinions on subjects where he was not the expert.

At the end of the programme the organisational sponsor fed back that all objectives had been achieved and he was ready to be considered for further promotion.

Using the Democratic style involves and engages others by giving them both a chance to provide ideas and be involved in how the decisions will be implemented. While the Democratic style is not about one person, one vote, it does give everyone a voice. Most people will accept and be committed to a direction they did not hold if they feel their views are genuinely listened to, considered objectively and then given an explanation as to why their opinion is not being followed. You may be thinking, "all this discussion takes an awful lot of time", and so it might, but the upfront investment in time invariably pays off in the long run.

So it is with all the supporting styles of Coaching, Democratic and Affiliative. It takes some up-front time to set in place but once operational, speeds everything up.

The *Affiliative* style is useful across the board as a team builder and supports all other styles. Any kind of team activity can achieve this from meetings and workshops to promote dialogue, to team activities that have nothing directly to do with the business of the organisation. Different companies organise various kinds of events from a drink down the pub, to team sports/activity events, to charity raising, to working in the community. What is important is that the range of activities (not necessarily each one) enables everyone to be involved and feel comfortable and to be in an environment where they don't feel inhibited. This requires sensitive organisation and a good general rule is to involve a cross-section of employees in the organisation of such events. In fact, the organising of events can be as useful for building harmony as the event itself. But finally, don't forget the water cooler! Impromptu meetings can also often provide opportunities for the Affiliative style.

The goal is about building relationships at the emotional level and understanding who the real person is so that when times are tough people can rely on each other. In our experience one of the best forms of affiliative leadership takes place during our leadership programmes or team workshops. Here we are purposefully delving below the surface for behavioural solutions. Often we are told that one of the unexpected but valuable take-aways was that the participants got to know each other better, to understand each other, and quite frequently people who did not get on well become much closer. The process also sometimes naturally identifies toxic individuals who are a block to team-building – they usually either change or leave.

Questions and actions for personal development

Using emotional intelligence to develop, use and improve the full range of leadership styles is a major milestone on the way to becoming an excellent leader.

1. What are the six styles of leadership, and:
   - Which is your natural default style? What do you notice about the impact it has on others?
   - Which do you use most often? Why?
   - Which do you use when stressed?
   - Which would you like to use more? Why?
   - Which do you feel most uncomfortable using? Why?
   - Which would you most like to develop? Why?

2. Let's see how you rate yourself on the two most important styles (Visionary and Coaching) and which granular behaviours you could work on to improve those styles. Take the form you have completed from Chapter 7, Table 7.2 and follow these instructions (Wall & Knights, 2013):

Complete the sub-totals and totals for each section as marked.

   Now complete the blank rows as follows:

X = *Coaching style leadership*　　　Y = *Visionary style leadership*
A = Emotional Self-Awareness　　　D = Self-Confidence
B = Empathy　　　　　　　　　　　E = Inspirational Leadership
C = Developing Others　　　　　　F = Change Catalyst
　　　　　　　　　　　　　　　　　G = Transparency

You can now observe your own assessment of your competence in seven EI Capabilities but also the two most impactful leadership styles, Visionary and Coaching.

You can rate your competence in the Coaching style as follows:
The maximum score is 60.
If you have 48 or above, you are a natural at the coaching style but may still need to learn specific techniques.
If you have 36–48, you are good but may need some further development.
If you score 24–36, some improvement is probably needed.
If you scored less than 24, a significant improvement is needed.

You can rate your competence in the Visionary style as follows:
The maximum score is 80.
If you have 64 or above, you are a natural at the Visionary style but may still need to learn specific techniques.
If you have 48–64, you are good but may need some further development.
If you score 32–48, some improvement is probably needed.
If you scored less than 32, a significant improvement is needed.

Note: Most leaders in our experience will have a better rating (e.g. "natural", "good", "some improvement" or "significant improvement") in the Visionary style than in the Coaching style.

Finally, take a look at the granular behaviours where you scored lowest compared to your other scores. What would it take for you to improve these scores? Choose 1–3 granular behaviours to work on to improve your leadership.

References

Goleman, D., Boyatzis, R. and McKee, A. (2002). *Primal Leadership: Realizing the Power of Emotional Intelligence*. Harvard Business School Press. Published in the UK as *The New Leaders*.

LeaderShape (2017). *Leadership and Emotional Intelligence Performance Accelerator*. www.leadershapeglobal.com/Leipa [accessed on:18/07/2017].

Wall, T. and Knights, J. (2013). *Leadership Assessment for Talent Development*. Kogan Page.

9 Coaching style of leadership

John Knights

> *Coaching is about developing someone's performance at a rate and to a level beyond their expectations.*
>
> *Many leaders don't realise that one of their major roles is to develop the people around them.*

Overview

All our research and experience, and that of others, has confirmed that of the six leadership styles (see Chapter 8), the Coaching style is the least used by leaders even though it is the second most impactful after the Visionary style. The good news though is it is the easiest to learn because there are many simple proven techniques that can be used to develop and implement this style. A key role of leaders – which is often missing – is to help develop the people they are responsible for. The Coaching style is the best style to use to help people learn in the workplace and develop their potential.

This chapter explains what the Coaching style is and when to use it, and provides several simple steps to become proficient enough to implement it successfully in the workplace.

Definitions

One of the most concise and accurate definitions of coaching is by Sir John Whitmore (Whitmore, 2002), "Coaching is the art of facilitating the development, learning and performance of another". Sir John was one of the most respected proponents and authors of executive and business coaching and his book is an ideal companion for anyone really interested in developing their coaching skills.

As you have read before in this book, there are many definitions of the words we are using. "Coaching" comes in all shapes and sizes: life coaching, executive coaching, career coaching, leadership coaching, sports coaching, etc., etc.

We like to use a stretching addition to Whitmore's definition in order to raise horizons:

Coaching is about developing someone's performance at a rate and to a level beyond their expectations.

Coaching style of leadership 95

The important thing to remember when we are discussing the Coaching style of leadership is that we are not referring to external professional coaches brought in to help individuals for particular reasons or to achieve specific objectives. Here we are referring to organisational leaders using the Coaching style to aid the development of other individuals in their organisation, most commonly those reporting directly to them. This creates an important different dynamic from the role of an external coach who can be totally objective and works in the focused interest of the individual, which experience shows will most likely be beneficial to the organisation as the sponsor of the assignment.

The leader has, as their prime responsibility, the success of the organisation or division or team s/he leads. That success will be aided significantly if each of the people in the organisation reaches their potential. So in Coaching style leadership, the company performance is the prime objective, whereas in external executive coaching, the individual performance is the prime focus.

Also in the Coaching style, mentoring can be an important ingredient if used in the right way. We define mentoring as "using your experience to enable the performance of another". As an aside, in our view all "mentors" should use the Coaching style when mentoring.

Coaching does *not* include discovering the roots of interfering behaviour or treating someone with any mental health issues such as depression. The best and only thing to do in such a case is to refer them to a medically qualified specialist for counselling and treatment.

There is, however, a continuum between mentoring, coaching and counselling as can be seen in Figure 9.1

An overview of the Coaching style of leadership as described in Figure 8.2 is repeated here for convenience in Box. 9.1.

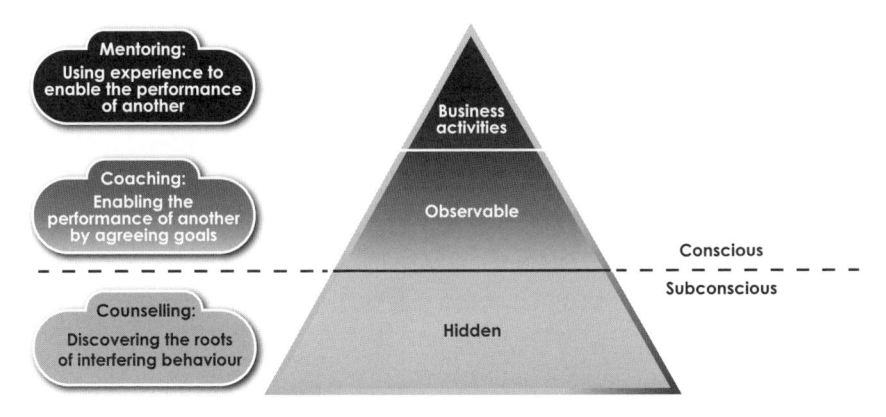

Figure 9.1 The continuum

> **Box 9.1 Coaching style**
>
> **Description:** Enables leaders to build capability in individuals that are consistent with organisation's goals by helping them solve issues and challenges through listening and asking open questions.
>
> **When to use:** To help individuals develop. It is a good default style to help individuals become more independent and engaged, and take greater responsibility as a result of building competence. The time spent coaching should be seen as an investment by the leader.
>
> **Potential weakness:** If not explained, followers can feel it is abdication of leadership. Alternatively, leaders without training can make the mistake of giving opinions and answers too early in the dialogue and thus undermining the process.
>
> **Key matching style:** Coaching tends to support other styles, especially *Pace-Setting*.
>
> **Impact:** Very positive, but needs leader to be trained in order to implement effectively. Usually used too infrequently.
>
> **Key EI Capabilities/Competency:**
>
>   1. Developing Others (Relationship Management)
>   2. Emotional Self-Awareness (Self-Awareness)
>   3. Empathy (Social Awareness)
>
> *See Chapter 7, Table 7.1 for description of EI Capabilities*
>
> **Note:** It is a very rare organisational leader who has been assertive enough to get to the top of an organisation and is also a natural in the Coaching style. Coaching is counter-intuitive for most people and needs to be proactively learned. As we learned in Chapter 7, Empathy is the EI Capability most often needing development in leaders, irrespective of gender or culture.

When to use the Coaching style

The Coaching style should be used to help individuals have the competence and confidence to take on more responsibility, to be empowered, to take more initiatives and to accept accountability. This is achieved by helping them become more aware of themselves and others, manage themselves better, and improve the building of relationships. This is consistent with building their emotional intelligence. How you do that is explained later in this chapter.

Many leaders don't realise that one of their major roles is to develop the people around them, especially their direct reports. In this context we are not referring to sending them on external programmes but how the leader can personally help and support an individual to develop to their potential on a day-to-day basis. For this to happen effectively the leader needs to remove any sense of fear of competition they might feel from their followers. By developing their people, leaders will increase the capability of the team they are in charge of and hence the performance of the organisation, which of course results in success for the leader too.

In many organisations from all sectors and types, we hear that the senior leadership agree on the vision and values of the organisation but that it is not getting through the middle management down to the "troops"; and of course, the middle management are blamed for acting as the barrier. The actual problem is usually with the senior leadership because they do not fully engage with the middle management by using a full range of leadership styles. The default is often a directive style from above to implement a certain new policy. In particular, there is an absence of the Coaching style to support the middle managers to both work out how to implement the changes and also make the commitment to actually do it.

We have also heard many leaders who have concerns that developing their people will cause them to want higher salaries. While this is always possible, greater capability delivers improved results and therefore, arguably, deserves better remuneration, so it should be a win-win for everyone. There are sometimes worries that good people will leave the company for a better job elsewhere as a result of having been developed. In our experience this is more usually the case as a result of an overall poor culture in the organisation or because there are no opportunities for promotion. However, another important consideration in this is if someone leaves feeling that the company has supported and developed them, they will be a good ambassador for the brand and possibly a future customer.

This just shows how important it is for the senior leadership in any organisation to ensure that the encouragement of this powerful Coaching style is combined with a culture and policies that enable these developed individuals to thrive through empowerment and responsibility (see Chapter 10).

There are also other times when the Coaching style can be very useful; with peers, when managing upwards, or even with clients or suppliers when there is a potentially contentious issue to be resolved, where a shared goal is required, or anytime when cooperation will be beneficial.

A really valuable time to use the Coaching style is when someone who reports to you comes to you for an answer to a question or to resolve an issue. Giving an answer may be the most expeditious route to a solution in the moment but, over the long term, it does not provide any development of the individual and they will continue taking up a lot of your time as that process is repeated every time they have a problem. Unless it is specific information that only you possess we recommend that whenever someone asks a question, you work on getting them to answer the question themselves. You can ask questions like:

- What would you do if I was not here?
- How would you solve the problem?
- What do you think we should do?

The answer to each of these questions can lead to a coaching conversation, which in turn will make the people around you more competent, independent and empowered, and over the long term allow delegation that gives you more time for the "important" rather than "urgent". Using a Coaching style is an investment of time that pays off in terms of improved capability in team members and freeing up the leader's time to focus on more strategic issues.

How to become proficient in the Coaching style

Explain what you are doing

To be effective, when you start to use the Coaching style make sure you explain what you are doing and why in advance. Remember, this is a style you have never used before so if you suddenly start only asking questions, and giving no answers, there is a danger that people will think you are suddenly and inexplicably abdicating any sense of responsibility. I have seen this happen and it can be very unsettling.

It is advisable to explain to those about to be involved in any new leadership style you introduce – but especially the Coaching style.

The six step process

The first thing to be aware of is that perhaps the most important aspect of coaching that allows people to come to their own solutions is in the act of speaking aloud and hearing themselves. Providing people the space and safe environment to speak aloud does not take great competence in the Coaching style so it is a great start to the process.

The essential components to become competent in the Coaching style are to learn:

1. a simple process – to avoid jumping to opinions and solutions before fully understanding the facts and the possible implications of these
2. the 1-to-1 communication process
3. to listen effectively
4. how to ask the right kind of questions
5. the use of silence
6. to avoid having an opinion.

Any leader can learn these six simple yet sometimes counter-intuitive steps to become a great coach. Always remember, the coachee should always be responsible for the content of the conversation, and the coach for the process.

Step 1: A simple process

The most well-known coaching model is the GROW model originally developed by Graham Alexander and promoted by Sir John Whitmore (Whitmore,

> **Box 9.2 The "ToGrow" model**
>
> TOPIC: *What issues would you like to discuss?*
> ✓ Make sure you are very clear about this before you move on
> ✓ The topic sometimes needs to be "redefined" later in the session, perhaps after the reality
>
> GOAL: *What do you want to get out of this session?*
> ✓ The goal sometimes needs to be "refined" later in the session, perhaps in the reality
>
> REALITY: *Tell me about the current situation/how do you feel about it?*
> ✓ Ask simple, obvious questions to gain detail
> ✓ Assume nothing
> ✓ Clarify the topic again before you move on
>
> OPTIONS: *What could you do about it?*
> ✓ Options are possible solutions
> ✓ What alternatives are there?
> ✓ What could be possible outcomes of the alternatives?
> ✓ Rate options in terms of practicality
> ✓ Assess any possible pitfalls and potential resistance from others or what support may be needed
>
> WRAP-UP (WILL DO): *So what are you going to do?/What are the next steps (and when)?*

2002). We prefer a variation called ToGrow, which has the elements described in Box 9.1. The essence of the process is to compartmentalise the various aspects of reaching a decision and in particular making sure there is no discussion about possible solutions until all the relevant facts are on the table.

At the start of the process the person coaching asks the coachee what they would like to discuss (Topic). When this is clear the next step is to establish the Goal for the session (this is not the goal for the outcome of the topic as this may not be known yet). It is a good idea for the coach to inform or agree how much time they have for the session so that can be used in judging what might be achieved. If it is a simple topic it may only require a few minutes in an operational setting whereas other topics might require a special meeting of an hour or more.

Note: Sometimes when coaching in an operational situation (as compared with a professional external coach) the topic or issue might belong to the leader. For example, if the follower has had trouble getting to work at a time that meets the organisation's requirements, the leader may want to put that subject on the table to ascertain the reasons behind the tardiness and how it might be resolved.

This approach is much more likely to achieve a good solution for both parties than just penalising the person in some way for being late.

Once the goal for the session is established, the coach starts to explore the Reality of the situation. What is the background and what are the facts? Try to keep to relevant information and if the coachee has a tendency to go into great detail, the coach may need to manage this. On the other hand other people may tend to give very short answers and they will need to be encouraged to expand. The most important thing to remember during the Reality part of the process is to avoid any discussion about possible solutions. The coach is responsible to help solutions develop later in the process rather than during the Reality. On average the Reality part of the session may take up 60–80 per cent of the total time and can include revisiting and maybe amending both the Topic and Goal as more information is revealed.

Once all the relevant facts have been described, the next section of the process is to start asking the coachee what the Options are to solve the issue or topic. The coachee will normally start off with those ideas s/he has already thought of. The role of the coach is to get the coachee to expand the list of options and then discuss their merits and risks. Such questions as, "if none of the options you have come up with were possible what else could you do?" can sometimes help people be more creative and move outside the box.

This is the time when it is very tempting for the coach to mention the options they have in their mind, especially if their ego believes it is also the best solution! The coach leader must resist this temptation at all costs. If, when all options have been listed and explored, you still have an idea that has not been surfaced, this is the time you can move to a more mentoring role. But don't just throw out your idea. Ask the coachee if s/he would like your input on a possible option.

That way even though it is the leader's idea, the ownership of putting another option on the list is with the coachee, who will feel less obliged to accept it just because it comes from the boss. It is important that the coachee believes in the eventual decision and way forward. The final step is to make the decision as to what SMART[1] actions the coachee is going to take to solve the issue presented as the Topic.

Step 2: The one-to-one communication process

It is a two-way communication in at least three steps:

1. The first person starts the conversation by saying something. It can be a statement of fact, a question, an opinion, an issue, etc.
2. The second person feeds back the essence of what they have heard by paraphrasing and using the same vocabulary for key words where possible.
3. The first person confirms either that the second person has heard correctly or corrects or adds to what has been fed back.
4. This can be iterated until there is full understanding.

This is a useful process to use when in any one-to-one conversation to avoid misunderstanding. In a coaching conversation it is particularly important. It does not matter whether the person doing the coaching is the first or second to speak but it is the coach that is responsible for using the process, particularly when there is any reasonable possibility of a misunderstanding or lack of complete understanding.

Step 3: To listen effectively

This is about listening attentively and focusing 100 per cent on listening to what the person being coached is saying. This needs practice but can be aided by making sure that you are not paying attention to anything else; the computer screen, your phone, someone shouting in the distance. Think of yourself being in the zone, focused totally on this individual and what they are saying and showing. Often, when in conversation the temptation is to think about what we want to say next. In doing so we could miss important information because we have actually stopped listening. Sometimes the last thing a person says may be the most important so we should listen attentively to the end.

In this context listening is broader than just taking in the words. As we learned in Chapter 6 (see Figure 6.2) only 7 per cent of communication comes from hearing the words themselves, the rest being the tone of the words and non-verbal communication (body language and expression). Our experience is if you know someone well and are proficient in this focusing, the Coaching style can be used over the phone even though some of the non-verbal communication is lost.

Most leaders can become effective listeners just by removing anything that could divert attention. If it is an important or complicated conversation, move to a meeting room where you will not be disturbed.

Step 4: How to ask the right kind of questions

The most important thing to remember is to ask open questions. Open questions are those that cannot be answered "yes" or "no". The easiest way to do this is to start each question with one of these four words:

1. How
2. When
3. Where
4. Who

We recommend caution in using the word "why" as this can be interpreted as trying to catch someone out or being aggressive rather than just gaining information. "Why" implies judgement, which can feed fear and anxiety, which stifles ideas, initiative and innovation.

By asking an open question you are not providing any information but just providing the coachee with a platform to expand on their thoughts. Remember the best questions are the simple ones, e.g. "How do you feel?"

102 *John Knights*

There are a few other recommendations how to handle questions:

1. Don't ask leading questions. It is very tempting to have an opinion or solution in your head and lead the person towards the same conclusion. But as explained below it is important not to have an opinion. Also, the individual might feel they are being coerced into your decision.
2. Don't keep jumping in with questions. Allow a few seconds between when the coachee stops talking and you asking another question. This allows thinking time and an opportunity for the coachee to continue.
3. Ask questions to clarify and flesh out issues. Don't be afraid to dig deep but only if relevant rather than just out of personal curiosity.
4. A good question to ask when you feel that you are coming to the end of a section of the discussion is, "what else would you like to add before we move on?"

Step 5: The use of silence

This can be very powerful and useful but it must be used with care to avoid it becoming a battle of wills. If both parties understand the power of silence there is always a danger that it becomes a competition. It is also advisable to remove direct eye contact during silence so the other person does not feel intimidated.

However, all that being said, silence can be very powerful in allowing people to speak at a deeper and more revealing level than they otherwise

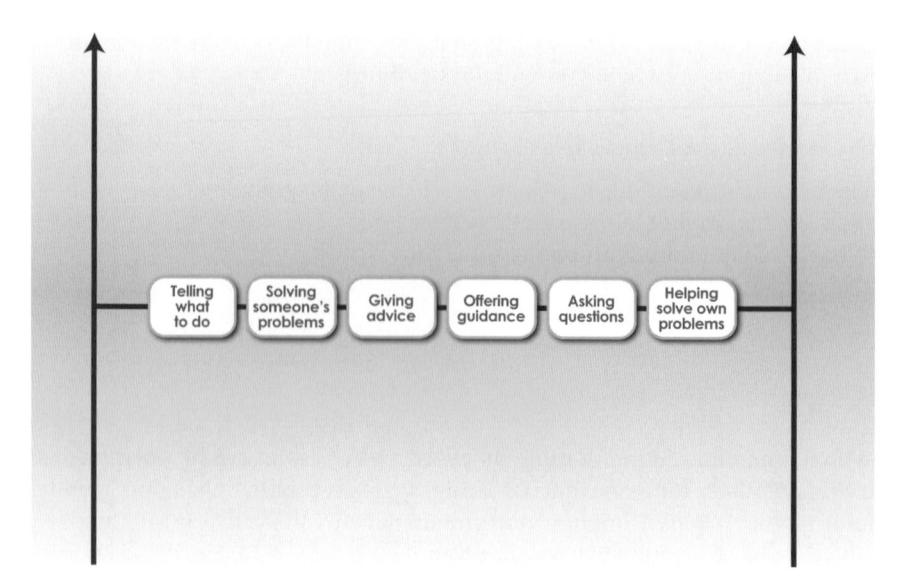

Figure 9.2 Spectrum of 1:1 styles

Source: © LeaderShape 2016. All rights reserved.

would. We as humans have a natural tendency to want to fill any gap in a dialogue and thus miss the opportunity to hear the more useful information that tends to come towards the end of a person's statement – often after they think they have finished, as that is when the subconscious brain processes comes into play.

If the coachee starts to play a game around silence, bring that issue out in the open, explaining that your reason to allow silence is to give more time for the coachee to think through what more they may have to say and that it is not being done to establish superiority.

Step 6: To avoid having an opinion

This is often the most difficult aspect of coaching to achieve, especially for a leader who is usually expected to give opinions and make decisions. But the process will be far more effective if first you can avoid letting your opinion jeopardise the process and second, when more experienced, avoid having an opinion altogether. Our experience is that this improves rapidly with practice.

What is your natural 1:1 style?

Take a look at Figure 9.2 and from the six white boxes decide which phrase most closely represents the style you use most during one-to-one conversations with the people who report to you.

Having decided, now go to Figure 9.3 to see how your most used style fits into the spectrum for you to develop the capability of the people in your organisation. Moving your style towards the right will enable the Coaching style to be used more frequently and successfully.

Challenge vs. nurture

Challenge = Robust + Stretching
Nurture = Supportive + Encouraging

It is important to know our natural default approach to coaching. Are we basically someone who likes to challenge and the nurturing comes hard to do or are we a natural nurturer? This is an important distinction, not only for you as the coach but also for coachees who will be more motivated by one of the approaches. You have probably heard top football managers say that some of their players need an arm around the shoulder whereas others need a kick up the backside. So it is when coaching in the workplace. It is important to understand what your own preference is and, more importantly, what is most likely to motivate the coachee. The best coaches provide a balanced approach and adapt their style depending on the coachee and their needs.

When the balance between nurturing and challenging is wrong, performance will decrease. Too much nurturing will encourage acceptance of mediocrity

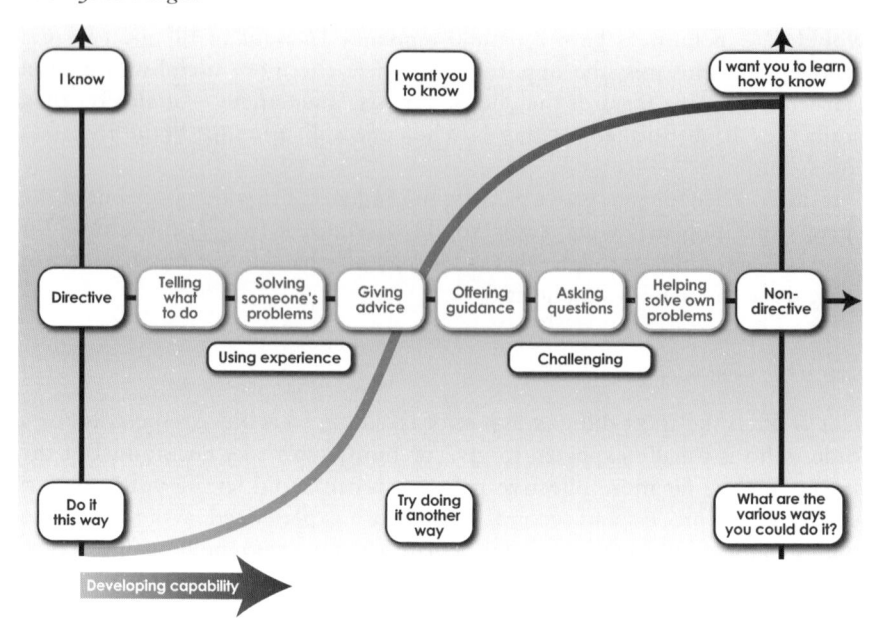

Figure 9.3 Spectrum of 1:1 styles

Source: © LeaderShape 2016. All rights reserved.

and complacency. Too much challenge will result in fear and anxiety. If in doubt, start with nurturing to bring confidence then challenge to bring performance. This cycle can be repeated, building confidence then applying stretch to continually build performance.

If you are a challenger then learning how to be more empathetic is well advised. Fortunately, as I found personally when I started to coach, the act of coaching is a great way to naturally develop your empathy because the process forces you to listen and really understand the issue and what lies behind the more obvious facts. If you are a default nurturer then the odds are you will find coaching more natural and comfortable in the beginning. But the danger is that the coaching process does not achieve its potential without some challenge built into the system. You may be empathetic but as you learn more about issues it may convert to sympathy, with you sharing the emotions rather than helping the coachee to deal with them. So you may need to force yourself out of your comfort zone into being more demanding in following the ToGrow process.

Good luck in developing your Coaching style – you will be amazed how learning to use the Coaching style will have such a positive impact on what you and your team can achieve.

> **Questions and actions for personal development**
>
> Answering the questions below will assist in you developing your coaching style skills.
>
> 1. Describe the Coaching style of leadership.
> 2. When is it useful to use the Coaching style of leadership?
> 3. What is the single most important act that enables people to reach their own solutions?
> 4. What are the six essentials of coaching you need to learn to become effective?
>
> Now for some practice:
>
> 1. Practise coaching, ideally in a triad where all three are learning the Coaching style. Take turns to coach each other on a real issue, with one person being an observer.
> 2. At the end of each coaching session, first the coach says how they think they did, then the coachee describes how it was for them and the value derived, and finally the observer gives their view, in particular referring to the six steps.
> 3. Complete two or three triad sessions over a couple of weeks and then start practising with your direct reports but remembering to explain what you are doing in advance. Ask for feedback on how it felt for them.
> 4. Continue this process until it starts to become natural – and then just use the Coaching style as an important part of your leadership style portfolio.

Note

1 Specific, Measurable, Achievable, Relevant, Timed.

References

Whitmore, Sir J. (2002). *Coaching For Performance: Growing People, Performance and Purpose (3rd revised edition)*. Nicholas Brealey Publishing.

10 Creating a performance-enhancing culture

John Knights

All leaders of organisations, divisions or teams set a climate whether they intend to or not.

Overview

"Culture eats Strategy for breakfast" is often attributed to Peter Drucker, the great management guru. Of course you need both but in our experience if a company does not have the right culture the strategy will neither be attainable or sustainable. With the right culture, strategy can be more emergent and flexible to respond to our fast changing world.

The first step in creating a performance-enhancing culture is for the leadership of the organisation, primarily the CEO, to establish the right climate by being consistent in its core values and behaviours. Actually changing the culture in any organisation takes longer and requires the engagement and commitment of most of its people.

We define culture in four parameters (Power, Structure, Achievement and Support) and each parameter is specifically related to one or two of the six leadership styles we covered in Chapter 8. So by identifying the "Actual" and "Ideal" cultures for an organisation using these parameters, we can first identify the leadership styles the leaders need to use and also the granular behaviours the organisation needs to focus on in order to move towards the Ideal. This is achieved using a unique culture survey. We demonstrate how the desired culture of an organisation can be created by focusing on a few granular behaviours.

In order to get individuals to buy into and own the commitment to the desired culture it is important that there is an explicit and understood contract between each individual leader and each person reporting to them.

Definitions

The two most important words to define in this chapter are climate and culture.

Climate: the philosophy, attitude, spirit, beliefs and values of the organisation that is set by the top leader or leadership team and communicated and received by the people in the organisation.

Daniel Goleman (Goleman, 2000) explains how Richard Litwin and Richard Stinger (Litwin & Stringer, 1968) and David McClelland (McClelland, 1998) developed a definition of climate as six factors that influence an organisation's environment:

1. *Flexibility* by minimising red tape
2. sense of taking *Responsibility*
3. level of *Standards*
4. aptness of *Rewards*
5. *Clarity* about mission and values
6. getting *Commitment* to a common purpose.

My view is that the first five are all firmly in the *climate* camp whereas getting commitment is the result of climate and more a desirable trait of the *culture*.

Culture: The simple standard definition used throughout the business world is, "how we do things around here". We have no reference for where it originated, maybe (Bower, 1966), but alone we believe it is insufficient. We think an organisation's culture should include an inbuilt desire to improve so our definition is, **"how we do *and improve* things around here"**. This implies a willingness to change continuously, not just for the sake of it, but with improvement always in mind.

Every organisation has its own culture, be it a business, a charity, the government, the local community or our family. We believe there are three prime purposes to culture:

1. to do what we do as effectively as possible
2. to continue to improve what we do and how we do things
3. to enjoy what we do.

One is not sustainable long term without the others and for each of us to perform effectively we need to understand the culture we work in both as individuals and as teams. Culture should be a means to achieving the goals of the organisation but as we shall see later in this chapter, the Ideal culture turns out to be remarkably similar across all organisations.

The difference between climate and culture

Climate is about setting the scene and the style and communicating and role-modelling the philosophy, attitude, spirit, beliefs and values of the organisation. Climate impacts culture, for good or bad, rather than the other way around. You can't change the culture without changing the climate first – which firmly rests with the leaders of the organisation. These are all aspects of Transpersonal Leadership that we cover in Part 2 of the book.

Culture, on the other hand, is primarily about behaviours, that is, implementing the climate into "the way we do and improve things around here". As we shall discover, emotional intelligence drives culture. Culture is changed by the influence of all the people in the organisation.

Climate can be very quick to establish, and is often changed rapidly when a new leader is appointed. Any incumbent leader can change the climate too (see Case study 1). Culture, however, takes time to change; more likely to be measured in years. The reason for this is the natural human resistance to change due to fear and because ingrained habits need to change, requiring a rewiring of the brain that is energy intensive.

Climate and culture are intrinsically linked.

The importance of climate

The easiest and best time to set the climate is when new in the post, but with effort it can be done at any time. It is not what a leader may think should be done but what they *actually* do and do consistently themselves. They can set the scene with words but they must quickly demonstrate the climate they wish to create by their actions and behaviours.

Case study 1 – true and anonymised

Raphael is the head of the international operations of a major European charity. He was brought on board because of his commercial experience and to drive a major initiative in Africa. He had excellent values in terms of integrity and courage and built a highly intelligent team around him. He was also a very nice person socially. But with his background in hierarchical cultures and organisations, he believed he should have the vision and albeit politely, tell people what to do. He preferred verbal dialogue to written reports and he had a one-to-one relationship with each of the project leaders in his team. Additionally, Raphael was very busy. The result was decisions were delayed, key staff were stressed because they were very busy, but not involved, and therefore had not fully bought into the decisions they had to implement. After the first two years he was ahead of schedule with his goals but the situation was not sustainable and he was considered unreliable by other senior executives, despite his enormous achievement.

He realised that to bring sustainable success to this 6-year project, he had to change the climate in order to build the right culture in the organisation. With the support of the CEO, he engaged himself and his team in a leadership programme and personal coaching. The first action he took was to tell everyone that he was not satisfied with his own performance and wanted to change his leadership style to become more democratic in decision-making and use the coaching style to help develop the capability of his bright team. In addition, he encouraged the project leaders to work more closely together and made an effort to better manage his time and ensure all decisions were recorded in writing. This created

> a climate where the whole team felt more valued and as a result felt ownership in the success of the venture.
>
> The project is not complete yet but this is a great example of how a leader with great potential was able to move away from his default modus operandi to change the climate through honesty, transparency and being willing to be vulnerable.

Perhaps the most recent globally publicised examples of how leaders set a climate are those of the US presidents Obama and Trump. Just compare the different climates they set when they first came to power, the impact they had, and in who they attracted to their cause and who disconnected.

All leaders of organisations, divisions or teams set a climate whether they intend to or not. It can be good or bad. It is best when the climate is consistent across the organisation. There will always be some variation because a climate will always depend to some extent on the unique character of each leader. Very different climates set by different leaders within one organisation can, however, be quite disruptive. But whatever the form, it must be authentic, credible and supported by actions.

As an example of the importance of climate, in a study of 19 insurance companies, climate created by the CEOs among their direct reports predicted the business performance of the entire organisation. In 75 per cent of cases, climate alone accurately sorted companies into high vs. low profits and growth (Goleman et al., 2002). According to Goleman (Goleman, 2000), climate alone does not determine performance, but overall, it can account for 20–30 per cent of business performance.

Creating and maintaining the right climate is the most important sustainable achievement of any leader. This will in turn enable the right culture to develop over time.

Culture: the link between leadership and performance

Culture plays a vital role in the relationship between leadership and performance, and this differs depending on whether the leadership is Transformational or Transactional.

Transformational Leadership involves the four positive leadership styles (see Chapter 8): Visionary, Democratic, Coaching and Affiliative. It was originally introduced as a concept where "the best leaders are those who inspire others to come together toward the achievement of higher aims" (Burns, 1978). Detailed research (Bass, 1985) showed that followers of such a leader feel trust, admiration, loyalty and respect for the leader and because of the qualities of the Transformational Leader are willing to work harder than originally expected. These outcomes occur because the Transformational Leader offers followers something more than just working for personal gain; they provide

110 *John Knights*

followers with an inspiring mission and vision and give them an identity, which creates intrinsic motivation.

Transactional Leadership comprises primarily of the Pace-Setting and Commanding leadership styles combined with a lot of management. This term was also developed by James Burns and Bernard Bass and is explained as providing reward in exchange for effort and good performance but punishing non-performers without considering the reasons behind the under-performance. The management might be active (checking deviation from rules and standards), passive (intervening only if standards and targets are not met) or laissez-faire (abdication of responsibility and avoiding decisions). There is significant evidence that incentive schemes do not work (Kohn, 1993; Fisher, 2016), which undermines the likely effectiveness of this equation for success.

As we can see from Figure 10.1, on the left hand side, Transformational Leadership comes from the leader setting a positive climate that enables the development and improvement of the right culture for the organisation, which in turn produces enhanced performance. Leaders may have direct impact on the performance of an organisation, for example when they are leading a major project such as an acquisition, partnership or client relationship, but generally, the leaders rely on the people at the sharp end of the business and those that support them to provide the outstanding everyday performance. And that only comes from an excellent culture.

In Figure 10.1, on the right hand side, we see the culture model for Transactional Leadership where the culture reacts to the performance of the

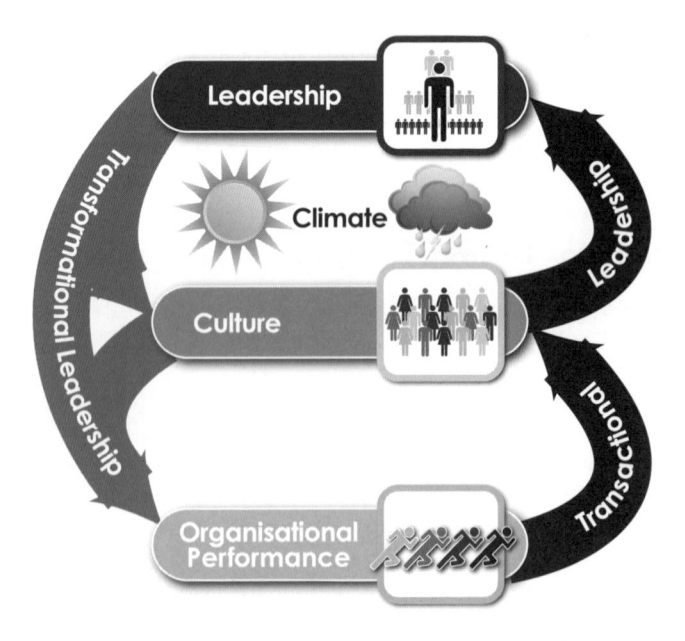

Figure 10.1 Transformational and transactional culture

organisation. This may be dependent on external events but also very often because the leaders are not setting a climate conducive to producing a transformational culture. Transactional leadership can be acceptable in times of crisis or where there is urgency for a short-term outcome but if it exists for longer periods, the leadership needs to reset the climate to reinstate the transformational leadership. Bass found that most leaders he came across in his research in the 1970s and '80s were primarily Transactional Leaders and this finding is totally consistent with our own current experience and research, which shows that Pace-Setting leadership is still dominant in most organisations (see Chapter 8). HR directors in the UK still rate performance management as the most important leadership skill/behaviour, which will continue at least until 2020 (CIPD, 2017).

The complete story of how leadership impacts performance as explained above can be seen in Figure 10.2.

The greatest impact that leaders can have on the culture after creating the right climate, and hence organisational performance, is through using the Coaching style of leadership with their direct reports. This builds capability, engagement, ownership and empowerment (see Chapter 9). We believe this should be repeated throughout every level in the organisation. One of the reasons most organisations do not perform at the level they could is because the Coaching style is still so rarely used.

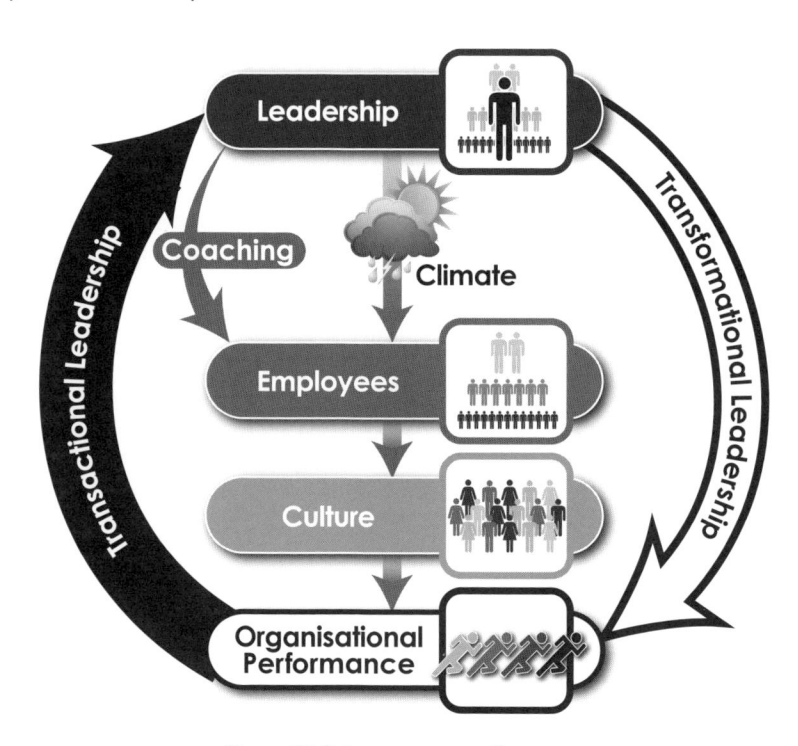

Figure 10.2 Impacts on performance

The four culture parameters

From earlier chapters we know that our genes and personal development can impact our performance, but so does the environment we operate in. So it is critical to develop a performance enhancing culture.

The way we achieve this is to establish the key factors (we call them "parameters") that define a culture and then link each of them to one or more of the six leadership styles we have identified and discussed in Chapter 8. If we measure the parameters for both the Actual and Ideal culture, we can identify the current leadership styles that dominate and the leadership styles that are required to achieve the Ideal. With the right kind of culture survey tool, we can identify specific granular behaviours within each parameter that will take the organisation from the current Actual state towards the Ideal.

The framework for linking leadership to performance via culture has been well demonstrated by Ogbonna and Harris (Ogbonna & Harris, 2000) when they investigated the responses from over 300 UK leaders of substantial organisations. We combined this with the findings of the original seminal article on organisational culture types by Roger Harrison (Harrison, 1972), which was popularised by Charles Handy with whom Harrison worked for a number of years (Harrison, 1987). This provided an appropriate concept for defining culture by different parameters and fitted into our framework, which included linking the parameters to the six leadership styles.

We identify the four parameters as Power, Structure, Achievement and Support (see Figure 10.3). An explanation of positive and negative traits of these parameters can be found in Table 10.1.

We have analysed the results of the LOCS Culture Shaper tool (LOCS, 2017) over 10 years. This tool identifies 60 distinctive, indicative behaviours for both the Actual and Ideal culture. When answering the questions online, participants are not aware that any of the behaviours described relate to a specific culture parameter so they cannot be influenced by the name of the

Figure 10.3 The four culture parameters

Table 10.1 Culture parameters: positive and negative traits

Positive traits	Negative traits

POWER
Based on inequality and control of access to resources

– Strength	– Rule by fear
– Justice	– Abuse for personal advantage
– Benevolence	– Intrigue/politics
– Depends on accepting legitimacy of hierarchy and inequality	– Knowledge is power

STRUCTURE
Based on structures and processes

– Stability	– Impersonal
– Efficiency	– Assumes people are not trusted
– Clear expectations	– Absence of empowerment
– Followers are protected from arbitrary exercise of authority	– Controls stifle innovation
– People know what is expected and are trained to perform	– Slow to make changes

ACHIEVEMENT
Based on rewards for achievement (rewards may be ego or non-ego based)

– Alignment to vision, values and purpose	– Burn-out
– Allows self-management	– Different visions may create confusion
– High morale and energy	– Lacks focus on planning
– Values are even more important than profit and growth	– Arrogance, elitism, lack of cooperation
– Failure provides learning opportunities, leading to innovation	– Overrides ethics

SUPPORT
Based on trust and empathy

– Sociable, helpful and understanding	– Conflict avoidance and need for consensus leads to paralysis
– Fosters warmth and caring	– Equality can swamp capability differences
– Lots of help and understanding	
– Non-judgemental of others	– Tough decisions avoided because of need for kindness
– Seeks harmony – avoids conflict	
– People make the extra effort	– May support anti-management behaviour

Adapted from the work of Roger Harrison (Harrison, 1987)

114　*John Knights*

parameter. All organisations we have analysed demonstrate that they are a blend of all four culture parameters. These are our key findings:

1. The Actual culture is usually perceived differently in different parts of an organisation, be it different locations (national or international), or across the hierarchy of organisations, divisions or departments within organisations. This is true for private, public and not-for-profit organisations.
2. Power and Structure are invariably higher than people desire, and Achievement and Support lower. By exception, Structure may remain at the same level between Actual and Ideal especially in situations where performance is highly reliant on safety or security (see Case study 2).
3. Power is usually the parameter that people would like reduced most and Achievement the parameter people would like to increase the most.
4. In general the higher up the hierarchy of the organisation, the perception of the Actual culture is closer to the Ideal. That is, the more senior the individual (except someone new to the organisation), the more likely they are to believe the Actual culture is closer to their expressed Ideal.
5. The most amazing finding though is that when it comes to the Ideal, the vast majority of individuals and virtually all organisations we have been involved with, irrespective whether these are in the Western World, India, Latin America or Africa, come up with a similar desired Ideal culture profile (see Figure 10.4). This Ideal profile shows Achievement as the most important, followed by Support, then Structure and, finally, Power. What this demonstrates, even though we do not at this time have results from China, Japan or the Middle East, is that this Ideal culture would seem to be driven by human nature rather than the influence of a business sector, or even a national or ethnic culture.

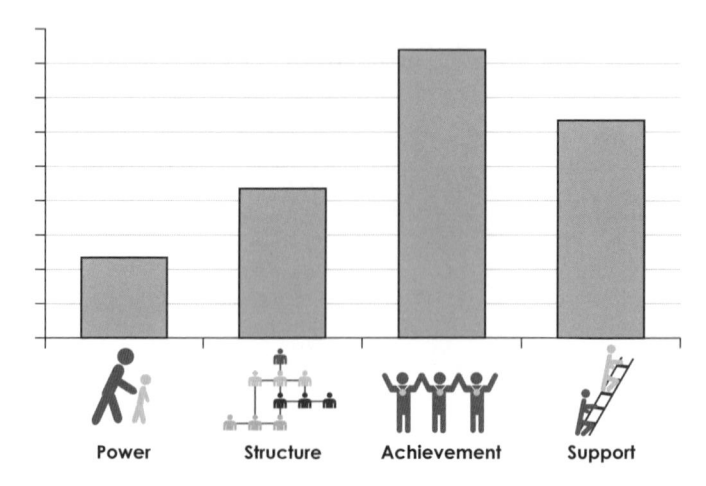

Figure 10.4 Ideal culture in the twenty-first century?

Of course there are differences in national, ethnic, religious and sector cultures but many of these are about customs, manners and morals as discussed in Chapter 18, and the White Papers on *Ethical Leadership* (Knights, 2016) and *Leading Across Cultures* (Plaister-Ten, 2017) published by Routledge. But here we are focusing on basic human behaviours, which we find seem to be universal and support the discussion in Chapters 3 and 4.

The benefit of identifying the Ideal culture for the organisation is that it gives the organisation a beacon to aim for. From this we can identify which leadership styles need to be used more and which less, and also which key granular behaviours need to be changed across the organisation in order to promote those leadership styles that will, in turn, enable the development of the Ideal culture.

Figure 10.5. shows which leadership styles relate to which culture parameters. These links between styles and culture parameters first came to our attention in the research of Ogbonna and Harris mentioned previously, which allowed us to develop our model of linking it with the work of Roger Harrison and Daniel Goleman. The results of our own research since 2005 support the findings of Ogbonna and Harris.

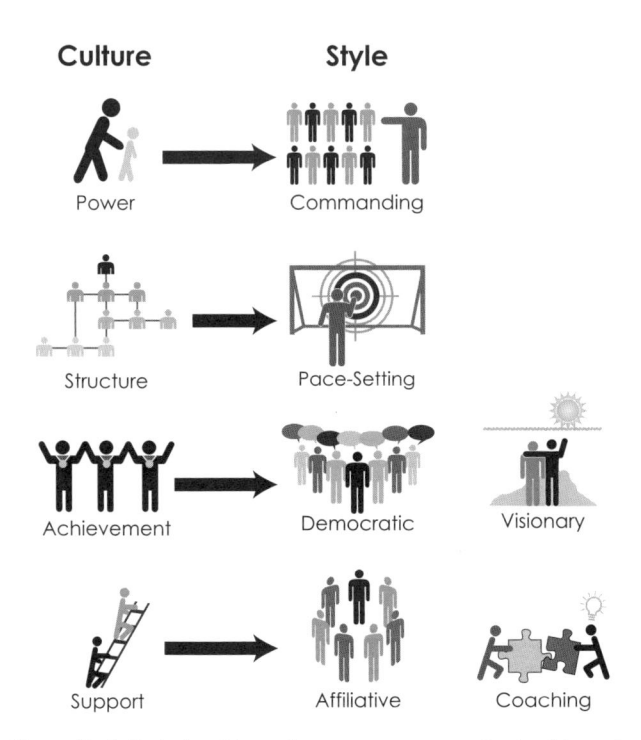

Figure 10.5 Relationship: culture parameters vs. leadership styles

Case study 2 – culture survey: true and anonymised

The natural gas storage division of a major energy company had a near disaster the year previously due to an accidental large release of gas, which fortunately did not explode. As a result of this event, and perhaps also because of a very stable and ageing workforce, the organisation had become extremely risk averse, not just from a health and safety perspective but also in meeting its strategic goals. There was a perceived need for more engagement and initiative.

In brief, the results of the LOCS© survey identified the following:

- A desire to significantly reduce the Power parameter (Commanding style of leadership).
- To keep the Structure parameter about the same (i.e. Pace-Setting style) – this is an unusual exception compared to most organisations because of the inherent safety risks.
- More or less equally increase the Achievement and Support parameters (thus an increase in Visionary, Democratic, Coaching and Affiliative styles).
- The two granular statements that most needed to be removed from the culture were: "Employees are treated as human machines to be directed from above", and "To survive in the organisation an employee must learn who is important and what behaviours are acceptable".
- The statement that most needed to become the norm in the Achievement parameter was: "One person has legitimate authority over another when using greater competence and knowledge to support the other."
- The statement that most needed to become the norm in the Support parameter was: "Different work groups are very friendly and responsive to requests for help."
- Overall there was a realisation that leaders needed to do more listening, that the different functions needed to work better together, that teams needed to function better at having collective responsibility and covering for each other, and finally that the leadership needed to engage the staff by involving them in the decision-making and through that, increase commitment.

The "Aha!" moment for the management came in the follow-up workshop when they realised that at the point of the incident they did what any organisation should do in a crisis: that is, use the Commanding style predominantly, backed up by adherence to processes and procedures.

However, what they had failed to understand was that as soon as the crisis was averted the leadership style needed to change. Instead they continued with the Commanding style, telling intelligent people what to do. This is a sure fire recipe for disengaging colleagues, which was in fact what resulted. The upshot of this was the leadership first of all fed back the findings of the survey and articulated not only why, but how things were going to change. The senior leadership received coaching to understand in turn how they could coach. The leaders of the organisation got out of their offices and walked the job, not to check but to listen. Gradually, the culture of the organisation shifted to one where safety was all part of everyday behaviour rather than a mindless adherence to process.

The performance-enhancing culture model

The last piece to the puzzle is to understand that the Achievement parameter can be divided into two sub-parameters, Competitive and Innovative.

The Ogbonna and Harris study shows that leadership styles are not linked directly to performance but that leadership styles are strong predictors of the culture. The Achievement parameter is directly linked to performance, with the Competitive sub-parameter being geared primarily externally. The Innovative sub-parameter can be internally and/or externally focused. On the other hand, the Support and Structure parameters are internal and are more indirectly linked to performance in their role supporting the Achievement parameter.

The results of our own research indicate that the generation of an externally oriented culture (as opposed to internally oriented) is significantly influenced by the extent to which the leaders are supportive of followers and include followers in the decision-making process. This reconfirms the importance of the Democratic leadership style in supporting the Visionary style to create and maintain a strong Achievement orientated culture, and in the value of the Coaching and Affiliative styles in providing the Supporting parameter.

As William Weldon, former chairman of Johnson & Johnson, a health-care giant, observes: "Innovation is no longer about money, it's about the climate: are individuals allowed to flourish and take risks?" (The Economist, 2007).

The culmination of linking these various models can be seen in Figure 10.6.

They show how the various leadership styles influence performance through the different parameters of culture. Although this diagram does not show every single link between leadership styles and culture parameters it does include the most significant ones. Dotted lines signify less influence than a continuous line. Black lines are generally negative influences, and grey lines generally positive.

As we discussed in Chapter 8, each of the leadership styles are made up of a few key EI Capabilities, each of which comprises four granular behaviours. Figure 10.7 shows two examples of granular behaviours directly influencing the performance of an organisation.

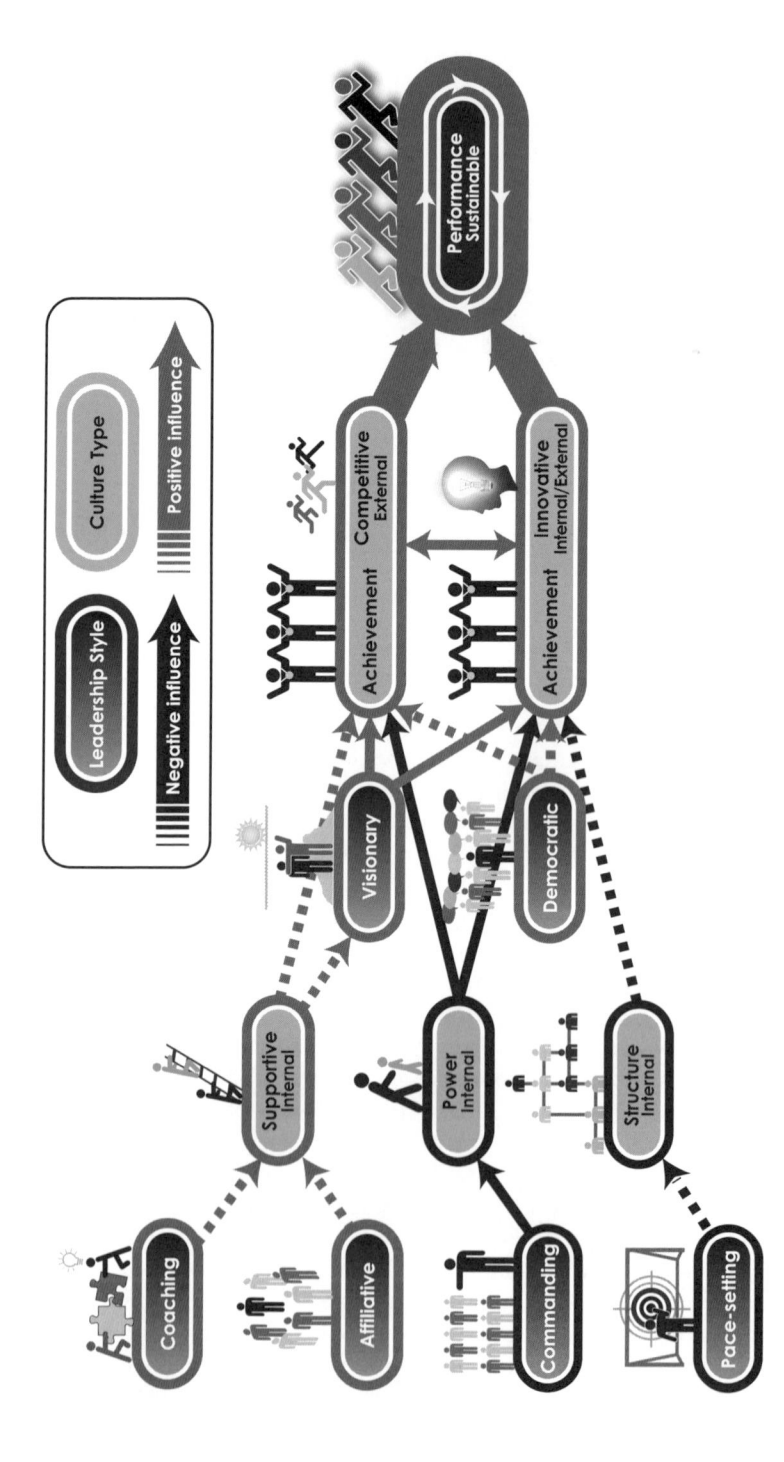

Figure 10.6 Relationship between leadership and performance

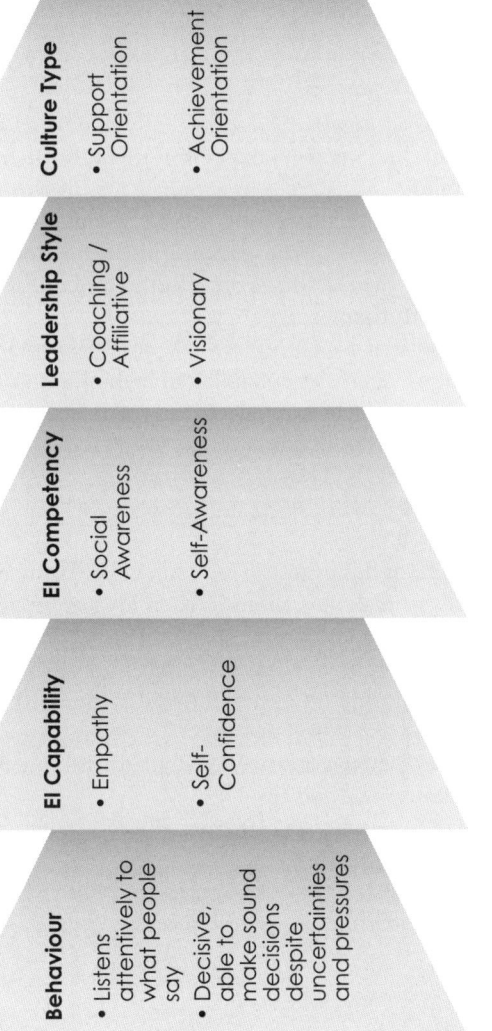

Behaviour	EI Capability	EI Competency	Leadership Style	Culture Type	Performance
• Listens attentively to what people say • Decisive, able to make sound decisions despite uncertainties and pressures	• Empathy • Self-Confidence	• Social Awareness • Self-Awareness	• Coaching / Affiliative • Visionary	• Support Orientation • Achievement Orientation	• Good Working Environment • Increased Productivity

Figure 10.7 Improved performance by behavioural change

Top tips how leaders can bring the Ideal culture to fruition

We now know all the characteristics of a performance-enhancing culture and we have the road map. Each organisation will have a unique Ideal culture but in our experience the vast majority of organisations will have a similar parameter profile, and for each Ideal culture there will be specific behaviours and recommended leadership styles that are identified. However, in addition to all that we have found there are two other areas that if handled properly will enable the Ideal culture to develop and be maintained. The first is contracting expectations between line manager and individual and the second is to understand the leader's role in implementing change successfully.

Contracting expectations

The truth is that most people in most organisations don't fully understand their role, what the organisation or their line manager expects of them, or their level of accountability and responsibility. So often too much is left in the foggy world of assumptions – on both sides. As a result most individuals will be conservative about their own level of decision-making but a minority will be optimistic and beg forgiveness if they get it wrong. Both can be disastrous and certainly negatively impact performance.

To address this we recommend that a "Contract of Mutual Expectations" (CoME) between individual and manager is essential. It can be built into the job description, personal development plan of annual objectives if desired. The CoME will vary with every pairing but we recommend the following framework of reference to enable that Ideal culture.

The line manager's responsibility:

- well communicated delegation of duties to the lowest level of competence
- empowerment to individuals to make decisions in their area of capability
- provide individual (Coaching style) and group (Affiliative) support
- provide the opportunity for everyone to maximise their potential
- share as much information as possible (as opposed to on a "need to know basis" as default)
- do-what-you-say-you-will-do-when-you-say-you-will-do-it; and if you absolutely can't, let people know in good time
- as far as feasible, involve everyone who will be involved in implementing a decision, in the decision-making process
- avoid a blame culture: criticise constructively and privately; praise publically
- communicate expectations of individual responsibilities.

The responsibility of both parties:

- taking personal responsibility
- accepting accountability

Creating a performance-enhancing culture 121

- being self-disciplined (including doing some mundane things regularly that we may not enjoy!)
- proactivity – showing initiative (this must be supported by the leaders).

Implementing change

As we have discussed, creating the Ideal culture is all about improvement and change, but:

> *New opinions are always suspected, and usually opposed, without any other reason but because they are not already common.*
>
> (Locke, 1690)

So how do leaders go about making change happen? A good place to start is with the Attitude Bell Curve (Seaman, 2003), which suggests that a good yardstick is that 15 per cent of a population are naturally supportive of change, 15 per cent resistant and 70 per cent neutral. There are various other versions of this curve that have different percentages. Our own experience suggests that about 10 per cent of the population are very resistant to change and 10 per cent will change at the drop of a hat (the so-called early adopters). But actually it is the other 80 per cent that is the most important to split into two categories, those somewhat reluctant to change and those somewhat willing to change, which split out at about 40 per cent each (see Figure 10.8). While it would

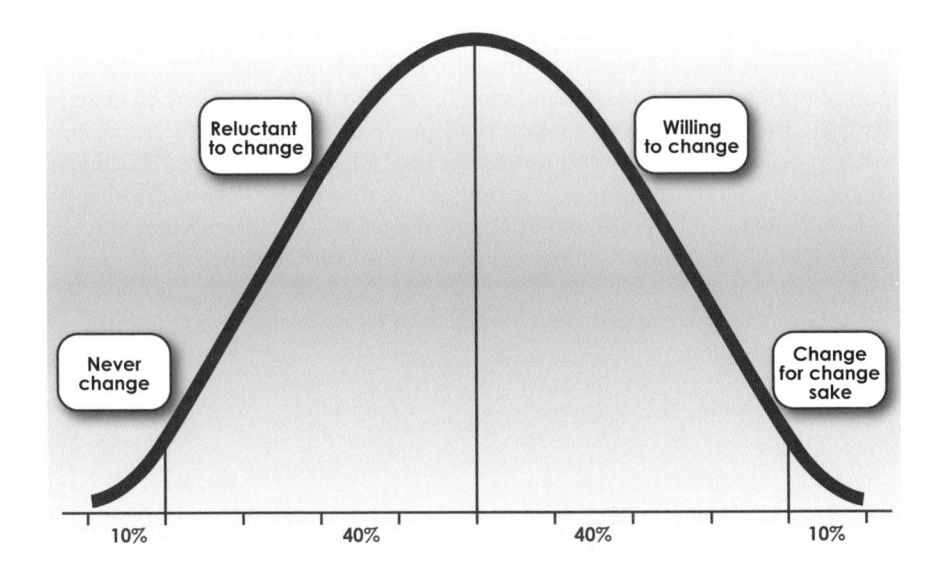

Figure 10.8 Making change happen
Source: © LeaderShape 2017. All rights reserved.

seem logical to perhaps focus on the 40 per cent reluctant to change, greater success is achieved by working with the 40 per cent willing to be converted. The conversion of this 40 per cent will then attract the reluctant 40 per cent, who will tend to want to be with the leading majority (default herd instinct of safety in numbers).

While this might be seen as manipulative to some, it is not when carried out with honesty and transparency. This approach will help to improve what numerous surveys confirm is a very difficult process (Strategy&, 2013).

The main requirements for success in our view are:

- remembering change happens when people respond at the EMOTIONAL rather than RATIONAL level
- understanding that individuals must commit to change emotionally
- accepting that the leaders must both understand and facilitate the change involved.

This requires the "ABO" COMMITMENT process:

Awareness: I am aware of the changes taking place.
Buy-In: I understand the personal implications of this change and believe it will benefit the organisation and me.
Ownership: I take personal responsibility for helping the company implement the change.

The ABO process can be best achieved by using the Contract of Mutual Expectations described earlier in this chapter. As this process continues to embed the cultural change, continue to acknowledge that most people are resistant to change and keep identifying those who are most willing to change. At the same time begin to replace rigid procedures with flexible guidelines where possible to increase empowerment and reduce bureaucracy. Be diligent to continue communication as it is vital to "oil the wheels" of culture change.

Remember, the greatest single reason for failure of culture change is the leadership of the company thinking it is only for everyone else.

The culture of an organisation is a reflection of the consciousness of its leaders.
(Barrett, 2006)

> **Questions and actions for personal development**
>
> Answering these questions will help you to understand the key issues around developing a performance-enhancing culture and how you might need to adapt personally to achieve success.
>
> 1. How would you define "climate"?
> 2. Think of a leader that is new in their post. What has s/he done to set a new climate so far?
>   a. What has been the initial response by the people around them?
>   b. What was s/he seeking to achieve? Was s/he successful?
>   c. Have you consciously set a climate? How would you describe it?
>   d. Have you unconsciously set a climate? How would you describe that?
> 3. What is culture and what is the connection and differences with climate?
> 4. How do leaders improve performance through culture?
> 5. Describe the four parameters of culture.
> 6. How does the Actual culture in your organisation differ from the Ideal?
> 7. What would you need to do to get to the Ideal?
>
> ACTION: What steps can you take personally to move your organisation towards an Ideal culture?

References

Barrett, R. (2006). *Building a Values-Driven Organization: A Whole System Approach to Cultural Transformation*. Routledge.

Bass, B. (1985). *Leadership and Performance Beyond Expectations*. N.Y. Free Press.

Bower, M. (1966). *The Will to Manage: Corporate Success Through Programmed Management*. McGraw-Hill.

Burns, J. (1978). *Leadership*. Harper Perennial Modern Classics; 1 edition (2010).

CIPD (2017). *HR Outlook – Views of the Profession – Winter 2016–2017*. Chartered Institute of Personal Development.

Fisher, A. (2016). Why Performance Bonuses and Merit Raises Don't Work. *Fortune Online*. http://bit.ly/2jZf3J3 [accessed on: 18/07/2017].

Goleman, D. (2000). Leadership That Gets Results. *Harvard Business Review* (Mar–April, 2000).

Goleman, D., Boyatzis, R. and McKee, A. (2002). *Primal Leadership: Realizing the Power of Emotional Intelligence*. Harvard Business School Press. Published in the UK as *The New Leaders*.

Harrison, R. (1972). Understanding Your Organization's Character. *Harvard Business Review*.

Harrison, R. (1987). *Organization, Culture and Quality of Service: Strategy for Releasing Love in the Workplace*. SOS Free Stock.

Knights, J. (2016). *Ethical Leadership: How to Develop Ethical Leaders*. Routledge. http://bit.ly/1sOmCWO [accessed on: 18/07/2017].

Kohn, A. (1993). Why Incentive Plans Cannot Work. *Harvard Business Review*. http://bit.ly/2kodNP3 [accessed on: 18/07/2017].

Litwin, G. and Stringer, A. (1968). *Motivation and Organizational Climate*. Harvard University Press.

Locke, J. (1690). *An Essay Concerning Human Understanding. Letter to the Right Honourable Lord Thomas, Earl of Pembroke and Montgomery*. Barron Herbert of Cardiff.

LOCS (2017). *LeaderShape Online Culture Shaper*. LeaderShape Global Website. www.leadershapeglobal.com/culture-shaper [accessed on: 18/07/2017].

McClelland, D. (1998). Identifying Competencies with Behavioral-Event Interviews. *Psychological Science* 9(5): 331–340.

Ogbonna, E. and Harris, L. (2000). Leadership Style, Organisational Culture and Performance: Empirical Evidence from UK Companies. *The International Journal of Human Resource Management* 11(4): 766–788.

Plaister-Ten, J. (2017). *Leading Across Cultures: Developing Leaders for Global Organisations*. Routledge. http://bit.ly/2mbDuYm [accessed on: 18/07/2017].

Seaman, R. (2003). *Managing Change Through the "Attitude" Bell Curve*. Publisher unknown. Indirect source: www.mentalgamecoach.com/articles/ManagingChange.html [accessed on: 18/07/2017].

Strategy&. (2013). *The 2013 Culture and Change Management Survey*. Strategy&.

The Economist. (2007). The Age of Mass Innovation: We Are All Innovators Now. *The Economist*, October 11.

11 Identifying strengths and improving development areas

John Knights

> *For most of us there are 2–5 granular behaviours that if developed will significantly improve our emotionally intelligent leadership.*

Jack Welch, the famous former CEO of General Electric, is quoted as saying, "Before you are a leader, success is all about growing yourself. When you become a leader, success is all about growing others" (Lowe, 2007). Although I don't know the context of this quote, standing alone it implies that not everyone is a leader, and more important that once you are a leader you don't need to go on learning and developing. We agree that helping to grow and develop others is a key role of a leader often forgotten, as discussed in Chapter 9, but the activity most commonly ignored by leaders is the need to continually develop ourselves regardless of our role or title. And in our view, everyone is a leader (see Chapter 3).

Overview

This chapter focuses on how you as an individual can maximise your development as a **Robust Emotionally Aware Leader** as defined in Chapter 2. For convenience we repeat the chart of Figure 2.1 as Figure 11.1, which shows the steps that the chapters of Part 1 of this book have taken us through. This chapter brings us to Stage 7.

The key is to identify our strengths and development areas and use those strengths to harness the development of the areas where improvement will have impact on our Emotionally Intelligent Leadership (EIL) performance. For most of us there are 2–5 granular behaviours that if developed will significantly improve our EIL. We have two specialised self-assessment tools you can use to identify these micro behaviours but to be sure you have identified the right ones we recommend using an appropriate 360° assessment tool with feedback from an accredited facilitator to ensure the report is understood.

Once identified, you need to complete an action plan and then start practising, ideally first of all in a safe environment, before practising and using in the work place. An excellent method to help you develop and embed these new

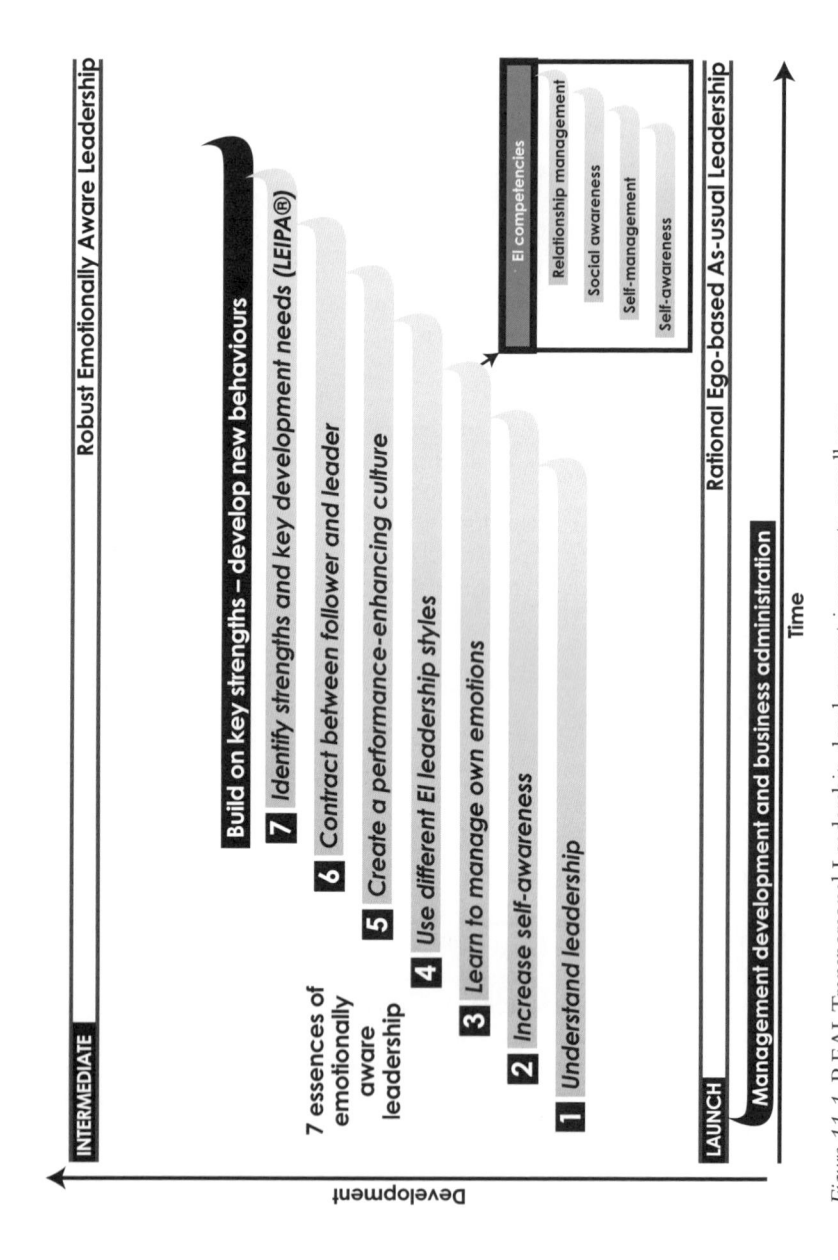

Figure 11.1 REAL Transpersonal Leadership development journey to excellence

Source: © LeaderShape 2012. All rights reserved.

behaviours is through a process known as Reflective Practice, which you will be introduced to in this chapter.

With your learning from Part 1 of this book and the development of these key behaviours, you will be ready and armed to move on to Part 2 of the Transpersonal Leadership journey.

Review what you have learned so far

In preparation for identifying your development needs, first of all review all the questions you have answered at the end of each chapter of the book so far. Think about how you answered those questions; were there any particular take-aways, and did you have any "aha!" moments? We suggest you make a list of those take-aways and special insights.

Identifying development needs and establishing an action plan

This can be done alone at a push but it is much more effective to work with a trusted colleague or small team who are perhaps sharing the process and have also learned the Coaching style of leadership or, best of all if budgets allow, also find yourself a good executive coach for a period of six months.

There are three routes you can use towards identifying the specific behaviours you need to work on:

1. Go back to the "Questions and actions for personal development" section of Chapter 8 and review the exercise you completed in Table 7.2. Make a note of the granular behaviours where you scored really high and those on which you scored the lowest.
2. If you did not do it at the end of Chapter 7 download and complete the LeaderShaper app available from Apple Store or Google Play – just search for "LeaderShaper". This will allow you to do a FREE self-assessment of your emotional intelligence and receive specific advice on how to improve those behaviours you believe need developing. You will see how the 19 EI Capabilities break down into 72 descriptive behaviour statements. When completed you can identify the three or so behaviours that you need to work on. For a small cost you can download a customised PDF report of your leadership styles.
3. The problem with a self-assessment is it does not show up your hidden strengths or blind spots, so we always recommend carrying out a 360° assessment where possible. Of course, we recommend you use our LEIPA® (*Leadership & Emotional Intelligence Performance Accelerator*) tool (LeaderShape, 2017) (http://leadershapeglobal.com/Leipa), but otherwise access any 360° that does the following:
    i. allows you to organise rater groups from your line manager(s), peers, direct reports and, preferably, others

ii. is confidential to you and anonymous for the raters
iii. asks questions about detailed emotional intelligence (EI) behaviours, rather than business skills or competencies
iv. includes verbatim statements from each rater about what they would like you to keep doing, do more of, do less of and start doing.
v. provides a detailed feedback session from an accredited facilitator that results in an action plan.

4. Preferably the assessment should also:

   a. measure the difference between observed and desired behaviours
   b. be contextual to your role rather than being related to a global norm that may be from a database that is entirely different from your own context
   c. connect the EI behaviours to leadership style competences
   d. measures the importance of each style in your role.

5. This will provide a matrix of your competence in each leadership style versus the importance of each style for your role. From that you can accurately identify those few micro behaviours that will have the greatest impact on improving your leadership performance.

Once you have identified the behaviours, the next steps are:

A. Go back to all your raters – except your line manager/mentors – one-by-one (or if you did a self-assessment, find some colleagues who will work with you) and tell them the two or three granular behaviours you most want to improve. Don't share your entire report and keep it short and sweet (max. 10 minutes, preferably face-to-face but remote is better than nothing). Just ask the same question for each behaviour: "What do you suggest I can do to improve this behaviour?" Note the answers of each rater. Many of us find this is a difficult process to face so our recommendation is to start with the person you feel most comfortable with and move on from there. Our experience is that in addition to being a very powerful way for you to really develop your action plan it will encourage others to be more open and hence is excellent for general team building. It is best to do this face-to-face or by phone but if you find this daunting or logistically challenging then doing it by email is better than not at all.
B. Then go to your line manager(s) and any in-organisation mentor who was a rater to ask them the same question and go through the same process as in point "A" above. Share with your managers as much information about the report and rater feedback as you feel comfortable with.
C. Complete a SMART[1] action plan and share it with your coach or trusted colleague/team. Figure 11.2 is a template action plan form you can use.

This is a process you can repeat with further behaviours you might have identified for development once you have embedded the first two or three and they are already becoming habits. We strongly advise that you work on a maximum of three behaviours at a time to avoid overloading the brain with rewiring.

Our strong belief is that any organisation's system for assessing performance should connect it with specific development and include objectives that are beyond just achievement of business targets. It should include behavioural objectives and development needs. The actions committed to in the action plan mentioned previously are ideal for including in the objectives to be achieved. This is how a 360° process can be both confidential and yet part of the HR development and assessment process. See Figure 3.2. to review how a personal development plan fits into the process from vision to performance.

Implementing the action plan

Of course, keeping on track and implementing an action plan can be accomplished alone but you are likely to achieve much more by doing it with the continued support of a close colleague, a small team on a similar journey and/or your line manager. As mentioned, that experience will be further enhanced through the involvement of a mentor or an external coach.

A particularly useful process to engage in to help you implement your action plan is Reflective Practice. Introduced by Donald Schon (Schon, 1983), Reflective Practice in its simplest form is thinking about and reflecting on what you do. It involves thoughtfully considering your own experiences as you make the connection between knowledge and practice, which becomes learning. This can then be channelled into development and improvement.

We discussed reflection as a part of the learning cycle in Chapter 5 and here is a technique to put it into practice, bearing in mind that most of us do not use reflection as much as we might, preferring to jump directly from action to conclusion. When we do reflect it is likely to be in a random or unstructured way, and even those who are natural reflectors often fail to convert reflections into actions. The technique we suggest is known as a "Reflection Note" and it provides the structure for developing the habit of rigorous reflection of learning experiences. The technique was originally developed for use by psychologists and so is well proven. Finally, it helps people become increasingly conscious learners, which in itself becomes more important as we move into the next stage of Transpersonal Leadership.

Some (especially those who have a strong preference for analytical thinking) will find the process difficult at first but with patience and perseverance the value will become apparent as you gain deep level learning from every day events as well as from more formal learning situations.

We recommend it to be used each time you are practising something during this action plan phase but also after a major event or where something very positive or very negative has happened. As you become more experienced and it becomes a habit you will be able to replace written notes with mental ones. Discussing your reflection notes with an experienced coach can help you uncover deeper insights.

There are four steps to a Reflection Note. Generally, write two or three concise sentences for each question, although you may need to write a little more to answer the first question. A good guide is the Reflection Note should not take up more than one A4 or standard letter page.

1. *Exactly what happened and why in that way?*
   This is not like a normal meeting report where the business facts are described. Here we need to describe more what we observed, how people were acting and behaving. How did people respond to you and each other when certain things were said or done? What senses or feelings did you pick up?
   This encourages greater self-awareness of events.
2. *How did you think, feel and behave?*
   This is often the most difficult section to complete as traditional learning and workplace cultures either ignore or suppress these "emotional intelligence" aspects of reflection. Make sure (based on what you have learned from this book so far, especially Chapter 6) that you are differentiating between, "think", "feel" and "behave".
3. *What were the main learning points?*
   This is very different to traditional learning, which tends to emphasise the need to memorise and regurgitate hard information "facts". The structure of the Reflection Note discourages the habit of recording chapter and verse or writing "book reviews".
   The aim is to encourage objectivity and awareness of the essence of the learning experience.
   Understanding "feelings" and "why" you felt them are a big part of the reflection technique.
4. *So what will you do differently (is that a SMART goal? Does it need to be?)*
   This is how the deep learning can be converted into everyday practice and implementation.
   Learning is of no use if you don't do something with it. Sometimes, future actions can be captured in a simple sentence. Making them SMART ensures the actions are measurable and within a specific time frame rather than just good intentions.

Once you have completed your SMART actions you are ready to move to Part 2 of the Transpersonal Leadership journey. Enjoy!

The SMART[1] actions I am committed to as a *first step* in my development programme are: 1: Specific, Measurable, Achievable, Relevant, Timed	
SMART actions	**Date**

Figure 11.2 List of SMART actions

Note

1 Specific, Measurable, Achievable, Relevant, Timed.

References

LeaderShape (2017). *Leadership and Emotional Intelligence Performance Accelerator.* www.leadershapeglobal.com/Leipa [accessed on:18/07/2017].

Lowe, J. (2007). *Jack Welch Speaks: Wit and Wisdom from the World's Greatest Business Leader – 2nd Revised Edition.* John Wiley & Sons.

Schon, D. (1983). *The Reflective Practitioner: How Professionals Think in Action.* Arena Publishing.

Part 2
The advanced journey of the Transpersonal Leader

12 Introduction of Part 2, "The advanced journey"

John Knights

> *In addition to bringing our values to full consciousness, we must gain a better understanding of our ego and how to manage it.*

As we have seen, the "intermediate journey" described in Part 1 of this book is essentially about increasing awareness of our brain defaults, our preferences, our senses and our emotions, and then learning to manage them through implementing new or improved behaviours. In this way we become **Robust, Emotionally Aware Leaders (REAL-2)**.

The "advanced journey" will take leaders towards becoming **Radical, Ethically Authentic Leaders (REAL-3)**, that is **Transpersonal Leaders** (see Figure 12.1).

This advanced journey is primarily about bringing our values, beliefs and purpose to full consciousness and then acting on them by using the new and improved behaviours we have already learned in Part 1, and other behaviours we still need to learn, in order to manage our ego.

For the purposes of this journey and to understand how we use the words, we think of ***Awareness*** as fundamentally about "observation" (knowing about self and others) whereas ***Consciousness*** is about "experiencing" (connecting with self and others), in the moment.

Awareness vs. consciousness

The difference is quite critical for our understanding but unfortunately there are many definitions of awareness and consciousness. Here is a standard one from the English Oxford Living Dictionaries (OLD, 2017):

Awareness: knowledge or perception of a situation or fact.

Consciousness: the state of being aware of and responsive to one's surroundings.

To get an impression of the various views of the difference between consciousness and awareness see the discussion, "What is the Difference Between Conciousness and Awareness?" (Taub, 2015) (available at www.quora.com/What-is-the-difference-between-consciousness-and-awareness). *These views are from philosophical, religious, neuroscientific and moral perspectives and show how lacking in precision the English language can be.*

There is more about the neuroscience and philosophy of consciousness in Chapter 14.

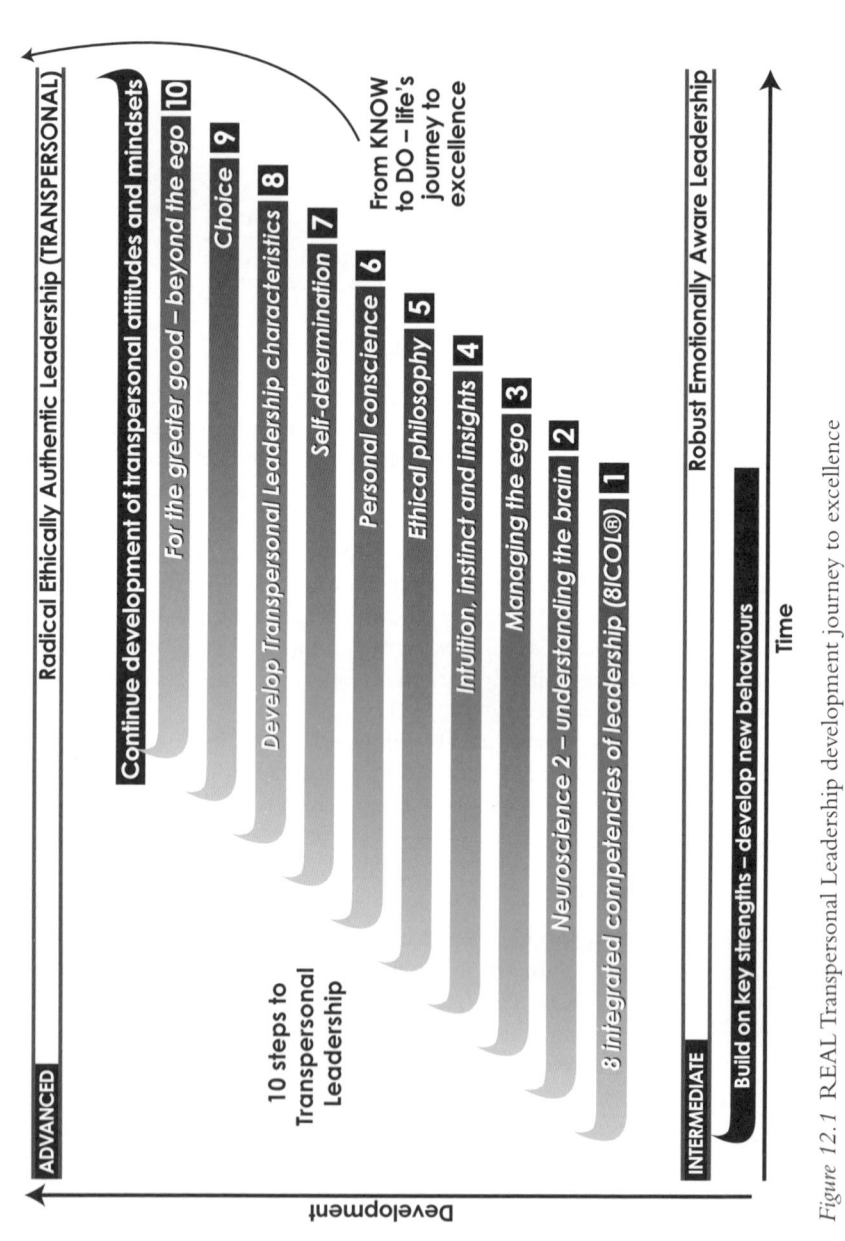

Figure 12.1 REAL Transpersonal Leadership development journey to excellence

Source: © LeaderShape 2012. All rights reserved.

Introduction of Part 2   137

This advanced journey (Figure 12.1) takes leaders on a voyage beyond emotional intelligence, beyond our ego to the ultimate state of Transpersonal Leadership. It is about increasing our consciousness and then learning and taking actions from that. In addition to bringing our values to full consciousness, we must gain a better understanding of our ego and how to manage it. Critically, we must also learn to improve our decision-making and judgement so it takes into account the emotional, ethical and authentic aspects of any issue or challenge as well as the logic-analytical ones we are often more comfortable handling. Learning that this journey has direction but no end point or ultimate summit, and is life-long, is the final important lesson.

A reflection on my own experience may bring some understanding to the journey ahead

Throughout my career I had been a successful senior corporate international business executive and then a serial entrepreneur, with more mixed results. I had lived in five countries, married a Swedish-Finn and carried out business in over 50 countries. So I had a lot of very varied experiences. However, it was only when I got the opportunity to learn to coach and put that into practice, moderating the development of a group of chief executives (see Chapter 1 for more detail of how that happened), that I suddenly started to realise the gaps in my own leadership capability. Even in hindsight I believe I was a better leader than many others I encountered – but I could have been so much better!

Coaching and group facilitating other CEOs at a level deeper than I had ever investigated before, threw up mirror after mirror as I recognised myself in the issues they raised. Through the programme I realised that these people were not aware of how their emotions were managing them rather than the other way around. Even more importantly, how in general their many "good" values (remember these were self-selecting CEOs who wanted to develop and improve) were not high up in their consciousness when making decisions. And they were to a large extent controlled by their egos.

My main responsibility was to nurture, support and challenge my clients through these issues and learnings. However, it also had a profound effect on me too. It made me realise that it is wrong to show up as a different persona at work and in our private lives, not to mention being stressful. I suddenly understood the values that we cherish in our relationships with family and friends are just as important at work if we are to achieve anything meaningful beyond fame and/or fortune. The single most important lesson I learned during this time was to learn to give without expecting anything in return – just as you would with your children or partner. I don't just mean not needing a quid pro quo, but also without expecting any reward for one's ego, "for being so nice", and without exploiting that "giving" at a future time. The amazing result is that by giving unconditionally, you build trust and then people give back. But to do that authentically and ethically, we have to bring our values to full consciousness and to be able to manage and control our ego.

Some people will say these things come more naturally with age and especially when you don't have the responsibility of a young family and a big mortgage. That has some resonance BUT I would not have wanted to wait until I was in my fifties to learn this

138 John Knights

*stuff. I have learned it by serendipity; many **never** get the opportunity. I would have liked to have learned it in my twenties and thirties – and then maybe I could have been a great leader. But better late than never! My colleagues have gone through parallel experiences, which in turn motivated us to develop the journey to becoming a Transpersonal Leader.*

Chapter 2 described in detail the meaning of the launch and REAL stages of the intermediate transpersonal journey:

Launch: Rational, Ego-based, As-usual Leadership
Intermediate: Robust, Emotionally Aware Leadership

The essence of that part of the journey was to build on the rational intelligence of the leader to enhance performance through adding emotional intelligence as shown in the diagram in Figure 2.2.

At the heart of the advanced part of the journey is the addition of spiritual intelligence to our rational and emotional intelligence as shown in Figure 12.2 (Figure 1.1 replicated). This will better enable us to define what "performance" really means to us.

So what is spiritual intelligence (SI)?

Once again there are a myriad of definitions, which range from the religiously oriented to the philosophical to the mystical. The following are perhaps the most useful definitions we have found when it comes to identifying the principle of SI:

> *Spiritual intelligence is a higher dimension of intelligence that activates the qualities and capabilities of the authentic self (or the soul), in the form of wisdom, compassion, integrity, joy, love, creativity, and peace. Spiritual intelligence results in a sense of*

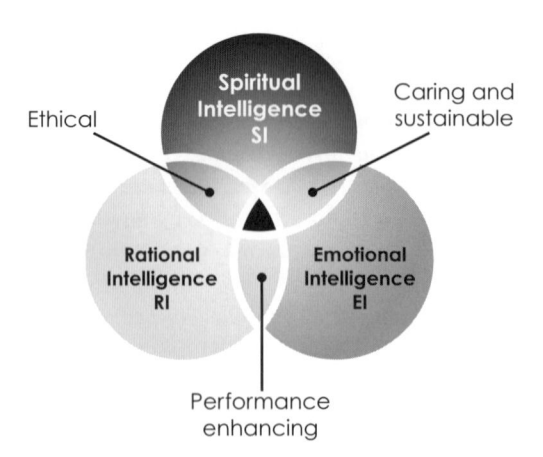

Figure 12.2 Transpersonal Leadership

deeper meaning and purpose, combined with improvements in a wide range of important life skills and work skills.

(Griffiths, 2017)

The ability to behave with Wisdom and Compassion while maintaining inner and outer peace (equanimity) regardless of the circumstances.

(Wigglesworth, 2013)

L. W. Fry (2003) defined "Spiritual Leadership" as "the values, attitudes and behaviours necessary to intrinsically motivate oneself and others so that they have a sense of calling and membership". He defined "calling" as the experience of how one makes a difference through service to others and, in doing so, derives purpose and meaning in life. He explained "membership" as involving establishing an organisational culture based on altruistic love whereby leaders have genuine care and concern together with appreciation and understanding for self and others.

These definitions and others have provided important guidance in developing our own definition of the Transpersonal Leader as given at the start of Chapter 1 and again here.

Transpersonal Leaders operate beyond their ego, continuing personal development and learning. They are radical, ethical and authentic while emotionally intelligent and caring.

They are able to:

- **embed authentic, ethical and emotionally intelligent behaviours into the DNA of the organisation**
- **build strong, empathetic and collaborative relationships within the organisation and with all stakeholders**
- **create a performance enhancing culture that is ethical, caring and sustainable.**

The first step (referring to Figure 12.1) in this advanced journey is understanding the Eight Integrated Competencies of Leadership (8ICOL®) – Chapter 13 – that take into account rational, emotional and spiritual intelligence and our innate personal preferences. We explain in detail the 8ICOL® model developed by LeaderShape to show how the different aspects of intelligence and competence provide a holistic template for leadership development that includes explaining how behaviours are the foundation for values and ethical behaviour. Uniquely, it introduces two new competencies of Personal Conscience and Self Determination, which help better appreciate the role and purpose in leadership of different kinds of values.

The second step, "Neuroscience 2" is discussed in Chapter 14 and together with some relevant philosophy focuses on consciousness and how the brain works to handle the spiritual, ethical and value-based aspects of leadership. Neurons connect in three different ways (see Chapter 4) but it's primarily the bonding through synchronous neural oscillations that we will address in this chapter.

The third step, "Managing the ego" is described in Chapter 15, explaining that we need to know what drives us in order to manage our ego. Whereas emotions can hijack our behaviours, drivers can hijack our ego. Moving beyond the ego as an organisational leader requires us to focus on the stakeholders we are serving and the order of priority of those stakeholders in different contexts. In the past, the shareholders of a private company were always the priority; more recently it seems to be the executives. But who really are the stakeholders that will determine the sustainable success of the organisation? And where is the ethical balance between a leader taking care of their own needs versus those of the organisation?

Chapter 16 covers steps 4 and 5. It discusses the importance of the 3Is (Intuition, Instinct and Insight) and ethical philosophy in decision-making and improving our judgement. We are taught throughout our education and most of our lives to make decisions rationally and logically, yet in actual fact, we tend to use logic for explaining our decisions rather than making them. The four other sub-, non-, un-conscious decision-making processes each come with their biases and prejudices that we need to be aware of and understand so that we can unpick and overcome them in order to make better judgements.

Steps 6 and 7 are covered in Chapter 17. We have developed a new framework for better understanding the role of values in leadership. We divide values into the areas of Personal Conscience and Self Determination. Personal Conscience is about "who I am" whereas Self Determination is "what I am going to do with who I am" and thus is very leadership focused. We will discuss the more common values that employees want in their leaders but also the softer values such as "forgiveness" and "humility", and the difficult ones like "vulnerability" that need to be developed and implemented in order to become a Transpersonal Leader.

Managing diversity is another area that is today critical for leaders to operate beyond their ego and in full consciousness, and through that establish creative, effective workplace cultures (see Chapter 18 authored by Jennifer Plaister-Ten). There have been huge changes in societies across the world in the last 20 years, whether it is gender, race, disability, sexual orientation, religion, ethnicity, etc. But also as globalisation increases, the challenges of geographical diversity and views about diversity itself are no longer reserved for the international business executive who flew around the world. Today, it is faced by increasing numbers of people in the workplace because of easy remote communication. Leading this increasing diversity brings a sharp focus on the importance of developing not only emotional intelligence but also values and ethical behaviour.

Developing Transpersonal Leadership characteristics, step 8 in the advanced journey, is explained in Chapters 19 (written by Sue Coyne) and 20. Transpersonal Leadership development is underpinned by an inner journey, which may include a mindfulness/meditation practice. Such practice supports the leader in being fully present and thus being aware of what is required in each moment from a leadership perspective. It also requires a growth mind-set and congruency of identity, values and beliefs. In addition, the leader needs to ensure that they are thriving as an individual so that they are able to create the conditions for their people to thrive. All of this ensures sustainable high performance and success.

Steps 9 and 10, "Choice" and "For the greater good" are examined in Chapter 20. At the end of the day, choice is much more important than our abilities, and ultimately, to be a Transpersonal Leader one has to make choices about what is right for all stakeholders, including the planet and the universe. To make those choices it is important to understand one's own purpose and spiritual belief system, and how that manifests itself into ethical behaviour. In the end, how will I, YOU, WE leave the world a better place?

Beyond the final step in the journey is continuous self-development, considered in Chapter 21, the final chapter of Part 2. There are five levels of self-awareness, the highest level being *"No longer a struggle between ego (what I want for myself) and the greater good"*. Reaching this level of self-awareness plus continually working to improve and develop those behaviours that are barriers to leadership competence, as well as raising one's consciousness to live one's values, is a life-long journey of development. The process in itself requires a number of emotional intelligence capabilities (e.g. initiative, achievement orientation and emotional self-awareness) and values (e.g. resilience, humility, motivation) to achieve. Continuous development can be aided by following transpersonal practices, which themselves are based on the complex-adaptive system of nature, by connecting with the various stages of human development and by using the evolution of intelligences as a guide.

With commitment and determination leaders can reach the advanced level of the REAL journey to become Radical, Ethically, Authentic Leaders. In our experience few leaders reach this level. Not because it is not possible for anyone with a slightly above normal IQ, but because very few will chance upon the experiences, learning opportunities and support that are required to get there. Our goal is to remove the "chance" element and make it a proactive choice for anyone who has the will.

Finally, let us review what the phrase "***Radical, Ethically, Authentic Leader***" means.

To be ***Radical*** is critical because we need a new kind of leadership. Current mainstream thinking on leadership is out of date for our times. We need to have the courage, fearlessness, conviction and ideas to move to a less materially oriented approach, to realise we might need an alternative to continuous growth and create a happier, fairer society. There may also be times when we need disruptive thinking for survival.

Acting ***Ethically*** means not only integrity but a social conscience and a willingness to follow the rules (or get them changed if that is what is needed). It means working for the greater good. And it is not only about "me" as an individual leader being ethical. We have a responsibility to create ethical cultures in organisations. Ethical leadership is defined in *How to Develop Ethical Leaders* (Knights, 2016) as:

> The process of influencing people to act through principles and values and beliefs that embrace ethical behaviour. Ethical Behaviour is about acting in a way that is consistent with one's own principles and values which are characterized by honesty, fairness and equity in all interpersonal activities, be they personal or professional, and by respecting the dignity, diversity and rights of individuals and groups of people.

A Transpersonal Leader must also be **Authentic** because a leader must act as they truly are. They must be honest with themselves and others. Excellent leadership is not a game, it is not something we can pretend to do and get right. The human being is very good at seeing through the falseness of others, although often not in a conscious way. "Authentic" also implies that the leader is the same person (though may behave appropriately differently) in all circumstances – their values are operating at full consciousness and they don't leave them at the door to the office when they come back from a quality weekend with the partner and/or children during which they have been a model family member (Knights, 2011).

To become this kind of **Leader**, an individual needs to be emotionally intelligent in order to have sufficient inner self-confidence, awareness and empathy to be able to take this advanced journey. To become a Transpersonal Leader we must bring our values, beliefs and purpose to full consciousness and act on them.

References

Fry, L. (2003). Toward a Theory of Spiritual Leadership. *The Leadership Quarterly* 14: 693–727.

Griffiths, R. (2017). *The Definition of Spiritual Intelligence*. SQI.CO. http://sqi.co/definition-of-spiritual-intelligence [accessed February 2016].

Knights, J. (2011) *The Invisible Elephant and the Pyramid Treasure*. Tomorrow's Company. www.leadershape.biz/invisible-elephant [accessed on: 18/07/2017].

Knights, J. (2016). *Ethical Leadership: Becoming an Ethical Leader*. Routledge. http://bit.ly/1Uh6vHL [accessed on: 18/07/2017].

OLD (2017). Oxford Living Dictionary. https://en.oxforddictionaries.com. [accessed on: 12/04/2017]

Taub, T. (2015). *What Is the Difference Between Conciousness and Awareness?* www.quora.com/What-is-the-difference-between-consciousness-and-awareness) [accessed July 2017].

Wigglesworth, C. (2013). *Integral Spiritual Intelligence: 21 Skills in 4 quadrants*. Inner Working Publishing. www.innerworkspublishing.com/news/vol32/reflections.htm [accessed on: 18/07/2017].

13 The Eight Integrated Competencies of Leadership (8ICOL®)

John Knights

A call to action to convert the characteristics of Personal Conscience from "think, feel and am" to "DO".

Overview

As we progress on this transpersonal voyage to the advanced stage that covers values, drivers, beliefs and purpose we need an extended competency framework from which to assess our status and progress, and to help us in our continued development.

As we explain in various chapters of Part 1, there are models to assess our rational intelligence (IQ), emotional intelligence (EI) and personal preferences (PP). However, there was nothing comparable to assess values, drivers, purpose, ethical behaviour and transpersonal practices, which are all connected to spiritual intelligence. So we set about building a model that incorporated these characteristics.

We investigated thoroughly cognitive, emotional, intuitive and spiritual concepts and competencies, together with reference to recent research in neuroscience. During our own research and analysis we realised that we could conveniently divide this area into aspects that respond to either "who I am" or "what I am going to do with what I am", the latter of which we felt was the ultimate leadership competency. These competency groups we called Personal Conscience and Self-Determination. These are described further in this chapter but also explained in greater detail in Chapter 18.

Having developed these two new competencies, we then integrated them with our four EI Competencies (Self-Awareness, Self-Management, Social Awareness and Relationship Management), rational intelligence (Intellect and Logic), and Personal Preferences, to provide an overarching Eight Integrated Competences of Leadership (8ICOL®).

8ICOL® (see Figure 13.1) thus provides a tool that can be used for assessment and development throughout the entire Transpersonal Leadership journey.

This model provides for all the different aspects of intelligence and competence within a holistic template for leadership development. In doing so, we clarify

144 John Knights

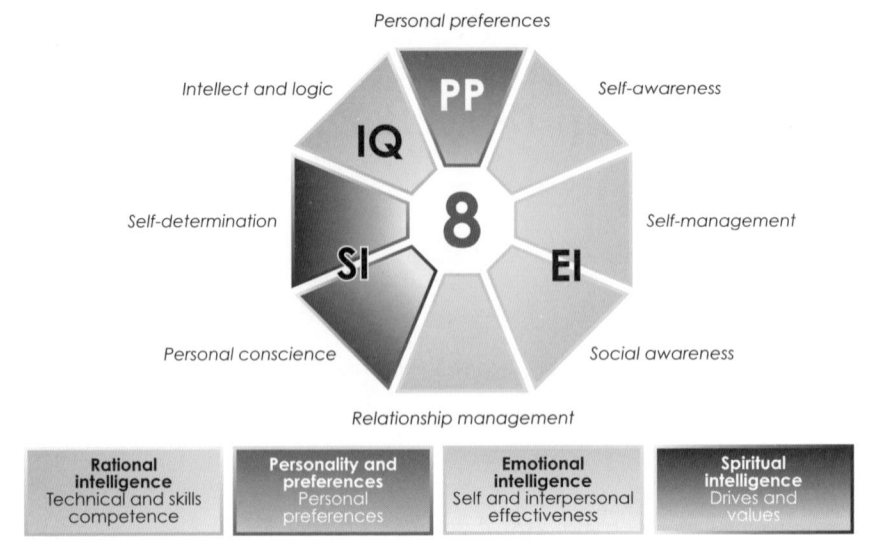

Figure 13.1 Eight Integral Competencies of Leadership (8ICOL®)

how behaviours are the foundation for values and ethical behaviour, and the link between rational and spiritual intelligence.

A brief history

There are many models that integrate competencies and/or intelligences. Howard Gardner was the first to develop the concept of multiple intelligences, first as seven intelligences[1] (Gardner, 1983) and then eventually adding two more, "naturalist" and "existential". However, not all these "intelligences" are directly relevant to leadership.

The next step in building a framework for leadership development was the Goleman/Boyatzis model discussed in detail in Chapter 7, which brings together four competencies of emotional intelligence. This was a progressive development from Gardner's interpersonal and intrapersonal intelligences, and specifically about identifying and developing behaviours. Danah Zohar (Zohar & Marshall, 2000) first introduced the concept of rational, emotional and spiritual intelligence as an integrated model based on neuroscience fundamentals. This was then further developed by ourselves and others including Richard Griffiths (Griffiths, 2017). When Gardner added the naturalist and existential intelligences it seems to be in recognition of the growing acceptance of and knowledge around spiritual intelligence.

Emotional intelligence has proven to be a powerful and important science in the improvement of leadership development. However, it has been realised that

EI alone is only part of the total picture, albeit a critically important one. LeaderShape has proven empirically, from the implementation of successful leadership programmes and analysis of its LEIPA® assessment tool that an EI approach when well implemented, can lead to much improved behaviours and sustainable leadership competence. However, it does not directly address the value-based, transpersonal and spiritual aspects of leadership critical in order to attain leadership excellence and provide the kind of sustainable organisations we need for the future.

Most of the granular statements in the 8ICOL® tool can best be assessed through the observation by others through a 360° process similar to LEIPA®. The assessment can be broken down into short segments and customised and carried out over a period of time so that the process is not too onerous for the raters.

Linking the three core intelligences (rational, emotional, spiritual)

Rational, emotional and spiritual are three intelligences that are core for development to becoming an excellent Transpersonal Leader (see Figure 12.2. in Chapter 12). Referring to the White Paper *Ethical Leadership: How to Become an Ethical Leader* published by Routledge (Knights, 2016), using the diagram from that paper replicated in Figure 13.2 and building on the neuroscience discussion in Chapter 4, we can build a picture of how these core intelligences fit together.

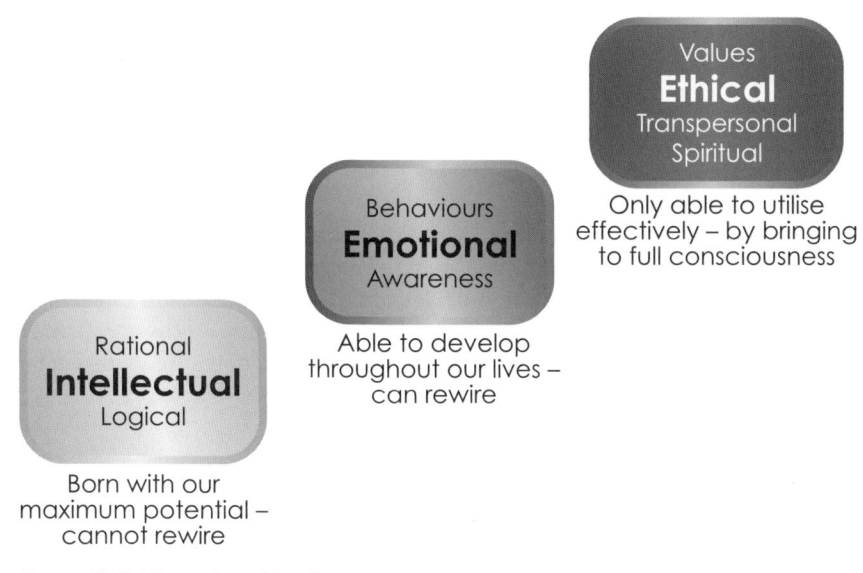

Figure 13.2 Hierarchy of intelligences

Quoting the White Paper

> We can see that the first level of intelligence is the intellectual; our rational and logical "thinking". The neural processes that enable this are through serial connections that are hard wired. To a large extent our potential intellectual capacity is fixed from birth (although most never reach anywhere near the capacity).
>
> The second level is emotional intelligence, which manages our emotions and impacts our "feelings" and behaviours. The neural connections that enable this intelligence are associative. That means billions of neuro cells are loosely connected but desirable connections can be strengthened through practice and repetition (this is often referred to as the "plasticity" of the brain).
>
> The highest level of intelligence is "spiritual" (which includes ethical), which manages, among other things, how we activate our values. Spiritual intelligence also has a unique way for our neurons to connect, known as synchronous oscillations. First discovered by Singer and Gray in 1989, every neuron in the localised part of the brain involved emits oscillations in harmony and unison in the 40 Hz range. Raising one's level of consciousness, for example through mindfulness exercises, activates this mechanism (Zohar & Marshall, 2000). Let's look at how these intelligences and the method of neural connections effect ethical (transpersonal) leadership.
>
> To be an excellent leader one needs a certain level of intellect. But an IQ of anything more than 15 per cent above the norm makes no difference (Goleman, 2004) to the likelihood of success as a leader. So whereas a reasonable intellect is a threshold necessity to becoming an excellent leader, it is not sufficient and certainly does not guarantee any competence in ethical (transpersonal) leadership as such.
>
> Having passed that threshold, the one thing anyone would accept is vital to be a good ethical leader is having good values, which involves the highest level of intelligence. However, we really need to investigate which values are critical for "ethical" leadership. LeaderShape has developed a model that divides values into two separate categories. Those that define Personal Conscience ("who I am") and those that categorise Self-Determination ("what I am going to do with who I am"). (Full details are provided in Chapter 17 of this book.)

It is often said that "values" are the core of the human being and the intellect is what differentiates us from all other animals. That may be true but it is only behaviours that can translate values into actions. As we have seen in Chapters 6 and 7, behaviours are primarily reactions to our emotions and how we manage them. The following case studies show how the right behaviours are so important in Transpersonal Leadership.

> **Two brief case studies (extract from the *Ethical Leadership* White Paper referred to previously)**
>
> Recently on a business trip to India I met the CEO of a major insurance company. He was an extremely intelligent and urbane man who had studied at Harvard and was interested in developing the next generation of leaders in their organisation. He was keen to better engage the people in the organisation (there was a high turnover of staff), wanted to genuinely improve customer service and was keen to increase the involvement of the organisation in the communities where they operated. All good values and principles. After about 15 minutes he phoned the HR director (who he had spoken highly about) and told her she would be interested in what we were discussing and to come to the meeting right away! She arrived soon after but was obviously not able to concentrate, perhaps because she had been taken away from something that she considered very important.
>
> Coincidently, during the same trip, I met the very mature CEO of a manufacturing organisation in the energy sector who had very similar issues. After about 15 minutes or so he phoned the HR manager (the HRD was away visiting one of their factories). The CEO asked him how he was and explained that I was visiting and talking about leadership development in their organisation, and thought the HR manager might be interested to attend if he was available although realised the CEO should have informed him earlier. After a few seconds of listening, the CEO said to the HR manager that he understood, it was important that he attended the other meeting that had been arranged and would brief him later.

In each case the leaders were transpersonal in the intent of their values but one of them did not have the awareness or know how to behave (the emotional intelligence) to put that person in the best frame of mind to do their job most effectively and to feel engaged, valued and of worth – all big motivators. Not surprisingly the turnover of staff in the second company was significantly lower. This very simple yet important lesson demonstrates the importance of integrating the three intelligences and that a good intellect and good values alone are not sufficient to be a Transpersonal Leader. It is the right behaviours together with full consciousness that enable the values to be an integral part of the how a leader operates.

The 8ICOL® model

The complete 8ICOL® model is shown in different formats in Figure 13.1. and Figure 13.3.

148 *John Knights*

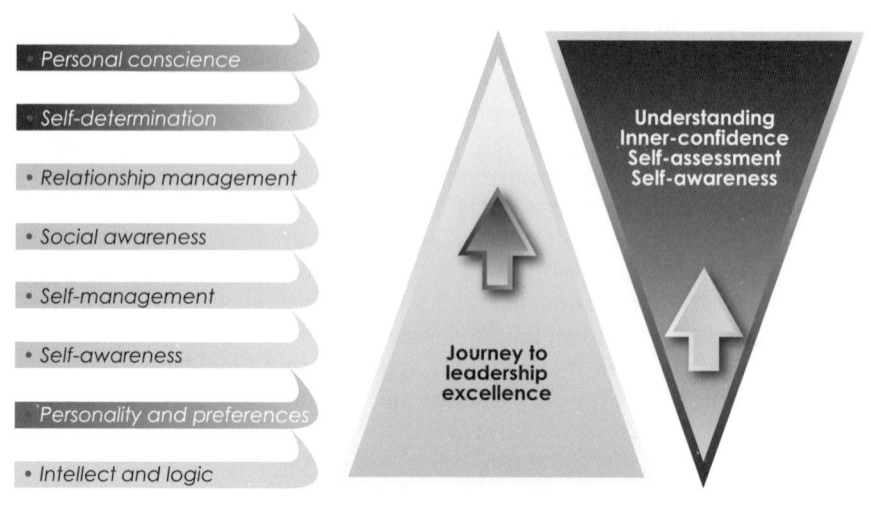

Figure 13.3 8ICOL®

Figure 13.3 shows the hierarchy of the eight competencies, which are explained in order as follows.

Intellect and logic: the rational intelligence. As discussed earlier in this chapter, to be the best a leader can be they need to have a rational intelligence or IQ that is about 15 per cent above the norm. A higher IQ than this has no bearing on success in leadership.

IQ varies in different parts of the world according to a controversial study (Lynn & Vanhanen, 2002), with North East Asian countries coming out on top (average 105) and the average for the developed world being about 100, and lower on average in developing parts of the world. The figures seem to broadly correspond to the level of mathematic and analytic education and culture, and we would expect the average maximum potential IQ to be similar across the world.

Intellect and Logic (I&L) can be further broken down into eight I&L Capabilities:

- Problem Analysis
- Verbal Reasoning
- Numerical Analysis
- Creativity
- Analytical/Logic Analysis
- Intuitive Judgement
- Practical Learning
- Strategic Thinking/Planning

Each Capability is defined by four statements. For example, Creativity is broken down into the following statements:

1. Comes up with imaginative ideas
2. Develops new ways of doing things
3. Searches to make job more effective
4. Provides others with good ideas to help them

In our view, I&L is a threshold Competency. You have no chance of becoming an excellent leader without a reasonable intellect but no amount of intellect will make you a great leader by itself – a mistake often made by those choosing who shall fill leadership positions.

Personality and preferences: There are many well-known tried and tested tools that measure personality traits and/or preferences so we are quite comfortable working with whatever the client is most familiar with. These kind of assessments were discussed in some detail in Chapter 5. The important thing to say here is that our personality and our preferences are generally innate characteristics of who we are but may also be influenced by our environment and, particularly, our upbringing. However, they must not be seen as putting us in a box forevermore. The importance of knowing these traits is so we can stretch ourselves and learn to overcome some of those characteristics that may sometimes be valuable but not always. As we discovered in Chapter 5, increasing our awareness and knowing ourselves is critical to succeeding in this competency.

For example, someone whose preference is to plan well ahead and to ensure that all "i"s are dotted and "t"s crossed before starting a particular activity might not fare so well if they are sailing single handed across the Atlantic where they need to be quick thinking and agile if there is a sudden freak wave or they hit flotsam. On the other hand, someone who likes to leave things until the last moment may also come unstuck in that same boat if they have not prepared in advance to make sure that all the equipment was delivered in time so it could be checked to make sure it was fully functional.

The four emotional intelligence Competencies: The Competencies of ***Self-Awareness, Self-Management, Social Awareness and Relationship Management*** cover the emotional intelligence Capabilities and behaviours reviewed in detail in Chapter 7. Alone they can be assessed through the LEIPA® tool but they now become an integral part of 8ICOL®. However, in addition to these standard EI Capabilities we have added a few extra Capabilities that fall into these four Competencies that can be added to the original EI model or that fall within the spiritual intelligence realm:

- *Self-Awareness:* spiritual Self-Awareness
- *Self-Management:* tenacity, decisiveness, vulnerability, spiritual Self-Management
- *Social Awareness:* compassion, universal awareness
- *Relationship Management:* delegation, empowerment, flexibility, spiritual relationship mastery

Again each of these added capabilities are defined by four granular statements. As an example, universal awareness:

- is aware of the "worldview" of others
- understands the power and limitations of human perception
- is aware of the spiritual principles of leadership
- has a sense of higher interconnectedness.

Personal Conscience and Self-Determination: Personal Conscience describes "who I am". What is *my* essence? To uncover this we need to understand our beliefs, morals, ethical behaviour and the subset of values we call "virtues".

Self-Determination defines "what I am going to do with who I am". This is the ultimate leadership competency, a call to action to convert the characteristics of Personal Conscience from "think, feel and am" to "DO". Salvador Dalí[2] is quoted as saying *"Intelligence without ambition is a bird without wings"*, which aptly explains the importance of this competency. Without it, the bird cannot fly!

Self-Determination is made up of our purpose and a series of special action oriented values that include:

- motivation
- aspiration
- drive (intense will)
- power
- energy
- courage
- resilience
- continuing professional development (CPD).

These final two competencies are explained in more detail in later chapters, especially Chapters 17 and 20.

Questions and actions for personal development

Please find below a few questions to help you ensure you understand the 8ICOL® model.

1. Why is 8ICOL® a useful tool for the development of Transpersonal Leaders?
2. How would you describe how the three intelligences used in 8ICOL® link together?
3. What are the Eight Integrated Competences?
4. Which is considered a "threshold competency" and why?
5. Which are the Competencies connected to spiritual intelligence?
6. Why is Self Determination so important for excellent leadership?
7. What broad areas are covered under Personal Conscience?

Note

1 Verbal-linguistic, logical-mathematical, spatial-visual, bodily-kinaesthetic, musical, interpersonal, intrapersonal.
2 Salvador Dalí, a famous Spanish surrealist painter (1904–1989).

References

Gardner, H. (1983). *Frames of Mind: The Theory of Multiple Intelligences*. Basic Books Inc..

Goleman, D. (2004). *Emotional Intelligence and Working with Emotional Intelligence*. Bloomsbury.

Griffiths, R. (2017). *The Definition of Spiritual Intelligence*. SQI.CO. http://sqi.co/definition-of-spiritual-intelligence/ [accessed on: 18/07/2017].

Knights, J. (2016). *Ethical Leadership: Becoming an Ethical Leader*. Routledge. http://bit.ly/1Uh6vHL [accessed on: 18/07/2017].

Lynn, R. and Vanhanen, T. (2002). *IQ and the Wealth of Nations (Human Evolution, Behavior, and Intelligence*. Praeger.

Singer, W. and Gray, C. (1989). Oscillatory Responses in Cat Visual Cortex Exhibit Inter-Columnar Synchronization which Reflects Global Stimulus Properties. *Nature* 338: 334–337; doi:10.1038/338334a0 [accessed on: 23/03/2017].

Zohar, D. and Marshall, I. (2000). *Spiritual Intelligence – The Ultimate Intelligence*. Bloomsbury.

14 The neuroscience of consciousness and how it applies to leadership

John Knights

> *Focus on specific things we want to bring into full consciousness, such as our purpose, our values and our ethics.*

Overview

The most important tool we have to help us develop beyond the emotionally intelligent leader of Part 1 of the book, to become a Transpersonal Leader, is our consciousness. As we discussed in Chapter 12, "consciousness" is about "experiencing" (connecting with self and others), in the moment. The purpose of this chapter is to understand more about consciousness so that we can better operate and manage it when we need to deal with our ego, make better judgements and be more ethical as explained further in Chapters 15–21. The more we understand what consciousness is and how it functions, the more likely it is we will be able to bring our decisions and choices to full consciousness and ensure our true values have a voice in everything we do.

In our experience some people really enjoy understanding the science that underpins our brand of leadership development as it provides more certainty to the theories. In this chapter we try to unravel and explain in layman's terms as much as possible the amazing and exciting science related to consciousness and spiritual intelligence. However, because research in this area is liable to rapid development what we present here may soon require updating. In addition to the science of consciousness is the question of what consciousness actually is: the ultimate question philosophers have been struggling with for millennia.

However, if science is not your thing and you are happy to "feel" your way through your development, then by all means continue straight to Chapter 15. You can always return here at any time.

"The neuroscience of leadership (part 1)" (Chapter 4) focused on the origins and reasons for our default behaviour, and perhaps most importantly the awareness of how our brain deals with emotions. This helps us develop emotional intelligence using the plasticity of associative neural connections. Those areas are relatively well understood in this new era of neuroscience.

In this chapter we will focus more on how the brain works to handle the spiritual, ethical and value-based aspects of leadership, which depends on bringing them to full consciousness.

It must be stated up front that the neural mechanisms that underlie consciousness are still not fully understood. However, the latest thinking and research shows that, although no-one knows all the answers, we can provide a good concept of how it probably happens.

David Chalmers, a well-known Australian philosopher and cognitive scientist explains, "within psychology and neuroscience, some new and rigorous experimental paradigms for studying consciousness have helped it begin to overcome the stigma that has been attached to the topic for most of [the 20th] century" (Chalmers, 1996).

Probably no facet of the mind is more a part of our everyday lives and yet so perplexing than consciousness and our conscious experiences. Even though there is no agreed theory of consciousness there is a general consensus that to understand the mind requires an understanding of consciousness and its place in the world. We also need to understand how it connects to non-conscious aspects of life (Stanford, 2014).

David Eagleman, an American writer and neuroscientist states, "Neuroscience over the next 50 years is going to introduce things that are mind-blowing" (O'Hagan, 2010). I think he is right. The research and hypotheses to date seem to suggest that one or more specific parts of the brain act as a modulator for sections of the cortex which provides our consciousness. The suggestion is that these act through synchronous neural oscillations and/or giant neurons as the main mechanism of communication.

Finally, according to recent research and thinking, neurons also exist in the heart and gut. So what might that mean for consciousness, spirituality and leadership?

What is consciousness?

The basics

We have defined it simply as "experiencing in the moment". Tennessee Williams wrote in *The Milk Train Doesn't Stop Here Anymore*, "Has it ever struck you that life is all memory, except for the one present moment that goes by you so quick you hardly catch it going?" In addition, a conscious experience is only available to the person who is experiencing it. It is very hard to express in words *exactly* what we are experiencing and it is impossible to experience someone else's consciousness. However, our own consciousness may relate to how another person is communicating their experience.

In some ways it is easier to describe consciousness by saying what it is not. We lose our "experiencing" consciousness when we are asleep, except when we are dreaming, although it might be more accurate to say we lose most of it as we might still be sensitive, for example, to the call of a child or partner (The Brain.McGill.ca, 2017).

Here are some common variations of the sense of "consciousness" (The Brain.McGill.ca, 2017):

- a state that can be changed by mental illness or drugs
- being aware of an external hurdle you need to overcome that stimulates your memory and emotions (as in "necessity is the mother of invention")
- personal consciousness; being who we are and knowing who we are, day after day
- being able to examine our own behaviours and through that decide our purpose and objectives
- making an ethical judgement about one's own and others' behaviour
- feeling that we have the free will to make our own decisions.

Ned Block, an American philosopher (Block, 2007), postulates four main types of consciousness:

- Access consciousness: a state where content is immediately available. It manifests itself in reasoning, analysis, control of actions, and speech.
- Phenomenal consciousness: results from sensory experiences such as hearing, smelling, tasting, and pain and includes sensations, feelings, perceptions, thoughts and emotions. He excludes anything cognitive.
- Reflexive consciousness: is when we check, review and reflect on thoughts and behaviours.
- Self-consciousness: is the representation of self that brings a wholeness to one's mental life.

As we can see, human consciousness is very hard to "nail down" exactly. It poses a very different kind of problem to scientists compared to say, understanding the solar system, explaining photosynthesis, or describing the splitting of the atom, which can be defined with scientific precision and does not have "subjectivity" attached. This just highlights the complexity we are dealing with. Various commentators use a paper by Thomas Nagel (Nagel, 1974) to explain this "subjective" side of consciousness.

Thomas Nagel: what is it like to be a bat?

"Consciousness is what makes the mind-body problem really intractable." He imagined a subjective viewpoint very different from a human one. He chose a bat because they orient themselves in space by emitting very high frequency sounds then locating obstacles or prey through the echoes (known as "echolocation"). Because we are incapable of echolocation we could never subjectively feel what it is like to operate in this way. Bats may receive the returning echoes as shapes rather than sounds, but it is something we may never know. Nagel concludes with, "It seems unlikely that any physical theory of mind can be contemplated until more thought has been given to the general problem of subjective and objective. Otherwise we cannot even pose the mind-body problem without sidestepping it".

As we have seen in Chapter 4 and will see again in this and future chapters, especially Chapter 16, most of the processes in the brain are actually unconscious, subconscious or nonconscious.[1] Our normal conscious state usually manifests itself through our five senses, often visual or auditory (verbal). But it is all of the un-sub-non-conscious processes (vision, memory, attention, emotions, insights, to name but a few) that make consciousness possible.

The goal for Transpersonal Leaders is to be able to bring more of the processes going on in our brain into full consciousness (see Chapter 19). Perhaps getting better at listening to that small voice in the background of our consciousness will help. But also we need to learn techniques that will help with this. It will enable us to focus on specific things we want to bring into full consciousness, such as our purpose, our values and our ethics (see Chapter 17). We also need to be more consciously attuned to our intuition, our insights, our instincts and how that impacts on our decision-making (see Chapter 16).

Connecting neuroscience to consciousness

Since Plato we have believed that consciousness is the "consciousness of something" but we were told that our minds were blank and only activated through external stimulation. Up until the 1990s scientists and biologists had been saying the same thing. Then in 1994, Nobel Laureate Francis Crick hypothesised that our emotions and memories and ambitions and free will are nothing but a huge group of neurons (Crick, 1995). As a scientist, however, he was at that time more interested in the neurons themselves than the effect of them.

Neural connections

So it would seem that Block's Access Consciousness relates to the serial neural wiring (see Chapter 4) of the brain in neuroscience terms, and his Phenomenal Consciousness correlates to associative neural wiring (see Chapter 4 for details).

So what about the third kind of neural connections, synchronous neural oscillations (SNOs)? They are wave motions that form across all the parts of the brain that relate to a particular event and sweep from the front of the head to the back, synchronising neural activity from every part of the brain (Zohar, 2016). SNOs were only discovered in 1989 by Gray and Singer when they identified that every localised part of the brain oscillated in unison at a frequency of 35–45 Hz when involved in perceiving an object (Gray & Singer, 1989). These are within the Gamma range of oscillations, which quickly became regarded as relevant signals of the brain's functionality, notably in connection with integrative functions (Basar et al., 1999). SNOs seem aligned to what Block refers to as Reflexive and Self-consciousness types of consciousness (see Table 14.1).

The SNO form of connection and networking is much more complex than serial or associative networks and research has only been possible really since the invention of the magneto-encephalograph (MEG). Serial wiring has been compared to a typical modern computer whereas associative networks can be compared to the most advanced computers in artificial intelligence with huge amounts of parallel processing that can learn. This is a useful analogy in today's

Table 14.1 Connecting the philosophy and neuroscience of consciousness

Block's types of consciousness	Types of neural connection
Access Consciousness	Serial neural wiring
Phenomenal Consciousness	Associative neural wiring
Reflexive Consciousness	Synchronous neural connections (SNOs)
Self-Consciousness	Synchronous neural connections (SNOs)

computer paradigm, although in reality the brain is an organism and does not actually process information like a computer (Epstein, 2016). There is no computer yet envisaged that can deal with meaning and beliefs. Unlike computers, we are conscious. We are not just aware but we are aware we are aware. We can change the rules and the boundaries. We are creative, intuitive and insightful. Only humans can ask "why"? The best guess is that SNOs are somehow involved with this extra dimension, this unity.

The brain is made up of many individual systems that process shape, colour, smell, feel, emotions, etc., yet when we look around our location we see it as a whole. This phenomenon is known as the "binding problem". How can we have a conscious, coherent, unified perception of an object, given that its various attributes are processed in different parts of the brain? Is there a place or places and/or a process where all the information about an object converges to become conscious?

Some technical detail

During the 1990s Rodolfo Llinás (the Colombian inventor of the MEG – and a founding father of neuroscience) with colleagues carried out research to progress knowledge of the function and processing of 40 Hz SNOs. The studies were centred around the interactions between the thalamus and the cortex (see Figure 14.1). They developed a theory to address the "binding problem", which showed that 40 Hz electrical current oscillations occur in phase between the different parts of the brain that correspond to a particular module of conscious thought (to bind the modules of content together) but also with the non-specific oscillations across the cortex. It has been shown that these cycles of oscillation correlate with conscious experiences continuously during being awake and dreaming, but not during deep sleep or when the brain is in a coma or anaesthetised. Day-dreaming, trance, meditation and hallucinatory states provide similar conditions and they all create 40 Hz oscillations. Llinás concluded that consciousness is an essential and fundamental state of the brain and that 40 Hz SNOs are an important contributor to consciousness

(Llinás & Paré, 1991; Joliot et al., 1994; Llinás et al., 1998; Llinás & Steriade, 2006; Llinás, 2015).

From Llinás's research described above, it was shown that consciousness can be varied by stimulus from outside the body or from within; which is closer to the view of Buddhist thinkers and the eighteenth/nineteenth-century German philosophers Kant, Hegel and Schopenhauer (Zohar & Marshall,

2000). Since Llinás's ground-breaking research there have been numerous studies on the synchrony between the thalamus and the cortex. In general, the message is that the thalamus has a role in consciousness but there is no confirmation that it is the sole modulator of consciousness. George Mashour and Michael Alkire's review of the subject (Mashour & Alkire, 2013), especially of research (Liu et al., 2013), demonstrated that for animals where their thalamus had been removed it was still possible to maintain a level of consciousness and they could even move around. However, these animals seemed oblivious to their surroundings, thus questioning whether they had any sensory awareness.

Francis Crick and his long-time colleague Christof Koch were the first to consider the claustrum (see Figure 14.1), an extremely thin sheet of neurons, as a part of the brain that might be involved with consciousness (Crick & Koch, 2005). Crick died in 2004 before the paper was published and since then Koch has taken over the mantle and is now President and Chief Scientific Officer of the Allen Institute for Brain Science in Seattle.

Subsequently, researchers developed a hypothesis (Smythies, 2012) that suggested the "binding problem" could be overcome by the claustrum connecting to the cortex in cycles using SNOs that may function as the neural correlates of consciousness.

Koubeissi et al. (2014) confirmed the importance of the claustrum as part of the network to the cortex that both serves and disrupts consciousness (Mathur, 2014).

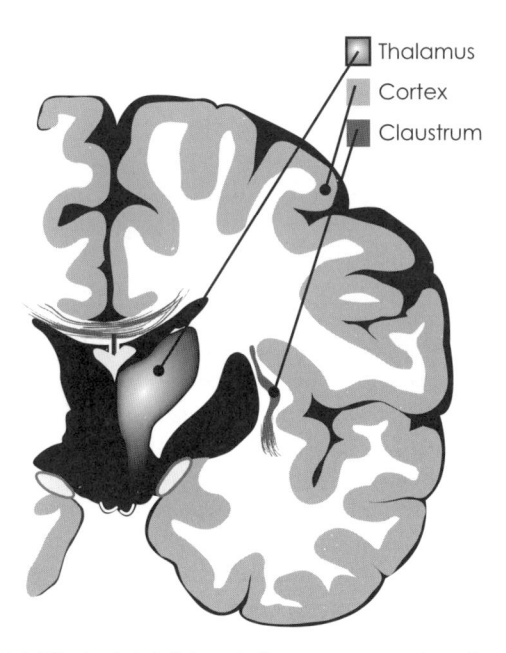

Figure 14.1 The brain's left hemisphere - cross-section, frontal view

Source: Gray's Anatomy / Wikimedia Commons.

On 14 February 2017, Koch and his team at the Allen Institute announced that they had traced three neurons in the claustrum of mice that send fibres throughout and around the entire cerebral cortex, one being described as like a throne of thorns (Reardon, 2017). As a result of this Koch believed the claustrum is the seat of consciousness for mice and humans.

However, in a study on the effects of the claustrum on consciousness in 171 combat veterans (Chau et al., 2015) it was indicated that the claustrum may have an important role in regaining, but not maintaining, consciousness.

So it would seem we have two different hypotheses of how consciousness works in the brain. The first is that the thalamus is the modulator that creates synchronous oscillations throughout specific areas of the cortex and the second that the claustrum is extremely interconnected to the cortex through long fibrous neurons. At the time of writing there are no confirmed neural connections between the thalamus and the claustrum (Mathur et al., 2009; Mathur, 2014), indicating there is still a way to go to solving the puzzle.

It is possible that both systems are necessary, but alone may be insufficient for consciousness. Using a metaphor, maybe in the end there will be several orchestral conductors like the claustrum and thalamus leading many musicians, each playing different instruments, in several orchestras but where each musician might be playing in more than one orchestra. Quite complicated!

Neurons in the heart and gut

With the revelation that the heart and gut also both contain many neurons it is very tempting to leap to the conclusion that these are the second and third "minds" after the "brain" with functionality beyond their own organ.

Several serious commentators believe that our emotions are influenced by the chemicals and nerves in our gut and that our state of mind, our happiness and our feeling of love are created by the chemicals and nerves in our heart (Rajvanshi, 2011). This thinking is consistent with ancient teachings such as Ayurveda and the chakra system originating some 5,000 and 3,000 years ago respectively in India, and favoured by spiritualists around the world. For those who have a belief in this ancient wisdom (and many similar teachings from around the world) it is also very tempting to project possibilities into probabilities or even facts, without the hard evidence. It also stimulates adversary rather than cooperation amongst the neuroscientists.

The heart does have a few (ca. 40,000) neurons and the gut has many more (ca. 100 million), but these are minor compared to the brain, which has around 100 billion, a thousand times more. The gut also has maybe 500 million nerve cells and the heart two billion muscle cells. They are complex organs. It is also important to note that there are hundreds of different types of neurons with different specific message carrying abilities. So the neurons in the gut and heart are different from those in the brain; they are not brain cells. However, research does seem to conclude that the neurons in the gut and heart do act like a brain in controlling some of the localised functions (Malone, 2013) and maybe sending messages to the brain.

Recent science strongly suggests that bacteria in the stomach also impact the function of the brain (Mastone, 2011) and we should be aware that bacterial cells outnumber human cells in the body by ten to one. It is also true that the vagus nerve, one of the longest in the body, has the central purpose to transmit information between the internal organs and the brain, in both directions, communicating through tiny electrical currents. But no-one is sure exactly what information is transmitted or in which direction, though there are many theories and suppositions.

Serotonin, a chemical known for producing a feeling of well-being, is produced primarily in the gut, with only 10 per cent of it produced in the brain. In the gut it affects appetite and digestion. A lack of it in the brain can cause depression. There is disagreement whether serotonin flows from the gut to the brain via the bloodstream. Dopamine is another multi-purpose chemical; in the brain it can increase stress and plays a role in reward-related behaviour. But in the intestines it stabilises the upper gut yet assists movement in the colon.

The heart secretes peptides that help in blood pressure modulation but also stimulate the pituitary gland (located in the base of the brain), which releases the hormone oxytocin known as the empathy or "love" hormone. It is also generally accepted that emotions, among other things, affect our heartbeat.

Steven Novella, President of The New England Skeptical Society, a non-profit educational organisation founded in 1996 to promote science and reason, has some interesting comments on this subject. In referring to the meme that the heart has a mind of its own, he comments, "there is a certain flavour of misconception that occurs when a cultural belief intersects a scientific factoid that superficially seems to support that belief". He concludes,

> *The heart does not contain brain cells. It contains neurons that comprise its own intrinsic system for regulating cardiac function. Further, neurons alone do not equal mind or consciousness. It takes the specialized organization of neurons in the brain to produce cognitive processes that we experience as the mind. This is all a complex and fascinating system. It is a shame that some gurus exploit this for a cheap mystical metaphor, distorting the very cool science.*
>
> (Novella, 2013)

So we can still use the term "gut instinct"; but don't take it too literally until the science proves it, and as we will discover in Chapter 16, there is a lot more to it than meets the eye.

Likewise "affairs of the heart" will remain connected to love in all our cultures, and why not? But the truth and "cool science" might be a tad more complicated.

Spiritual intelligence in terms of neuroscience and consciousness

As we quoted in Chapter 12, spiritual intelligence can be defined as

> *a higher dimension of intelligence that activates the qualities and capabilities of the authentic self (or the soul), in the form of wisdom, compassion, integrity, joy,*

love, creativity, and peace. Spiritual intelligence results in a sense of deeper meaning and purpose, combined with improvements in a wide range of important life skills and work skills.

(Griffiths, 2017)

Danar Zohar (Zohar & Marshall, 2000; Zohar, 2016) and Richard Griffiths (Griffiths, 2017) have both given excellent explanations of why serial neural oscillations (SNOs) is the system of neural connectivity that relates to spiritual intelligence. However, Griffiths is of the opinion that consciousness is not a product of the brain, based on "post-materialist" science that shows that consciousness continues in the absence of brain activity. Post-material science is gaining in popularity and credibility among some eminent scientists (Beauregard et al., 2014) but as much of this kind of science is based on personal experiences and recollections, such as near death experiences (Atwater, 1994), it cannot be explained by currently known science or evidence-based research. Whatever the final answer on the source of consciousness, it is surely closely linked to spiritual intelligence.

Personally, I believe spiritual intelligence is a foundation of the human mind (as is rational and emotional intelligence) and can be referred to and used effectively in searching for our further personal development. But, as this chapter shows, there are still far too many unknowns which tends to make me sceptical of those who think they have all the answers. However, I do think the technology is "cool" and the subject "awesome".

Questions and actions for personal development

Here are a few questions to check your understanding of the neuroscience around consciousness and spiritual intelligence, and the complexity of our brain:

1. What does consciousness mean for you personally?
2. How do you feel spiritual intelligence connects to consciousness?
3. How do you think this chapter might help you increase your level of consciousness?

If you want to check how much of the relevant science you have taken in:

4. What are the four suggested types of consciousness?
5. Explain synchronous neural oscillations.
6. What did Rodolfo Llinás and his colleagues conclude?
7. What is the latest thinking on how the claustrum connects to the cortex?
8. What can you say about neurons in the gut and heart?

Note

1 Nonconscious describes any mental process that goes on, in which the individual is unaware. Nonconscious can be subconscious or unconscious. Subconscious is information that is not currently being thought about but can be retrieved fairly easily once you direct your attention to it. Unconscious processes are those that we are unaware of.

References

Atwater, P. (1994). *Beyond the Light*. Birch Lane Press.
Basar, E., Basar-Eroglu, C., Karakas, S. and Schuurmann, M. (1999). Brain Oscillations in Perception and Memory. *International Journal of Psychophysiology* 35(2000): 95–124.
Beauregard, M. et al. (2014). *Manifesto for a Post-Materialist Science*. Open Sciences http://opensciences.org/about/manifesto-for-a-post-materialist-science [accessed on: 18/07/2017].
Block, N. (2007). *Consciousness, Function, and Representation: Collected Papers: 1 (Bradford Books)*. MIT Press.
Chalmers, D. (1996). *The Conscious Mind In Search of a Fundamental Theory (Philosophy of Mind)*. Oxford University Press.
Chau, A. Salazar, A., Krueger, F., Cristofori, I. and Grafman, J. (2015). The Effect of Claustrum Lesions on Human Consciousness and Recovery of Function. *Consciousness and Cognition* Nov; 36: 256–264.
Crick, F. (1995). *The Astonishing Hypothesis: The Scientific Search for the Soul*. Simon & Schuster.
Crick, F. and Koch C. (2005). What Is the Function of the Claustrum? *Philosophical Transactions of the Royal Society B: Biological Sciences* 360: 1271–1279.
Epstein, R. (2016). *The Empty Brain – Edited by Pam Weintraub*. Aeon.co. https://aeon.co/essays/your-brain-does-not-process-information-and-it-is-not-a-computer [accessed on: 18/07/2017].
Gray, C. and Singer, W. (1989). Stimulus-Specific Neuronal Oscillations in Orientation Columns of Cat Visual Cortex. *Proceedings of the National Academy of Sciences, USA* 86: 1698–1702.
Griffiths, R. (2017). *The Definition of Spiritual Intelligence*. SQI.CO. http://sqi.co/definition-of-spiritual-intelligence/ [accessed February 2016].
Joliot, M., Ribary, U. and Llinás R. (1994). Human Oscillatory Brain Activity Near 40 Hz Coexists with Cognitive Temporal Binding. *Proceedings of the National Academy of Sciences, USA* 91(24): 11748–11751.
Koubeissi, M., Bartolomei, F., Beltagy, A. and Picard, F. (2014). Electrical Stimulation of a Small Brain Area Reversibly Disrupts Consciousness. *Epilepsy & Behaviour* 37: 32–35.
Llinás, R. (2015). Mindness as a Functional State of the Brain. In Blakemore, C. and Greenfield, S. (Eds) *Mindwaves*, pp. 339–258. Basil Blackwell.
Liu, X., Lauer, K., Ward, B., Li, S-J. and Hudetz, A. (2013). Differential Effects of Deep Sedation with Propofol on the Specific and Nonspecific Thalamocortical Systems: A Functional Magnetic Resonance Imaging Study. *Anesthesiology* 118: 59–69.
Llinás, R. and Paré, D. (1991). Of Dreaming and Wakefulness. *Neuroscience* 44(3): 521–535.
Llinás, R. and Steriade, M. (2006). Bursting of Thalamic Neurons and States of Vigilance. *Journal of Neurophysiology* 95: 3297–3308.
Llinás, R., Ribary, U., Contreras, D. & Pedroarena, C. (1998). The Neuronal Basis for Consciousness. *Philosophical Transactions of the Royal Society B: Biological Sciences* Nov 29; 353(1377): 1841–1849.

Malone, D. (2013). *Of Hearts and Minds*. Top Documentary Films. http://top documentaryfilms.com/of-hearts-minds/ [accessed December 2016].

Mashour, M. and Alkire, M. (2013). Consciousness, Anesthesia, and the Thalamocortical System. *Anesthesiology* 1(118): 13–15.

Mastone, R. (2011). The Neuroscience of the Gut. *Scientific American*, April 19, 2011.

Mathur, B. (2014). The Claustrum in Review. *Frontiers in Systems Neuroscience*. https://doi.org/10.3389/fnsys.2014.00048 [accessed on: 04/04/2014].

Mathur, B., Caprioli, R. and Deutch, A. (2009). Proteomic Analysis Illuminates a Novel Structural Definition of the Claustrum and Insula. *Cerebral Cortex* Oct; 19(10): 2372–2379.

Nagel, T. (1974). What Is It Like to Be a bat? *The Philosophical Review* LXXXIII(4) (October 1974): 435–450.

Novella, S. (2013). *Brain Cells in the Heart?*, Neurologica Blog. http://theness.com/neurologicablog/index.php/brain-cells-in-the-heart/ [accessed March 2017].

O'Hagan, S. (2010). David Eagleman: 'We Won't Die – Our Consciousness Will Live Forever on the Internet'. *The Guardian online*. www.theguardian.com/science/2010/apr/04/david-eagleman-40-afterlives [accessed on 27/02/17].

Rajvanshi, A. (2011). The Three Minds of the Body – Brain, Heart and Gut. Published as an article in *Speaking Tree (Times of India)*, 29 May, 2011.

Reardon, S. (2017). A Giant Neuron Found Wrapped Around Entire Mouse Brain. *Nature*. www.nature.com/news/a-giant-neuron-found-wrapped-around-entire-mouse-brain-1.21539#/ref-link-1 [accessed on: 01/03/2017].

Smythies, J. (2012). Consciousness and Higher Dimensions of Space. *Journal of Consciousness Studies*. 19 (11–12): 224–232.

The Brain.McGill.ca. (2017). *What Is Consciousness?* http://thebrain.mcgill.ca/flash/d/d_12/d_12_p/d_12_p_con/d_12_p_con.html [accessed March 2017].

The Stanford Encyclopedia of Philosophy. (2014). *Consciousness*. Center for the Study of Language and Information (CSLI), Stanford University. https://plato.stanford.edu/entries/consciousness/ [accessed on: 18/07/2017].

Zohar, D. (2016). *The Quantum Leader*. Prometheus Books.

Zohar, D. & Marshall, I. (2000). *Spiritual Intelligence: The Ultimate Intelligence*. Bloomsbury, London.

15 Beyond the ego
Working for all stakeholders

John Knights

Moving beyond the ego as an organisational leader takes on an extra dimension.

Overview

Managing one's ego and moving beyond it is a critical aspect of Transpersonal Leadership. Whereas Part 1 of this book was primarily related to managing emotions to develop emotional intelligence, the focus in Part 2 is about managing our ego and moving beyond it, to develop our spiritual intelligence. This is not only to stop our ego impeding our personal performance as a Transpersonal Leader, but also to help us make the best decisions for the organisation we work for and the stakeholders who depend on the organisation's success.

As individuals, our human default is to survive and prosper by taking care of number one. How this manifests itself will depend on how we were brought up, the culture we live in and our environment; be it our immediate family, our greater family, the community, or maybe our country. It will also depend on how we have developed as a human being.

But what is "ego"? As with many important things that we need to understand, it is complicated! There are various understandings of what ego is, so we need to define what we mean. Although we discuss it in some detail in this chapter, perhaps the easiest way to define "ego" is to consider what your mind conjures up when you think of someone being "egotistical". They are self-important, self-absorbed, defensive when criticised, compare themselves favourably to others (secretly if not in public) and intimidate others to get what they want. They need attention and need to show how brilliant they are. Basically, they are only considering outcomes for their own benefit. Often this is an unconscious process – and all very human.

They are driven by a desire for power, prestige, recognition and personal reward.

The consequences of a leader with a powerful ego is that they will make decisions for their own benefit rather than in the best interests of the organisation. Organisational cultures have "egos" too, resulting in them giving preference to particular stakeholders, which might not be in the long-term interest of the organisation. It is important for Transpersonal Leaders to be fully conscious of their own egotistical tendencies, as well as their subjective preferences of stakeholders, in order to make decisions in the best interest of the organisation.

What is ego?

Definitions

The word "ego" is literally from the Latin for "I" and probably re-entered the English language in the early nineteenth century. Other than the above definition, dictionaries tend to add something along the lines of, "A person's sense of self-esteem or self-importance" (Oxford English Dictionary).

The general psychoanalytical definition of "ego" is, "the part of the mind that mediates between the conscious and the unconscious and is responsible for reality testing and a sense of personal identity". This of course refers to Sigmund Freud's psychoanalytic personality theory that dates back to 1923 (Freud, 2010). Although it is impossible to discuss "ego" without some reference to Freud, he has been discredited in many circles. He is rarely referenced in modern science, mainly because many of his conclusions based on the observations he made are not acceptable, either scientifically or morally. However, he got a few things right which have informed our modern understanding of the unconscious mind; that the mind operates in different ways and has defensive mechanisms. The box below summarises Freud's theory and shows the connections we would make to modern neuroscience.

Sigmund Freud's psychoanalytic personality theory (Freud, 2010)

Freud's most important idea was that the human psyche has three aspects. They are the **id**, the **ego** and the **superego** and they develop at different times in our lives. They combine to create the complex behaviour of humans. It should be thought of as a psychological system rather than anything physical in the brain, but there are analogies to neuroscience.

According to Freud, the "id" is the instinctive part of the mind we are born with, what we would call the unconscious, hardwired, default brain.

The "ego" develops in order to resolve the conflict between the demands of the id and the real world. Both the id and the ego are driven by pleasure but the ego uses the brain's cognitive power to develop realistic strategies to satisfy the id's demands. Although not identical, we can relate this to the conscious associative rewiring of the brain and the managing of emotions.

The "superego" acts as the moral compass to control the impulses of the id. The superego includes the conscience and the ideal self. In Freud's

> theory, the conscience is used to punish through a feeling of guilt, whereby the ideal self is the standard of how we ought to be in terms of how we treat others and generally behave as a good member of a society. This has its parallel in the synchronous neural connections that are linked to our spiritual intelligence: what some might call the "soul".

The way we like to define "ego" in the context of the Transpersonal Leader is to refer to the negative part of one's personality that we must overcome:

> *The ego is that part of our self that is based on our self-image and only interested in our own personal benefit.*

(see Figure 15.1)

Moving beyond the ego

As a human being we can start to look beyond our ego by considering the important people in our lives and how we can manage our own ego for the benefit of others. This is a natural, even automatic process for many, but not for all. We must ask ourselves honestly in the situation when we want the best for our partner or our children (or other close relative or friend), are we genuinely serving their best interest or because their success will satisfy our own ego in some way? Very few of us will be at one extreme or the other along the ego parameter. We can all improve.

Figure 15.1 Ego self image

To identify where you are, you might ask yourself questions such as:

- When I see my child/partner being successful, to what extent do I feel deep inside that it would not have happened without me?
- Does it make me feel more successful when my partner/child is successful?
- Does it make me reactive negatively when my child fails to achieve something?
- Do I feel jealous when someone is interested in my partner?
- Does it make me feel a failure when my child/partner does something stupid in public?

These are questions we don't normally ask ourselves. We just react and respond subconsciously when they arise. Whatever you answer, it is affected by your ego. You might ask yourself why you respond the way you do and how it might feel to move along the spectrum towards just being delighted for the other person rather than for yourself, and what change in you that would take. These questions are deep and personal and may benefit from support from a coach or therapist.

However, moving beyond the ego as an organisational leader takes on an extra dimension. The cultures we often operate in teach us to think that organisational life is about the survival of the strongest, that it is competitive, and that there is no room for values and ethics at the sharp end of business. If we want to get to the top we have to be tough and think of number one first. All these factors stimulate our ego, and it is very difficult to discern the difference between the real me and my ego.

To move beyond the ego we need to move our focus towards the survival and prosperity of the organisation and its stakeholders, we need to be collaborative, and we need to have a touchstone for making decisions that is based on our core values. We have to think about others first, and if we do things correctly our success will come in the wake.

It is also worth highlighting the connection between ego and self-confidence. As we explained in Chapter 7 we do not define self-confidence as being the best or demonstrating a dominant persona as one might expect from an alpha male. That would be self-confidence overtaken by ego. In our context the transpersonal kind of self-confidence is an inner feeling of being comfortable with who you are, about liking yourself, being able to show humility and vulnerability and always looking to develop yourself further. It is a self-confidence beyond the ego.

Managing our ego

If we are to move beyond our ego, we must learn to manage it. Based on our experience of working with hundreds of senior leaders and the related research, we have identified four main drivers[1] of a leader's ego:

- Power
- Prestige
- Reward
- Recognition

Power is about the need for control and to be in charge. The need for power can arise from insecurities or as a result of being brought up to think you are better than anyone else. The need for power manifests itself in having to be right, being considered the most important. We learned in Chapter 10 that there are both good and bad aspects of power but it always requires an acceptance from others that the leader has the discretion to distribute resources and rewards as they see fit.

Prestige is about being admired or respected for one's achievements. This is about what people think about you as a result of what you have succeeded in. As an outcome of your prestige you might be invited to important meetings or to speak at a function; or to be admired by your peers.

Reward is about being given something in return for one's services and achievement. Usually in a financial form.

Recognition is the appreciation, acclaim, praise and commendation for one's achievements. Recognition may result in a medal, a title or an honorary position.

As might be noticed, there is an overlap between the last three drivers but they do have subtle differences. In essence they are all about receiving something in return for what we achieve. All these drivers require that the ego be stroked with some kind of reward. Referring to Chapter 10 we learned that transactional leadership provides reward in exchange for effort whereas transformational leadership creates intrinsic motivation by providing an inspiring vision. From this we can see that the leader with a high ego is destined to remain in transactional mode.

Power is something different. Power puts *me* in charge so I can reward *myself*. I am not dependent on others to have an opinion in the same way as the other three drivers. It is noteworthy that a need for control is a key attribute of a sociopath and while about one in 100 of the general population is a sociopath this increases to one in 25 for CEOs (Babiak et al., 2010; Dutton, 2012). Other recent but incomplete studies put the ratio as high as one in five. This suggests that sociopaths are attracted to leadership because of the power and control it gives them. They possess anti-social and manipulative attitudes and, lacking empathy, basically only care about themselves (Knights, 2016). They are primarily driven by power.

To develop as a Transpersonal Leader we must each bring all these drivers to full consciousness so that we are in mindful control and aware when they are impacting our decision making. These drivers are not immoral or unethical in themselves but if we make decisions in service of these drivers when it is to the detriment of the organisation or even not for its maximum benefit, then we are not being transpersonal.

Self vs. organisation

There is always a danger for organisational leaders that we won't get the balance right between what is best for "me" versus what is best for the organisation.

Further, when we think about what is best for the organisation, how does that impact the various stakeholders?

As we discussed in Chapter 2 it is natural in our early careers, both from a human maturity perspective and one of economics and sustainability, to focus more on our personal needs. We want to find the right partner, earn more money, get a nice car, buy a house and take care of the children.

However, to get most of these things we need a good job, and here starts the balance between our responsibility to ourselves and our families compared to our responsibilities as a member of the organisation we work for. As we gain experience and responsibility, and develop as a leader, we need to become even more focused about making the right decision for the organisation and its stakeholders. We should remember that as a leader we are remunerated by the organisation to act for its benefit.

But how do we do that? The battle is ultimately one between the drivers of our ego and our responsibility to the organisation.

Every time we make a decision we should ask ourselves, "am I making this decision primarily for personal gain or for the benefit of the organisation?" Again, it must be stressed that this is not necessarily a moral issue, it is just about doing it in full consciousness and in an authentic and transparent way. It is not complex, but it is difficult. We are used to just getting on with the day job and not consciously thinking of these issues – but we need to.

For example, if you are looking for a promotion and genuinely think you are the right person for the job then there is nothing unethical about declaring yourself and trying to convince others of the merits of appointing you. However, there are many cases where individuals will manipulate a situation for their personal gain when it is not in the best interests of the organisation. See the case studies below for examples.

Case study 1 – putting promotion ahead of the organisation's prosperity (true and anonymised)

At a large consultancy partnership it was coming up to the time for the election of the managing partner, a post that would be held for four years. The incumbent Moustafa was running for re-election and another senior partner, Mathias was running against him. Moustafa had done a good steady job, with the organisation growing faster than the national economy. Mathias had bigger plans for getting into new businesses and growing at twice the speed of the previous four years under Moustafa. Mathias was very ambitious and decided the best way to beat Moustafa, who was highly respected throughout the industry though introverted, was to discredit his competency.

During Moustafa's tenure, about 3 years earlier, another partner with the strong backing of Mathias had persuaded the partnership to invest in a new kind of digital business. Mathias saw this support as something that would build his credibility. It required a large investment and would not make a profit for at least 5 years but could transform the business. Moustafa with the backing of the required majority of the partnership approved the project.

Although this new business was developing well in general and was now seen as key to the future success and transformation of the organisation, there had been some short-term set-backs particularly because of the illness of the partner in charge. As a result after 3 years there had been a huge investment and the expected returns were more than 6 months behind schedule.

Mathias made the case that the investment in the new business had been Moustafa's responsibility, was losing huge amounts of money and needed to be sold off as soon as possible. Mathias's charisma, determination and political nous won the day and he was voted in as managing partner. He sold the digital business to a competitor and over the next 4 years the organisation stagnated. However, in that 4 years he managed to sideline his potential challengers for the top job and centralised his control. He was re-elected for a further 4 years before retiring. The organisation continued to stagnate while the competitor the digital business was sold to gained greatly from its purchase.

This is a clear case where personal gain motivated by power and reward was to the detriment of the organisation.

Case study 2 – putting one's standing in the profession ahead of the good of the organisation (true and anonymised)

Deidre had been CEO of a large public sector service organisation for 16 years. She was all powerful and had seen off two chairpersons in the previous 5 years who wanted to develop the business model and attain a more independent status. This was so the organisation could make decisions without requiring government approval. Having come up the ranks, her main source of pride was the high regard in which she was held within the professional organisation to which she belonged.

Susanne was then appointed as chair, a non-executive part-time role, with the clear mandate from the government to obtain this more independent status. Having reviewed the situation with the board and other executives throughout the organisation, she decided it was necessary to develop a new agreed vision and strategy, to make the executive board more accountable at board meetings and to improve their behaviours and attitudes. She had the firm support of the non-executives but all but one of the executive directors were either silent or lined up behind the CEO in opposition to these changes. To make the right changes and break the deadlock she realised she needed external help to bring objectivity to the situation.

After not making the progress she needed to and many emotional discussions with her coach, Susanne realised that the only solution was to remove the CEO and replace her with the only executive director who had remained independent. The problem was the government were not happy with this decision because of the status and prestige of Deidre. Susanne really loved her job as chairperson and as a relatively young person saw it as an important step in her career. Nevertheless she was willing to put her job on the line in order to remove the CEO and after threatening to resign finally persuaded the government who then found a prestigious but non-managerial role for the CEO in another organisation.

This story shows how one egotistical person put herself before the organisation, driven by her desire for prestige and recognition, and how the other was willing to risk her job and reputation to do the right thing for the organisation – beyond the ego.

There are many examples like this and I am sure you know of some yourself. The question we each have to answer is do we want to be like Mathias or Deidre, or do we want to be transpersonal?

Working for all stakeholders

Organisations have egos too, embedded in their culture. Once we are conscious of the drivers of our own ego and feel we can manage them, the next step as a leader is to think and act beyond the ego of the organisation.

Although any organisation may have a unique set of stakeholders, most will be covered in the following list – in alphabetical order:

- customers
- community
- employees (collective, teams and individuals)
- planet
- senior management team
- sponsors
- suppliers
- shareholders (or partners)
- universe

Every organisation has its own culture, and every culture has its own sub-conscious priority for its stakeholders. Many private sector organisations would claim the customer is the most important, though quite often we know this is not actually so. From observation we know that many public sector organisations have a priority of their employees over customers. The financial sector in particular is renowned for giving a priority to its senior executives, and many other organisations refer to the roots of capitalism in describing their mission as "to maximise the return for shareholders".

Case study 3 – stakeholder priority (true and anonymous – under Chatham House Rules[2])

Here is an extract from the interview of the Chairman of a large water utility that has a monopoly of a region of the UK).

INTERVIEWER: Who is the key stakeholder for your organisation?
CHAIRMAN: Our client
INTERVIEWER: And who is your client?
CHAIRMAN: OFWAT, the regulator!
INTERVIEWER: And what about your customers?
CHAIRMAN: Who do you mean?
INTERVIEWER: The people and companies you sell your water and sewage services to.
CHAIRMAN: Oh, we don't really consider them as customers, except some of the big companies we have to deal with. We don't have any interaction with them. The only organisation we need to satisfy is the regulator.

Case study 4 – stakeholder priority (true and anonymous)

During an early session of a Transpersonal Leadership programme for the clinical leadership of a large hospital, we were discussing the importance of their stated vision that puts patients at the centre of everything. However, during the discussion about what this really meant for each individual in the room, it became apparent that really, the loyalty of a number of these leaders was to their colleagues. They felt an obligation to protect each other, as that was the culture they had been brought up with since they were students. While laudable in some ways, we asked how that put patients first. It manifested itself by showing that some operational processes were actually designed for the benefit of the doctors rather than the convenience and welfare of patients.

With this new insight, these very intelligent individuals with basically noble intentions, realised how their subconscious group ego had undermined their prime role, and set about changing many procedures with the patient in mind.

A growing number of companies include taking care of the community they operate in as part of their ethos. One of the most famous is the Indian conglomerate, Tata, who state in their purpose that "at the Tata group we are committed to improving the quality of life of the communities we serve" (Tata, 2017). This ethos goes back to their founder, Jamsetji Tata, when he established the company in Bombay (now Mumbai) in 1868. However, it is becoming increasingly more complex to maintain such a purpose as the organisation becomes more global. More and more organisations are taking their commitment to their communities and the planet more seriously but still many others perceive their obligations to community and the planet as being covered by their CSR marketing budget.

When working with leadership teams in organisations we always ask them to declare the order of priority of their stakeholders. It is amazing how usually there are a range of views within the team and how often it is mentioned that they have never thought about this question before. Once they agree what the pecking order is, the next question is, "what *should* the order of priority be?" The final reality is that the priority will change depending on the context of a particular situation and each stakeholder's need at a particular point in time.

Part of the answer has to relate to the importance of each stakeholder to the survival and sustainability of the organisation (i.e. the egotistical reasons) but the rest of the answer has to be related to the value your organisation is bringing to each stakeholder its transpersonal purpose. As a starting point we advise that a checklist is developed for each stakeholder stating what it brings to the organisation and what it needs from it. From there you can develop a comprehensive stakeholder document that can become an integral part of the organisation's strategy.

Questions and actions for personal development

The questions below will help you understand your ego and how you can be sure you are managing it.

1. What is your understanding of what "ego" means in the context of Transpersonal Leadership?
2. What can you do to understand the impact your ego is having on your decision-making?
3. What steps can you take to manage your ego more effectively?
4. Think of an example when you put yourself before your organisation and why – and vice versa.
5. Can you think of a decision you have made where you got the balance right between you and the organisation?
6. Who are the stakeholders in your organisation and what is their order of priority – and what is the justification for this order?
7. What should the order of stakeholder in your organisation be?

Notes

1 In this context, a "driver" is an instinctive need that feeds the ego.
2 Chatham House Rules: when a meeting, or part thereof, is held under the Chatham House Rule, participants are free to use the information received, but neither the identity nor the affiliation of the speaker(s), nor that of any other participant, may be revealed.

References

Babiak, P., Neumann, C. and Hare R. (2010). Corporate Psychopathy: Talking the Walk. *Behav Sci Law* Mar–Apr; 28(2): 174–193.
Dutton, K. (2012). *The Wisdom of Psychopaths: What Saints, Spies, and Serial Killers Can Teach Us About Success*. FSG Books.
Freud, S. (2010). *The Ego and the ID. Originally published in 1923*. Createspace Independent Publishing Platform.
Knights, J. (2016). *Ethical Leadership: Becoming an Ethical Leader*. Routledge. http://bit.ly/1Uh6vHL [accessed on: 18/07/2017].
Tata Group (2017). *About Us*. www.tata.com/aboutus/articlesinside/Values-and-purpose [accessed March 2017].

16 Improving judgement and decision-making

John Knights

Proactively use intuition, instinct, insight and ethical philosophy to support rational logic.

Overview

On the one hand we are taught throughout our education and most of our lives to think rationally and make decisions based on sound logic. On the other, we are advised to trust our gut instincts and our intuition. We are also informed that our conscious rational brain responds far slower to information than our unconscious brain and because of this we make many biased and prejudiced decisions (known as "unconscious bias"). Many commentators and even experts refer to gut feeling, intuition and instinct as if they all meant the same thing whereas they are actually all quite different.

The purpose of this chapter is to clarify the processes our brain uses to provide the information that enables us to make decisions. We will also learn how bringing these processes to a greater level of consciousness can improve our judgement and hence help us make better decisions.

Together there is one *conscious* and four *non-sub-unconscious* decision-making processes (see Figure 16.1) that impact our judgement:

- *Rational/logical*
  A conscious process to consider the relevant variables of a situation and to access, organise and analyse relevant information to arrive at a sound conclusion (Richetti & Tregoe, 2001).
- *Intuition*
  A *nonconscious*[1] process that is judgemental, rapid and involuntary. It is based on personal experience but liable to be affected by emotions, bias and prejudice (Sadler-Smith, 2007).
- *Instinct*
  An *unconscious* process that is innate and a result of something learned by our forebears. Also liable to be biased and provide an incorrect reaction when confronted with new information that provides a different perspective or perception (Sadler-Smith, 2009).

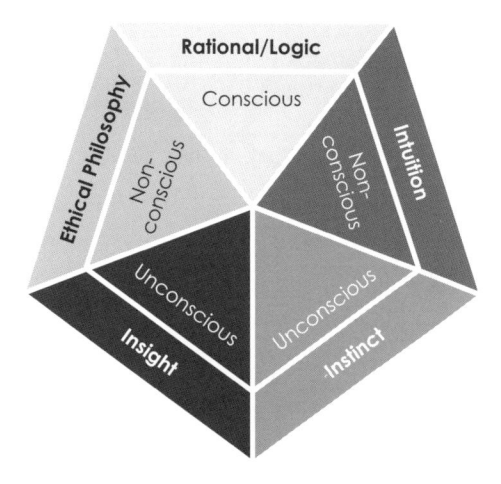

Figure 16.1 Five decision-making processes

- *Insight*
  An *unconscious* voluntary act from external stimulation that may happen immediately or be delayed until it is triggered by a brain process or another external event. It is an "aha" moment when the neural cells start to reconfigure (Klein, 2017).
- *Ethical philosophy*
  The basic motivation behind what makes us want to be ethical, to do what is consistent with our values (good or bad), whatever the context (Knights, 2016). It is usually a nonconscious process.

Each process has its own bias, which we need to be aware of and understand if we are to make decisions based on good judgement. The key to succeeding, then, is to identify and consider all the relevant information in full consciousness to reduce bias and prejudice. Figure 16.2 shows the two main routes to decision-making as we shall discover during the rest of this chapter.

Finally, there is luck, for which there is no brain process!

The importance and limitations of the nonconscious processes

Nonconsciously, we process about 200,000 times more information per second than we do consciously, although only a small proportion will be related to decision-making. Typically our unconscious biological reactions engage about 250 milliseconds before our conscious processes (Shire, 2010). Most of the research on unconscious bias has been connected to issues of gender, race and ethnicity (see Chapter 18), which shows its results from our exposure to the

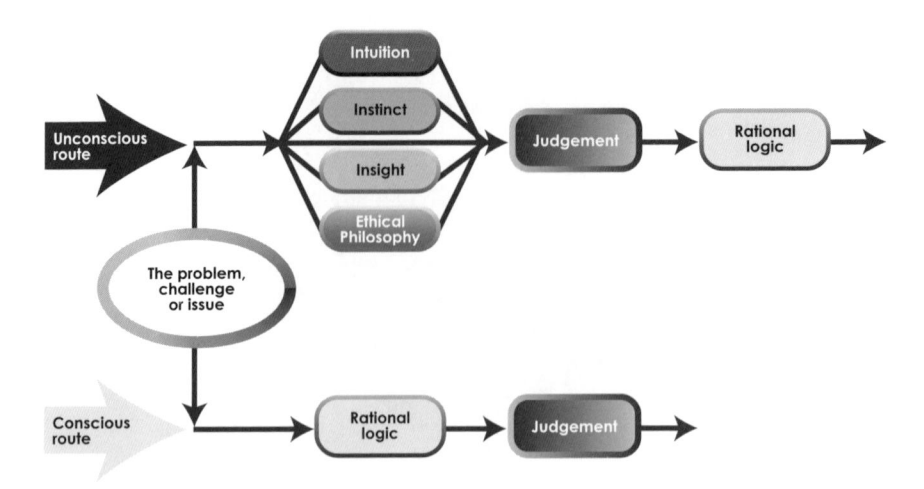

Figure 16.2 Decision-making routes

attitudes of others, images and stereotypes throughout our lives from an early age. This impacts our intuition and, over time, also our instincts. Our unconscious bias resulting from our instincts is more likely to be connected to the differences between life in the Stone Age and today, such as default leadership styles as discussed in Chapters 3 and 4. Although unconscious bias from these causes will impact our leadership, there are many more areas based on our individual nature, nurture and very personal experiences that have not yet been well researched.

Consider this example

You are in a board meeting and the executive vice president of international operations (Heather) brings a non-board member into the room, the vice president of Asia (Chen). She asks him to present the proposal they have been working on to invest US$50 million to expand operations in China. The president (Jasper) – the chair of the meeting – asks Chen to explain why he thinks the company should invest so much money in such a high risk market where they have already had problems with IP and other legal issues. Chen explains the plan and then, when asked by Jasper why he is so sure it is a good investment, Chen answers, "My gut feeling tells me it is the right thing to do". Jasper responds, "I need facts. I am not interested in your gut feeling and won't put the company at risk based on it". Chen answers, "Why did you give me this job if you aren't going to trust me? You know I have more experience working in China than everyone else in the senior management put together, and I just know it's the right thing to do!" The meeting concludes with Heather admitting they have to go back and do more homework, thinking to herself that she needs to get to the bottom of this "gut feeling" so it can be communicated to the board in a rational way.

What are you thinking having just read the example? Chen is out of his mind? Jasper should trust the expert? Heather makes sense?

There are two basic problems with this event. First, Jasper, the CEO, does not rate intuition. Second, Chen has not brought his intuitive decision-making to full consciousness, so while he is able to explain the logical reasoning why they should proceed, he is not able to communicate the intuition that has caused this. Most importantly, he has not investigated his potential unconscious bias and/or prejudice.

Having witnessed this kind of situation many times over my career where unconscious decision-making processes don't get a look in, here is a personal example with a positive outcome.

Example: where nonconscious processes were invaluable, valued and understood!

In late 2010, I was asked by the then CEO of Tomorrow's Company, Tony Manwaring, if I would write a report about "Tomorrow's Leadership – the transpersonal journey", a subject I had been researching with colleagues for a few years. We called the report "The Invisible Elephant and the Pyramid Treasure" (Knights, 2011). Especially important for this example, the prime sponsor was the Tata Group, initiated by the then corporate vice president of group corporate sustainability, Anant Nadkarni. Anant and Tony invited me to participate at a national conference on sustainability in Mumbai, India, in November 2011, where they would launch the publication. I would also have an opportunity to run a workshop on Transpersonal Leadership to the gathering of some seventy senior executives from the largest organisations in India.

How I actually came to being there you can certainly put down to karma, serendipity or just raw luck depending on your preference! What happened during the workshop was that these senior executives as a group were more engaged and energised than any similar group I had come across anywhere else at the time. Out of the 70 participants, I was contacted personally afterwards by no fewer than 40 who were interested in following up. At that time we had no other contacts or representation in India, and I had not gone to India expecting it to be the start of LeaderShape's international business. But the evening after the event, lying in bed, it suddenly came to me (insight) that we had to be in India to take this opportunity and meet the needs of the leaders of India.

Thinking more about it, I drew on 30-plus years of doing international business in a large number of countries to start to work out how we could do this (partly intuition and partly rational – but also bias because of my natural optimism and love of different cultures). I had also visited India several times in the 1970s and '80s and so knew something of the culture, but that was before India's business was opened up to the rest of the world. I also knew that our financial resources limited our strategic options.

On returning to the UK I had an excellent, open conversation with my board colleagues at LeaderShape. Based on my previous international experience I felt that the only way forward was to find the right partner in India who shared our values (ethical philosophy) and our belief about leadership but who also had access to the organisations that would be interested in our services (intuition). Of the other three members of the board, two – both with their own international experiences – had their own intuitive feeling that this was the right thing to do for the future of the organisation, while one was much more cautious.

Logically, we saw it as the biggest democracy in the world, and soon to become the most populous, growing reasonably fast but with the potential to grow much faster (as it is now). The educated middle class, while still a small percentage of the population was larger than the total population of the UK, and most senior leaders had been educated in a top Indian business schools and/or at a world class institution abroad.

However, one of our board members was more cautious and referred us to a mutual colleague who had lost millions in India due to choosing the wrong partner. We then had a discussion about whether working in India was too big a risk (instinct with prejudice). This caution proved valuable however, because it focused our minds on being sure we got a partner we could trust, first and foremost (which is actually true of business anywhere in the world).

Through our various networks we were finally directed to someone who had an outstanding reputation in India for being an ethical and caring leader, Nikhil Nehru, and who really got what we were about, but who was semi-retired. There was no doubt we could trust this man (instinct, intuition, ethical philosophy). Over a period of 4 years he established our presence in India and through his network found and supported our current partner Prime Meridian, led by Pavan Bakshi (intuition), who we discovered had the same values set as Nikhil, as well as an exceptional military and business career background (rational).

If we had relied only on rational logic and not taken into consideration our unconscious biases and prejudices we would probably still be a UK-only business. As it is, only 6 years later, we are now operating in a number of countries on four continents but we retain the same intuitive mantra, "number one is find a partner who shares our values".

As we can see from these examples, most complex decisions will require integrating several if not all of our decision-making processes to reach a sound judgement. We need to be aware of the processes being used, be able to bring them to full-consciousness and carefully review the biases and prejudices. We tend to think of biases and prejudices being only negative but they can also be over-positive. This might, for example, be due to a lack of experience (naivety) or perhaps being too optimistic as a result of a life with few setbacks.

Now let's look at the five processes in more detail.

The five decision-making processes (from Figure 16.1)

Rational/logical

We can use rational logic alone when a problem is very simple or purely numerical/analytical, when all the facts are known, and when there is no time pressure to work out the answer (see the conscious route in Figure 16.2).

Economics is a good discipline to consider the limitations of rational/logic thinking. Economists are excellent at explaining the past once all the information is available but notoriously poor at predicting the future. More recently, new sub-disciplines such as behavioural economics and neuro-economics have evolved that include in their predictive formulas how humans behave in certain situations and how the brain functions. The most famous proponent of behavioural economics is Daniel Kahneman, who won the Nobel Prize for Economics in 2002 and is perhaps even more famous for his best seller, *Thinking, Fast and Slow*[2] (Kahneman, 2012). In his language, "Slow Thinking is slow, deliberate, and logical. It usually takes more time, often includes numerical or factual information that our brain needs to process and is void of emotion".

The other vital role of the rational/logic process (and often forgotten) is to analyse, organise and enable communication of the decision-making judgements that come from the four nonconscious processes (see Figure 16.2).

Intuition

Apart from being nonconscious, judgemental, rapid and involuntary, "intuition is based on holistic associations, has impact (both perilous and powerful) and is pervasive across cultures and languages" (Dane & Pratt, 2007). It is also very associated with emotions and feelings, and is primarily non-verbal.

The superior capability of cognitive experts such as chess players largely depends on automatic, quick information processing, which is referred to as intuition. Intuition develops following extensive long-term training enabling players to nonconsciously and instantaneously "think" several moves ahead without processing the moves rationally.

> *Neuroscience experiments training novices in shogi (also known as Japanese chess) showed that the caudate nucleus activated more strongly than in other parts of the brain. The **caudate nucleus** plays a vital role in how the brain learns, specifically the storing and processing of memories. It works as a feedback processor, which means it uses information from past experiences to influence future actions and decisions.*
>
> (Wan et al., 2012)

This is basically the same process as when we unconsciously recall our experience (our memory) to make an unconscious judgement or decision.

Intuition, supported by instinct and ethical philosophy, plays a vital role in making decisions where there is a shortage of data and quick decisions are required, or problems are too complex to decipher by logic alone.

A simple experiment explained by Professor Sadler-Smith of Surrey University demonstrates this

When we purchase shampoo, the decision-making process is balanced between conscious and unconscious. However, when we purchase a camera, a much larger percentage of the decision is unconscious. This might sound counter-intuitive with a camera being more technical but the reality is that while shampoo is a fairly simple item, a camera is too complex for most of us to make a decision rationally.

Instinct

As explained in the Overview above, instinct is something we are born with, part of our genetic make-up and an unconscious process. It is a result of the intuition of our ancient forefathers in Darwinian terms. Instinct is equally liable to be biased and incorrect (a simple example is the natural fear of snakes – whether they are poisonous or not). More importantly for the role of the leader is that the human brain instinctively tends to amplify the negative resulting in our tendency to keep doing the same, preparing for the worst and exhibiting powerful emotions. While these traits are highly suitable for life threatening situations they are often counter-productive in today's society where crisis is the exception, not the norm (see Chapters 3 and 4 for further detail). We have mentioned that the fundamental instinct of leadership – "to know everything and tell people what to do" – is ineffective in most situations except in emergencies. Yet most people will follow that instinct especially when stressed, until and unless their neurons have been rewired.

Insight

Insight is something quite different but is again often confused with intuition. The *Oxford Dictionary* defines it as "the capacity to gain an accurate and deep understanding of someone or something". Well, first of all, an insight is quite liable to bias so it is certainly not always accurate. Second, I am not convinced that an insight necessarily provides a deep understanding. So defining "insight" is quite difficult. In the advertising world it has been described as a "magic elixir".

In my view an insight is where you suddenly see a solution to a problem that is not based on any singular process but on an amalgam of processes in what seems like a random manner. As individuals we get those "aha" moments in personal and different ways, sometimes in the moment and sometimes delayed. For example, while I have been writing this book there have been several occasions where I knew what I wanted to say in a chapter but just could not arrange my thoughts in the right way or could not think of a suitable example to highlight a point. But I knew (from experience – intuition!) that if I just left it and did something else I would wake up in the middle of the night or while having a relaxing shower or sitting in the sauna, and suddenly the answer would come to me. This example shows how by increasing our awareness and consciousness of the insight process, we can prime our mind to continue to work on the problem unconsciously, thus increasing the chance of an insight.

As leaders we must remember what we discussed in Chapter 4. An insight is an unconscious voluntary act, which enables the brain to overcome its desire to limit the energy being used. It does this by releasing adrenaline-like chemicals and it has been shown that happy people have more insights, especially when in a calm frame of mind. We also learned that insights are best created by providing the right environment, which should be free of fear and anxiety.

However, insights are of little value unless they are acted upon; first by checking the potential bias, then by committing to do something about them and finally following a plan of action. Gary Klein (Klein, 2017) demonstrates how insight can be positively encouraged through employing these key strategies:

- noticing connections, coincidences and curiosities
- investigating contradictions
- creating breakthrough solutions through the force of desperation (i.e. "necessity is the mother of invention").

Ethical philosophy

Ethical philosophy plays a major role in our decision-making and hence our development as a Transpersonal Leader. We don't know for sure whether ethical philosophy comes directly from those instincts, intuition or insights but they may well play a part. First of all, we need to understand the difference between ethics and morals. Unfortunately, there are many varying definitions but to understand the subject we need some clarity. The following definitions come from *Ethical Leadership: Becoming an Ethical Leader* published by Routledge (Knights, 2016).

> *Ethical behaviour: acting in a way that is consistent with one's own principles and values, which are characterised by honesty, fairness and equity in all interpersonal activities, be they personal or professional. Also respecting the dignity, diversity and rights of individuals and groups of people.*
>
> *Moral behaviour: understands there are rules of conduct of any group or society, which may differ from one to another, but are based on conviction rather than proven evidence and may or may not be ethical as in the definition above.*
>
> *So in essence ethical behaviour is of a higher order than moral behaviour and this is very important for any leader operating in a culture (be it a country or organisation) where what is accepted morally is not ethical in the view of that individual. Just think about how capital punishment or gay rights are treated in different societies and what your view is – and how you might need to act.*

Before reading further, I suggest you carry out this quick exercise to get an idea of what your personal ethical philosophy is.

> **Exercise: identifying your ethical philosophy**
>
> You work as a technician for a major car manufacturer and you discover that one of the development teams have installed software that incorrectly lowers the readings of noxious chemicals coming out of the exhaust when under test conditions (sound familiar?). You decide to blow the whistle (in this exercise you do not have the choice **not** to blow the whistle!).
>
> Is the prime reason you blew the whistle:
>
> 1. because it is just the wrong thing to do?
> 2. because this will harm lots of people and increase the death rate, especially in major cities where car pollution is already a major problem?
> 3. it is against the law?
>
> Remember whether you chose 1, 2 or 3 so you learn to understand your prime ethical driver.

Roger Steare, in his book *Ethicability* (Steare, 2006), takes a very interesting approach to philosophy and how it can be used practically by the organisational leader. He defines the three dominant philosophies as "Principled Conscience", "Social Conscience" and "Rule Compliance". Principled Conscience (answer 1 in the exercise above) is about "ethical behaviour" – inner integrity and acting virtuously. Social Conscience (answer 2 in the exercise above) is about deciding what is good or bad by the consequence of our actions on others. Rule Compliance (answer 3 in the exercise above) is simply that – obey the law, follow the rules. Steare's research shows that about one-third of people completing a questionnaire opt for each of the three philosophies as their prime driver but the percentages vary depending on profession and sector (go to http://moraldna.org/ to take your personal test).

He argues that Principled Conscience is the philosophy of the highest order and makes us "moral grown-ups". The danger of being ruled by a Social Conscience is that it may be used at its worst to justify the means and act against minorities, or simply be directed to the pursuit of happiness and conflict evasion, rather than what is right. Rule Compliance tends to make us lazy about taking responsibility for our own actions and, in specific circumstances, can be used in an unprincipled way.

It is very powerful to learn to understand what our own dominant philosophy is because it is a fundamental basis of how we make decisions.

> **Another quick exercise to consider your ethical philosophy**
>
> When you read a contract do you focus on the intent, on how its implementation will affect other people or on the "letter of the law"?

We need to bring to full consciousness why we respond the way we do and work out how we might change it – if we wish to. Excluding the sociopaths, most top leaders would consider themselves people of principle and most would generally follow the rules. The one area where we find the biggest gap is the area of Social Conscience – this is not a reference to corporate social responsibility (CSR) or the social issues around company strategy but about how leaders relate to and deal with other individuals. It brings us back to empathy, that often-missing ingredient in emotional intelligence (see Chapter 7 for more details). It shows how emotional intelligence is so connected to a leader being able to actually demonstrate ethical behaviour rather than it just being in the mind. Any leader will be much better able to make sound decisions once they have worked out their own ethical philosophy and embedded the behaviours that allow them to communicate it effectively.

To be a Transpersonal Leader we need to be influenced by each philosophy but with more focus on the Principle and Social Compliance ones. Rules should be the result of a philosophy, not driving it.

Using the five decision-making processes effectively

So now we understand what the processes are, how can we actually make better use of all five in our decision-making? Here are some suggestions:

- use reflective practice (see Chapters 5 and 19)
- find a good coach (or colleague with coaching skills) to support you and if you are to help others to become Transpersonal Leaders, learn to coach them (see Chapter 9)
- continuously seek feedback on the outcomes of decisions and judgements you have been involved with
- create a learning environment around you and your people
- practise mindfulness (see Chapter 19).

These techniques are important in assisting us to make the transition from "Robust Emotionally Aware Leadership" to "Radical Ethically Authentic Leadership".

> **Questions and actions for personal development**
>
> Answer the questions below to better understand how you make decisions and how you might improve your judgement.
>
> 1. What are the five decision-making processes and which one do you use most in your work? Does that need to change?
> 2. How does unconscious bias affect your decision-making? Give an example where it caused you to make an incorrect decision.
> 3. What do you think is your most common unconscious bias?
> 4. Think of a situation where you used all five processes to reach your final judgement. How did you convince other people in the decision-making process?
> 5. How do you normally get insights and how does your work environment impact the frequency of them?
> 6. How did you feel when you discovered your prime ethical philosophy? Why? What, if anything would you like to change?
>
> As a result of reading this chapter what is the most important action you are going to take?

Notes

1 (Repeated from Chapter 14 for convenience.) Nonconscious describes any mental process that goes on in which the individual is unaware. Nonconscious can be subconscious or unconscious. Subconscious is information that is not currently being thought about but can be retrieved fairly easily once you direct your attention to it. Unconscious processes are those that we are unaware of.
2 The fast thinking is what we refer to in this chapter as "Intuition". Kahneman refers to it as the "gut" telling us what to do, being emotional and done with little thought or effort.

References

Dane, E. and Pratt, M. (2007). Exploring Intuition and Its Role in Managerial Decision Making. *Academy of Management Review* 32(1): 33–54.
Kahneman, D. (2012). *Thinking, Fast and Slow*. Penguin.
Klein, G. (2017). *Seeing What Others Don't: The Remarkable Ways We Gain Insights*. Nicholas Brealey Publishing.
Knights, J. (2011). *The Invisible Elephant and the Pyramid Treasure*. Tomorrow's Company. www.leadershape.biz/invisible-elephant [accessed on: 18/07/2017].
Knights, J. (2016). *Ethical Leadership: Becoming an Ethical Leader*. Routledge. http://bit.ly/1Uh6vHL [accessed on: 18/07/2017].
Richetti, C. and Tregoe, B. (2001). *Analytic Processes for School Leaders*. Association for Supervision & Curriculum Development.
Sadler-Smith, E. (2007). *Inside Intuition*. Routledge.

Sadler-Smith, E. (2009). *The Intuitive Mind: Profiting from the Power of Your Sixth Sense.* Chen Wiley and Sons.

Shire Professional (2010). *Unconscious Bias.* Innovative Research Solutions. www2.cipd.co.uk/NR/rdonlyres/666D7059-8516-4F1A-863F-7FE9ABD76ECC/0/Reducingunconsciousbiasorganisationalresponses.pdf [accessed on: 18/07/2017].

Steare, R. (2006). *Ethicability: How to Decide What's Right and Find the Courage to Do It.* Roger Steare Consulting Limited.

Wan, X., Takano, D., Asamizuya, T., Suzuki, C., Ueno, K., Cheng, K., Ito, T. and Tanaka, K. (2012). Developing Intuition: Neural Correlates of Cognitive-Skill Learning in Caudate Nucleus. *Journal of Neuroscience* 28; 32(48): 17492–17501.

17 The values of leadership
Personal conscience and self-determination

John Knights

As a leader you also have deep responsibility to bring out and maximise the motivation of others.

Overview

"Values" is another of those terms that are critical to leadership development yet difficult to define in the English language. Whereas some would say they are "important and lasting beliefs or ideals shared by the members of a culture" (BusinessDictionary.com, 2017), others suggest that in decision-making we should keep values and beliefs very separate (Barrett, 2006).

Fundamentally, a "value" is a measure of the worth or importance a person attaches to something and as such we define "values" in our personal lives as "a set of personal beliefs, principles and standards that guide an individual on how to evaluate right versus wrong".

There is no doubt that our values are strongly impacted by our parents and many other influences as we grow up, which will be a mixture of good and bad, but in the end, only we as individuals can determine what we believe is right and wrong. That is why in developing the Eight Integrated Competencies of Leadership (8ICOL®) model (see Chapter 13), "values" needed to be unpicked into its various elements and influences. The conclusion was to separate values into two aspects, personal conscience and self-determination. This makes them more manageable to explain and understand, and hence more accessible to work on in full consciousness.

Our personal conscience is about "who I am" as an individual and is a reflection of our beliefs, morals, ethical behaviour and the sub-set of values that we call "virtues". There is also our dark side, the part of our nature or nurture that is the barrier to acting virtuously and in full consciousness.

Our self-determination, on the other hand, expresses "what I am going to do with what I am". These are the values that convert our personal conscience into action and as such the ultimate competency of leadership that must be enacted through ethical behaviour.

Personal conscience in more detail

> *There is a higher court than courts of justice and that is the court of conscience, it supersedes all other courts.*
> —Mahatma Gandhi, the preeminent leader of the Indian independence movement in British-ruled India [1869 –1948]

Our personal conscience derives from a number of influences that can impact our values. These include our beliefs, our ethics, our morals – and results in our ethical behaviour.

Beliefs

Beliefs are non-rational and without proof. It is the acceptance of something through faith or trust or just plain confidence. They may be based on religion (e.g. belief in a higher power and their impact on the world) but can also be innate or nurtured, such as believing individuals have a responsibility towards future generations or to do good is reward in its own right. Beliefs can also have a negative effect on values such as believing "I am the best" or "the world does not treat me fairly". In whatever form, they are a huge driver of our values. We all need to bring our positive and negative beliefs to full consciousness from time to time to analyse whether we still have the faith or trust about something unproven or whether they need to be reassessed.

Ethics and morals

We discussed ethics and morals in Chapter 16 based on the White Paper published by Routledge *Ethical Leadership: Becoming an Ethical Leader* (Knights, 2016). In essence ethics is based on honesty, fairness and equity in all interpersonal activities and by respecting the dignity, diversity and rights of individuals. Morals, on the other hand, are the accepted rules of conduct of any group, society or culture, which may or may not be ethical. The difference between ethics and morals can sometimes create confusion and again needs to be brought to full consciousness. There are many examples in our attitude to diversity where actions taken a few decades ago would have been accepted morally but in hindsight can be seen to have been unethical (by our contemporary definition). For example, 100 years ago in the UK it was considered morally OK that women were not given a voice to elect the government of the day – New Zealand led the world where women voted in a general election for the first time in 1893. There are many similar situations around a whole range of diversity issues where one minority part of the population were or are considered and treated unequally.

There are still many situations in today's work place, including in socially progressive nations, where the accepted morals are unethical and often based on unconscious bias (e.g. 87 per cent of women surveyed received demeaning comments from men in Silicon Valley [Elephant in the Valley, 2017]). As Transpersonal Leaders we must make ourselves conscious of these situations and use our good values (virtues) and self-determination to weed them out.

Values/virtues

Beliefs, ethics and morals are the key drivers of our values. Values can be good or bad so we refer to good values as "virtues". From our research, experience and observation we have developed a core list of virtues, which we believe are fundamental to Transpersonal Leadership. These are shown in Table 17.1.

The four virtues shown in bold italics in the table (**trustworthiness, truth and honesty, excellence** and **integrity**) are by far the most common values cited by individuals attending our leadership programmes when asked to state the most important characteristics of the best leader(s) they had reported to. This is consistent with the most important traits of a leader from surveys across the world over the last 20 years and the list of values in value statements made by organisations. However, it is also worth noting that often the term "values" is used very loosely in such reports and surveys to include such terms as "customer service", "teamwork", "people" and "customers", which dilutes their credibility and shows that the essence of values and virtues is not clearly defined or understood.

Humility has always been recognised as an important value of leadership going back to Confucius ("Humility is the solid foundation of all virtues") but it is only in the last 20 years or so that humility has become considered an important value in business and organisational leadership. A 2014 study of more than 1,500 workers from Australia, China, Germany, India, Mexico and the US showed that humility is one of four critical leadership factors for creating an environment where employees from different demographic backgrounds feel included (Prime & Salib, 2014). The other three were empowerment, courage (see below under self-determination) and accountability.

Table 17.1 Personal conscience

Virtue drivers	Beliefs, ethics and morals
Virtues	• **Trustworthiness** • **Truth and honesty** • **Excellence** • **Integrity** • Humility • Fairness • Conscientiousness • Patience • Forgiveness • Altruistic Love

More recently, we are noticing that values such as "**fairness**" are becoming much more important to Millennials (born 1980–93) compared to previous generations (Deloitte, 2016). It is this generation that is beginning to take leadership positions and will be the senior leaders of the future.

Conscientiousness is another value that is so important to good leadership. It is one of those values that provides such an important role model to create an effective organisation that helps enable all those processes and procedures to actually work. Consider these statements:

- demonstrates good attention to detail
- is well organised in his/her work
- always delivers on any commitment
- is considered to be reliable.

How many leaders do we know who are strong, bold, visionary leaders who could help their organisations be so much more effective by showing more attention to these traits?

The last three most important virtues for leaders are patience, forgiveness and altruistic love. These are pure human values, which tend to be underrated and overlooked in modern organisational leadership. These virtues, if used in an authentic way, enhance loyalty, engagement and appreciation. There is a potential downside if these virtues are overused, for example if the leader has a need to be liked or confuses empathy with sympathy. On balance, however, they are underused because of our likely default that we think they might be seen as a sign of weakness.

Patience is a particularly important attribute for the Transpersonal Leader bearing in mind we have established that "developing others" is a key EI capability and Coaching is the second most impactful leadership style. Both need patience and a realisation that time invested supporting people to get things right will pay dividends in the long term. It is not only the EI aspects of dealing with other people that is important but also in decision-making. While procrastination can be a vice (the opposite to a virtue), patience can be a very useful asset to allow reflection, gather all the facts and to bring those unconscious biases to full consciousness. There is always a balance to make between being patient and procrastinating or wasting time, so you need to be aware of your own tendency and introduce mechanisms to help you move in the opposite direction.

A personal reflection on patience

Patience is probably the leadership virtue I struggle with the most. In the past I was especially impatient when people did not get what I was trying to communicate or did not do something I thought was obviously part of their responsibility. I also wanted to make decisions even if they weren't urgent rather than give time to reflect. I still struggle with these things and always will because it is my nature. However, being aware of this issue and the impact it can have on others I am now much better (though by no means perfect) at managing my default preference. *I avoid telling people what to do by going into Coaching style mode to ask questions and make sure they understand, and that I understand where they are coming from. I force myself to put off decisions that are not urgent to give time for reflection.*

Forgiveness is another valuable virtue of the Transpersonal Leader, which can bring great rewards in future performance but needs to be handled carefully. Whereas patience can be done quietly without bringing attention, forgiveness often needs to be communicated in detail not only to the person forgiven but also to observers who may not feel the forgiveness is fair. It requires both judgment and reflection to assess whether the level of seriousness or the frequency of the action warrants forgiveness, and to ensure that there is a learning process that is adhered to. Forgiveness is usually best administered in a Coaching rather than a Directive style. The opposite side of the coin is where people find it difficult to forgive, which might result from a bruised ego, a feeling of self-righteousness, or a desire to punish. It is important we understand our drivers and preferences and bring balance into our reactions.

A personal reflection on forgiveness

I find it easier to forgive people I like or feel sorry for! In the past this has resulted in retaining people when they should have been let go for the sake of the organisation. I have learned to be more objective and listen more to others and my own intuition.

It is most difficult for me to forgive people who have taken advantage of my trust for what I consider their own selfish advantage. The result is I have no time for them and want to disown them. While this is not unreasonable, in an organisational leadership role it is important to consider what is best for the organisation and its stakeholders.

The final important virtue in our list is "**altruistic love**". In our definition this is a particular unromantic, non-sexual kind of love in which care, tenderness and affection is given freely while expecting nothing in return. It is not about being a martyr, and in fact sustainable altruistic love is dependent on a high level of self-esteem, which requires loving oneself in the same way. It includes showing a deep understanding of others' needs and accepting them as they are, accepting their individuality. Finally, it is about appreciating the gifts and contributions others bring to the world. Fundamentally, it is about acceptance and appreciation of others and self and it is particularly important to overcome diversity prejudices.

A personal reflection on altruistic love

Of course I love my family, even though there may be members I do not particularly like, and I have an altruistic love for my close friends. However, I have discovered the real power of altruistic love for a leader is when it is beyond those closest relationships. In my days as a corporate leader my mind set was much more about being fair – balance, win/win, expect something in return for what I give and vice versa. Coaching provided the platform for me to give without expecting anything in return and then it developed into a mind set of giving where one can, for the pleasure and benefit it brings to others. The amazing thing, as many have experienced, is that one does actually get much more in return, in very unexpected ways, quite often in commercial benefit. The secret for me was to be able to remove the expectation of something in return. One simple example was when I was the founding chair of the Oxfordshire Learning and Skills Partnership (a voluntary position), which among other things helped young adults who were not in employment, education or training to find a way forward. As a result of building relationships with several organisation leaders to persuade them to help, a few who had leadership development needs asked if I could help them on a commercial basis.

For each of us, some of these virtues are more natural to us than others and we will work on them depending on our self-determination (as explained in the next section of this chapter). At the end of the chapter you can carry out a mini self-assessment on a few of your virtues.

Self-determination (the ultimate leadership competence)

Self-determination is not a mere phrase. It is an imperative principle of action, which statesmen will henceforth ignore at their peril.
—Thomas Woodrow Wilson, 28th President of the United States from 1913 to 1921 [1856–1924]

Self-determination is the combination of having a purpose in life powered by the values (see Table 17.2) that enable us to best use our personal conscience in order to make a positive contribution in whatever sphere we choose. For a Transpersonal Leader, this self-determination must be executed using the ethical behaviours listed in Table 17.3 at the end of this chapter.

Table 17.2 Self-determination

Value drivers	Purpose
Values	• Motivation • Aspiration • Drive (Will) • Power • Energy • Courage • Resilience • Continuous Personal Development (CPD)

Purpose

To be a Transpersonal Leader we need a purpose. To do that we need to understand ourselves, our passions and our motivations, and we need to have an environment in which our purpose can have a positive impact. Finally, our purpose must be consistent with that of the organisation in which we are a leader.

Few leaders give much thought to their purpose as they are usually motivated by the drivers of their ego – power, prestige, recognition and reward – as described in detail in Chapter 15. Without purpose, leaders are indeed at the mercy of their egos.

Personal reflection on purpose

I worked out my purpose a number of years ago when I started to work with other leaders and reflected on my own leadership failures, successes and philosophy. My colleagues and I discovered from our research and experience that what we now call Transpersonal Leadership is what the world needs in the twenty-first century.

My purpose is to "support leaders on their journey to become excellent Transpersonal Leaders".

If you have not yet worked out your purpose, then start asking the question, "what contribution can I make to improve the world, even if just a little bit?" There is no reason why your purpose should not change or become clearer over time, but if you don't start thinking about it you will never have one, and that would be a shame and a loss – read more about purpose in Chapter 19.

Self-determination values

> *Real leaders are ordinary people with extraordinary determination.*
>
> —Anonymous

Peter Drucker's quote, "It's impossible to motivate people.... all you can do is to provide the environment in which they can motivate themselves" has been around many years but is still just as true. If you are not motivated don't expect anyone else to motivate you. It won't work. Likewise you can't motivate other people. **Motivation** can be stimulated or dampened by the circumstances and environment in which we operate, but it can only come from inside us.

We can be intrinsically or extrinsically motivated. It is extrinsic when we are motivated to perform in order to earn a reward or avoid punishment, which are often ego-based drivers (see Chapter 15). Intrinsic motivators on the other hand are connected to doing things for their own sake because they are enjoyable or rewarding in their own right and hence more likely to be transpersonal (Ryan

& Deci, 2000). Consider the executive who joins the board of a charity because he wants to help the children it serves versus the one who does it to include in their CV to help with their political ambitions and ultimate recognition. Of course, many times the motivations overlap but it is well worth being conscious of where our motivation originates.

Most organisational leaders are motivated at least while they are on an upward path towards reaching their career goals. Leaders tend to be competitive and want to win, which also provides motivation; but the best motivation is when you have a clear purpose (also see Chapter 19 for more on motivation).

As a leader you also have deep responsibility to bring out and maximise the motivation of others. This is not achieved by the power of your vision, your compelling logic or wonderful incentives but by creating the correct environment and removing barriers that inhibit the natural motivation of others. Sometimes that might be by removing a sense of fear (see Chapter 6), by changing your leadership styles (see Chapter 8) and perhaps giving them more genuine responsibility (Nicholson, 2003).

Aspiration is more specific than purpose or motivation and is about the ambition to achieve something, usually quite specific, which can change depending on circumstances. It is important for each of us to have at least one aspiration at any point in time and then as specific next steps, such as the next role in my career, improving my Coaching style of leadership, developing a better work-life balance or spending a certain amount of time working in the community. An aspiration is not a done deal, it is something you have to work on as to how your will achieve it. It is the pre-cursor of an action plan, but useless if it does not become more concrete.

Drive, **power** and **energy** can be grouped together in this context. These values all provide the raw fuel to enable us to achieve. Power in this context is different than the ego-driven power described in Chapter 15. Here we are referring to a power that comes from within to give you inner confidence to keep going. Drive can be defined as an innate, unconscious urge to attain a goal or satisfy a need. Energy as a value is about having the force and stamina to keep going.

Ultimately, **courage** is following one's own ethical standards despite the consequences. But courage from the best leaders will not be foolhardy when faced with overwhelming odds but creative and with confidence. Of course in today's world an organisational leader is far less likely to face physical danger but rather such things as the emotional stress of disapproval or uncertainty, which challenges the ego, or financial insecurity. The ethical resolve is, however, no less important and while it may result in short-term pain is more likely to provide longer-term happiness.

Resilience is currently an in vogue management term. Everyone needs to be resilient. To be resilient one needs to be able to withstand shocks while maintaining functionality, to endure a high level of stress and to recover rapidly.

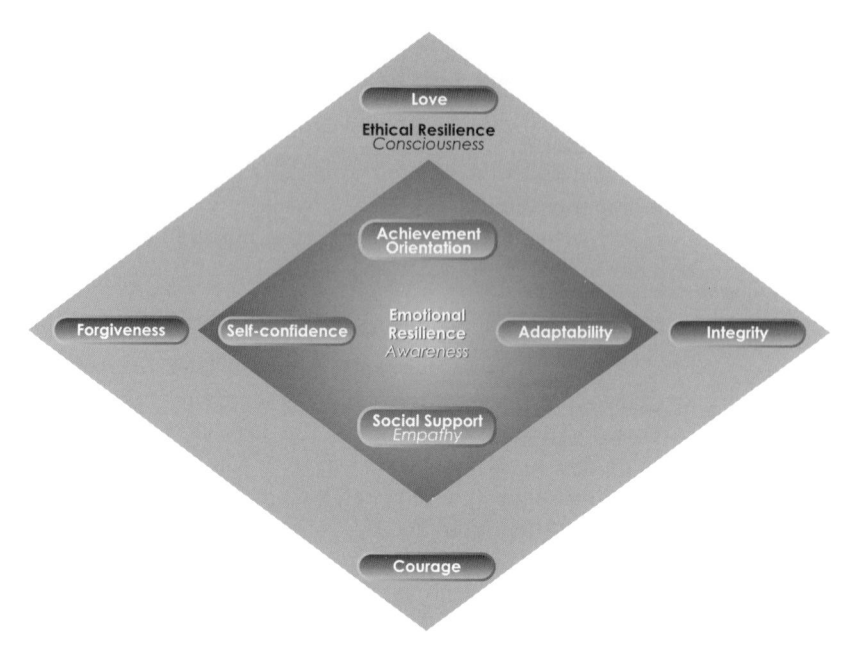

Figure 17.1 Transpersonal resilience

It is a popular term in management speak because so many of our organisations are plagued by (dis)stress. The more sensible leadership role is to develop a culture that has less distress. Resilience is an easily prescribed "medication" to combat the illness of stress when prevention has not been a priority.

As such, resilience is not a pure value but made up of a complex of EI Capabilities and values. As we can see from Figure 17.1, the emotional level of resilience is made up of achievement orientation, adaptability, self-confidence and the social support (requiring empathy), a model adapted from Cooper et al. (2013) to synchronise with the EI Capabilities in our emotional intelligence model (see Chapter 7). The transpersonal level involves love, integrity and forgiveness from the personal conscience stable and courage from self-determination. This diagram was developed with the support of Tony Wall who is also the author of Chapter 23. What it shows is that resilience has both a behavioural and values-based component and therefore requires both awareness and consciousness as explained in Chapter 12.

The final self-determination value is **continuous self development (CPD)**. This is a true value that underpins the maintenance and continuation as a Transpersonal Leader. It is a good leader's duty and responsibility to maintain that inner development both as a human being and as a leader. This is discussed further in Chapters 19 and 21.

Developing a set of core values

There are many more virtues and values than those listed and described in this chapter. We have just focused on those that we believe are the most important in the leadership context. Likewise, an individual or organisation may conclude that even this list is too large as a set of core values to use as a touchstone that can be focused on in living your life and when making a decision. You might want to consider developing a smaller list that challenges you in those areas where you might naturally have most difficulty but know are important in your role and to develop further as a Transpersonal Leader. It is important that these core values include a balance from personal conscience and self-determination.

Here are two examples where personal conscience and self-determination values have been used together:

1. "Courageous integrity", which was used by HSBC Bank after the financial crisis
2. "Power and love" applied by the negotiators in the peace talks between Palestine and Israel. As Martin Luther King put it, "Power without love is reckless and abusive, and love without power is sentimental and anemic" (Kahane, 2010, p.8).

Developing the core values of your organisation as an inclusive project can be very rewarding and developmental in its own right, and as an inclusive project, the values that are then listed on the website or in reception might actually become an important foundation for developing the ethical culture of the organisation. Unfortunately, for many organisations the "core values" are developed by the marketing department with a nod from the CEO – resulting in most people not knowing what they are. Values should be lived – not laminated (Stone, 2004).

Ethical behaviour

However, unless these virtues and values are transformed into the correct ethical behaviour, nothing good will come of them. Table 17.3 provides the four necessary criteria for ethical behaviour which need to be followed.

Table 17.3 Criteria for ethical behaviour

- Acts personally in a way that is consistent with own values
- Does her/his best to ensure the organisation follows its stated values
- Addresses and corrects situations when unethical behaviour is observed
- Is willing to be a "whistle blower" when ethical behaviour is not observed

Questions and actions for personal development

Answering the questions below is an important step in enabling you to further develop your personal conscience and self-determination.

1. Can you describe your core beliefs?
2. How about beliefs that may prejudice your path towards becoming a Transpersonal Leader?
3. Which of the listed virtues are part of who you are?
4. Which virtues do you struggle with and why?
5. What is your purpose?
6. Which self-determination values are your particular strengths and which do you struggle with?
7. What are your core values and why?
8. Are you willing to blow the whistle if ethical behaviour is not observed?
9. Complete the questionnaire (Table 17.4) following the instructions provided in the top right hand box of the questionnaire. Then follow the instructions provided after Table 17.4 to understand what the results mean to you. Decide what actions you are going to take.

As a result of reading this chapter and answering these questions what is the most important action you are going to take?

Table 17.4 Values self-assessment

	VALUES SELF-ASSESSMENT			
	How often do you perform/achieve the statements described below?			
1	Never or Almost Never	1	**Instructions:** Against each statement below score yourself from 1 to 5 in the WHITE boxes according to the chart to the left. Only you will see these scores so try to be objective.	
2	Occasionally	2		
3	Quite Often	3		
4	Usually	4		
5	Always	5		

X				
A				
1	Treats people with respect and dignity			
2	Trusts others to do a good job			
3	Can be trusted to keep a confidence			
4	Cares about the people in the organisation			
5	Has high moral standards and can be trusted to be ethical			
6	Can be trusted to do a good job for the company			Sub–Total
B				
7	What he/she says is believed			
8	Encourages others to give timely and honest feedback			
9	Discusses with people in advance of decisions that will affect them			
10	Communications to all stakeholders give a true and complete account			Sub–Total
C				
11	Acts in a way that is consistent with stated values			
12	Does not make commitments unless s/he strongly believes it will happen			
13	Does what s/he says s/he will do when s/he says s/he will do it			
14	Provides early full communication if a commitment cannot be kept			Sub-Total
D				
15	Acknowledges own limitations			
16	Accepts and appreciates negative feedback from others			
17	When he/she makes a mistake, accepts it gracefully, proactively and learns from it			
18	Happy to recognise he/she is only one of the players in the group/team			
19	Believes own importance/success comes from luck and timing as well as own capabilities			Sub–Total
				Total A - D
Y				
E				
20	Believes in carrying out duties as well as possible			
21	Feels there is value and worth in his/her role			
22	His/her role gives real satisfaction and enjoyment			
23	Actively provides environment to motivate others			Sub–Total
F				
24	Has determination to strive for goals that have been accepted			
25	Encourages and supports others to reach agreed goals			
26	Actively takes on barriers and hurdles to reach goals			
27	Usually finds a win-win way around obstacles			Sub–Total
G				
28	Applies resources in creative ways when faced with overwhelming odds			
29	Confronts situations with the confidence to ultimately succeed			
30	Has the ability to confront despite or without fear of the consequences			
31	Follows own ethical standards regardless of the result			Sub–Total
				Total E – G
	© LeaderShape 2009 – 2017 – this document is the intellectual property of LeaderShape Global Ltd			

Complete the sub-totals and totals for each section as marked.
Now complete the blank rows as follows:

X = *Personal conscience values*   Y = *Self-determination*
A = Trustworthiness   E = Motivation
B = Truth and honesty   F = Drive (intense will)
C = Integrity   G = Courage
D = Humility

You can now observe your own assessment of your competence in seven value-based capabilities but also how your level of personal consciousness compares to self-determination.

You can rate your competence in personal consciousness as follows:
The maximum score (total A–D) is 95.
If you have 76 or above, you are performing at a very high standard but may still need to develop specific aspects.
If you have 57–76, you are at a high level but may need some further development
If you score 38–57, some improvement is probably needed to become a Transpersonal Leader
If you scored less than 38, a significant improvement is needed to become a Transpersonal Leader

You can rate your competence in self-development as follows:
The maximum score is 60.
If you have 48 or above, you are performing at a very high standard but may still need to develop specific aspects.
If you have 36–48, you are at a high level but may need some further development
If you score 24–36, some improvement is probably needed to become a Transpersonal Leader
If you scored less than 24, a significant improvement is needed to become a Transpersonal Leader

Note: Most leaders in our experience will have a better rating (e.g. "very high standard", "high standard", "some improvement", "significant improvement") in Self-Development than in Personal Conscience.

Now compare how your scores for each of these seven virtues/values compare to whether you thought they were strengths or not in the earlier questions.

Finally, take a look at the granular statements where you scored lowest compared to your other scores. What would it take for you to improve these scores? Choose 1–3 granular statements to work on to improve your Transpersonal Leadership.

References

Barrett, R. (2006). *Building a Values-Driven Organization: A Whole System Approach to Cultural Transformation.* Routledge.

BusinessDictionary.com (2017). *Definition of "Values".* www.businessdictionary.com/definition/values.html [accessed April 2017].

Cooper, C., Flint-Taylor, J. and Pearn, M. (2013). *Building Resilience for Success: A Resource for Managers and Organizations.* Palgrave Macmillan.

Elephant in the Valley (2017). www.elephantinthevalley.com/ [accessed April 2017].

Deloitte. (2016). *The 2016 Deloitte Millennial Survey: Winning Over the Next Generation of Leaders.* Deloitte. www2.deloitte.com/content/dam/Deloitte/global/Documents/About-Deloitte/gx-millenial-survey-2016-exec-summary.pdf [accessed on: 18/07/2017].

Kahane, A. (2010). *Power and Love: A Theory and Practice of Social Change.* Berrett-Koehler.

Knights, J. (2016). *Ethical Leadership: Becoming an Ethical Leader.* Routledge. http://bit.ly/1Uh6vHL [accessed on: 18/07/2017].

Nicholson, N. (2003). How to Motivate Your Problem People. *Harvard Business Review*, January, 2003.

Prime, J. and Salib, E. (2014). The Best Leaders Are Humble Leaders. *Harvard Business Review*, May, 2014.

Ryan, R. and Deci, E. (2000). Self-Determination Theory and the Facilitation of Intrinsic Motivation, Social Development, and Well-Being. *American Psychologist* 55(1): 68–78.

Stone, B. (2004). *The Inner Warrior: Developing the Courage for Personal and Organisational Change.* Palgrave Macmillan.

18 Managing diversity

Jennifer Plaister-Ten

> *Nuances surrounding diversity are too complex to reduce to a set of competencies or a 'tick-box' compliancy.*

Overview

There have long been attempts to manage diversity. But is diversity really manageable? Amid calls for greater minority representation, global mindsets and improved intercultural skills (British Council, 2013), organisations have intervened. Organisations have implemented unconscious bias training and quotas for increasing the amount of women on boards have been recommended by the Davies Review (Davies, 2015). New legislation has meant that discrimination on the grounds of racial or ethnic origin, religion or belief, disability, age and sexual orientation is prohibited by law in many countries. Still problems persist.

Key elements, such as gender, racial and ethnic diversity, account for issues in the workplace and in society at large. Furthermore, as we have seen in the recent political arena, polarised views about what is right or wrong, good or bad, fair or unfair, normal or abnormal, good practice or bad practice can become entrenched and even become the cause of divided nations. However, it does not yet appear to be widely recognised that we all have natural unconscious bias, which triggers automatic judgments (see Chapter 16 for more details). This means that we are all wired to make snap decisions about key attributes such as a person's gender and also their race. Thus, in actual fact we could be legislating against something that is natural to human beings.

Social scientists (Tajfel & Turner, 2004) have long recognised that we are 'wired' to like and to trust people who we perceive to be the same as us; a concept that has now been substantiated by neuroscience. This means that we have tendencies to quickly look for allegiances to groups to which we identify as being 'like me' and at the same time, mistrust people from groups that are 'not like me'. This approach can be very useful in times of potential or actual danger, but can have undesirable or unintended consequences. Fearing people from a whole group can lead to stereotyping, to blame and to unjust attributions.

In the workplace this can lead to unfair treatment and processes or interpretation of the rules, depending upon which group you belong to.

This chapter suggests that approaches to diversity very much depend on the perspective of the person or the organisation or even the nation doing the managing. It questions whether or not interventions actually help those they are intended to help and finally explores what, if anything, can be done to further the diversity 'cause'. In so doing, we shall briefly explore the areas mentioned above; gender, racial and ethnic diversity, before exploring the advantages and disadvantages of four approaches to managing diversity. These are the unity perspective, the matching perspective, the learning perspective and the integration perspective. The chapter concludes that the nuances surrounding diversity are too complex to reduce to a set of competencies or a 'tick-box' compliancy. This is reflected in the Rosado's definition of managing diversity:

> *Managing diversity is an on-going process that unleashes the various talents and capabilities which a diverse population bring to an organisation, community or society, so as to create a wholesome, inclusive environment, that is 'safe for differences', enables people to 'reject rejection', celebrates diversity and maximises the full potential of all, in a cultural context where everyone benefits.*
>
> (Rosado, 2006)

This definition raises questions such as:

- Is the management of diversity a process?
- How does an organisation 'unleash' talent?
- What is a wholesome, inclusive environment and how would we know when we are in it?
- How do we know when it is safe – or unsafe – for differences to co-exist?
- What are the means by which it is acceptable to 'reject' rejection?
- How does everyone benefit and by what measures?

It is therefore suggested that with one definition alone, the range of interpretations could be so vast and indeed could be the source of misaligned assumptions and conflicting expectations and beliefs. Consequently, a call is made for all individuals and practitioners to take personal responsibility and some tips are offered here to help enable that.

The context

Gender diversity

Here are just some facts surrounding the diversity issue when looking at it from the point of view of gender. According to the United Nations, World's Women (UN, 2015), women work an average of 30 minutes more than men per day in developed countries, when unpaid work is taken into account. This figure increases to around 50 minutes per day in developing countries. Globally, about 75 per cent of men and 50 per cent of women are participating in the labour market. Pay parities continue to be uneven, with women earning 70 to 90 cents for every US dollar earned by men.

There is a persistent gender bias in the choice of disciplines in which girls become qualified. Girls are less attracted to scientific or engineering careers where there are higher economic returns although, when they do select such subjects, they can be found to outperform boys according to AAUW (2010). There also tends to be an under-representation of women in 'decision-making positions' such as leaders, managers and politicians. Correspondingly, an over-representation persists in jobs such as support and care work or those where low pay, long hours and lack of social protection persist, such as domestic work.

Davies (2015) reported that there were 12.5 per cent of women on boards in the United Kingdom in 2011 and in 2016 that figure had increased to ca. 26 per cent, with a call for growth to 33 per cent by 2020, although many are currently in non-executive roles. The '30 per cent club' (https://30percentclub.org) aims to provide women from the FTSE 350 with opportunities to experience a board level position for 12 months.

A quote from the then Prime Minister of Iceland, Bjarni Benediktsson, in a speech for International Women's Day 2017, is pertinent:

> *When it is no longer news to have women in leading positions, then – and only then – will we have gender parity.*

Racial and ethnic diversity

In the workplace, research conducted in the USA by David Thomas (Thomas, 2001), has shown that black and minority ethnics (BMEs) are subjected to a two-tier system, whereupon they have to prove themselves to be highly competent *before* getting promotion. Their white colleagues, on the other hand, are promoted on the basis of their potential. This reflects the assertion from minorities that they have to work 'longer and harder' to prove themselves.

In the current climate of widespread migration and the political swings to the right, stereotyping seems to be on the increase. This triggers survival instincts and a fear of 'outgroups'. According to news reports (International Business Times, 2015), people with a Muslim background in the UK experienced attacks rising by 300 per cent after the Paris atrocities in November 2015. Furthermore, we saw racial crimes increase by 42 per cent in the UK after Brexit, compared to the same figure the previous year (*The Independent*, 2016).

Perspectives on managing diversity

Managing diversity therefore rather depends on the perspective of the people doing the managing.

I have explored and identified the following four approaches to managing diversity. These are highlighted below in more detail:

- a unity perspective
- a matching perspective
- a learning perspective
- an integration perspective.

The unity perspective

This perspective tends to come from a fundamental set of beliefs that we are all the same in our 'humanness'. It suggests that differences do not matter at all and potentially do not even exist, because we are all a part of one big family; the human race. Diversity, therefore, is likely to be seen as a moral imperative when looking at it from the lens of 'unity'.

Advantages to this approach:

- suppressed or undervalued groups get a voice
- 'normalises' a diverse workforce
- non-discriminatory processes are built into the organisation system such as recruitment and retention, with 'penalties' attached to failure to adhere to them; for example, failing to meet quotas or targets
- it can suppress discrimination – and argue that discrimination does not exist; this makes it easier to manage on a surface level.

Disadvantages to this approach:

- there is a pressure for minorities to assimilate – people can feel 'preached' to
- people can feel torn between their values, but are not able to express them
- disagreements are not brought to the surface, and therefore there is the perception that there are no problems
- differences are not explored and best practice is potentially put at risk, therefore the performance and innovation of the organisation can be undermined.

The matching perspective

This perspective tends to accept difference and places a certain value upon it, in certain circumstances. Thus, in organisations where there is a valid 'business case for diversity', even if it is an implicit one, then this approach may be found. Therefore, a company wishing to extend its market reach geographically may recruit people from that country. This perspective can extend to sustainability programmes, as long as it fits within the meaning, purpose and overall strategy of the organisation. For example, a company selling new water purifying solutions may be found to be supporting communities experiencing water quality issues in Africa and may in turn recruit more people from Africa.

Advantages to this approach:

- a valuable resource to make connections with certain marketplaces or similar groups
- a 'matching' approach may provide the perception of a diverse workforce for example, matched to a certain segment of customers
- brings a voice to identified groups or marketplaces, that may otherwise be an excluded 'outgroup'
- creates a community of like-minded people within the segment, which, depending on its size and power can become a commercial or political 'vehicle'.

Disadvantages to this approach:

- can discriminate against others who have the skills but are not members of the targeted segment
- participants' experience within the group or segment may be regarded as limited or specialised, therefore their future career is also limited
- people may feel exploited for commercial or political gain
- diverse viewpoints from those who are outside of the segment (outgroups) may be overlooked, or even in the blind spot.

So it may be seen that both the unity and matching perspectives are successful to some extent, but neither provides effective approaches to learning from the benefits of diversity. The unity group tends to overlook difference completely in the belief that we are all the same and the matching group tends to believe that difference has a value, with the latter group believing it has a value in identified segments or groups; where ironically, everyone is the same.

Let us now have a look at a perspective that suggests we can all learn from our respective differences, regardless of which group we may or may not belong to.

The learning perspective

This perspective requires a mindset such as 'we work together *with* our differences, not in spite of them'. It requires that when a person takes the time to explain their position, they are not judged in return. Yet, as we have explored in the first part of this chapter, we know that each and every one of us judges. It is a natural human condition. When difference is treated as a learning resource it can be a powerful tool.

Advantages to this approach:

- identifying how best to work as a team
- exploring different perspectives about expectations from the leader and of colleagues

- diverse experiences that can lead to new ways of working, new processes and greater innovation
- people feel more valued and respected
- work and life is enhanced by insights and knowledge, and new skills are grounded in people's experiences.

Disadvantages to this approach:

- progress is often defined by learning from each other, rather than by generating change and is generally determined by the most powerful group; as represented by the shareholders of the company, the leaders or in some societies, by its elders
- it falls to traditionally under-represented groups to influence change
- power-dynamics, personal egos or the commercial-imperative fail to allow another the 'space' to allow their voices to be heard
- it takes more time and a degree of patience is required
- people from under-represented groups can eventually feel undermined and underperform or eventually leave.

The integration perspective

Finally, we will turn to explore the integration perspective that tends to believe there are many lenses from which to see a situation. Even from the point of view of one's own life and work experiences, there are often many ways to look at things, and even more so when we introduce the perspective of the other or others. An integration approach would acknowledge the many influences and changes people naturally face as they mature and/or move about in the world and would embrace the fact that each person has a unique set of experiences upon which to draw. It also looks outside the organisation and acknowledges that where people grew up, how they grew up and in what circumstances, or with what influences, profoundly impacts the way they work. Critically, when put together with another's unique set of experiences, this approach can generate a solution that is 'greater than the sum of its parts'. It is therefore an approach that can elicit best practice more readily than the others but even here there are hurdles to be overcome.

Advantages to this approach:

- respects the fact that each and every one of us is different
- best practice is sought from 'difference' as an expectation, a widely held belief that is part of the culture
- provides a structure for complexity (if using a model or tool)
- explores factors outside of the team or organisation that have a bearing on 'the system'
- reduces the potential for bias and judgment, because each person's narrative is unique to them.

Disadvantages to this approach:

- requires an acknowledgement that we are all different; not all the same
- requires accepting that we all have biases and judgments and therefore discipline in reflective practice is necessary to not only acknowledge this, but to work on overcoming it
- can take more time than the fast-paced world of work provides for
- may require training, as can on first impression appear complex
- may require an approach to thinking about problems and solutions in a way that is not available to everyone; for example, critical analysis or complex adaptive systems (see more on complex adaptive systems in Chapter 21).

We have so far explored the pros and cons of four approaches to managing diversity. However, it may be safe to assume that not all individuals within the corporate system or community are aligned in their thinking and in their approaches. In fact, it may even be safe to suggest that these types of approaches are often determined by human resource practitioners and may not even filter through to the workforce. Conversely, they may be debated at the 'top table', while not heard or acknowledged further down the organisation.

So in each taking responsibility for our own positive intentions in the area of diversity, we can individually work more effectively amongst diversity. Exactly how can we do that? Here are some ideas:

1. We can be prepared to learn and to reflect on the ways that our own unconscious bias affects the way we work, along with our attitude to the working practices of the organisation we are employed by. Only with this self-awareness will we be able to recognise subversive, destructive failures to comply with the 'system' and to recognise blind spots.
2. We can learn to stop imposing our own 'map' onto others. This can be tricky if it is the organisation's culture that is demanding a certain code of conduct and even more so if legislation is in place. We can stop compounding this by being very aware of our own unconscious bias as stated above but even more importantly, to find a way to make it explicitly known that you have realised you are, or have been, operating from a blind spot.
3. This next point concerns 'unlearning'. As global citizens we need to unlearn even faster than we learn; but it takes a lot of time to unlearn deeply entrenched views and habitual responses. We need to be aware, however, of those patterns that were formed in a different country or age, era or context that are no longer appropriate.
4. Use a tool such as the Cross-Cultural Coaching Kaleidoscope (Plaister-Ten, 2016) in order to integrate perspectives. Using this tool (see Figure 18.1) means taking a systems approach by exploring an issue through one or several external lenses. These external lenses are then related to the inner world of a person's identity, by exploring the links with values and

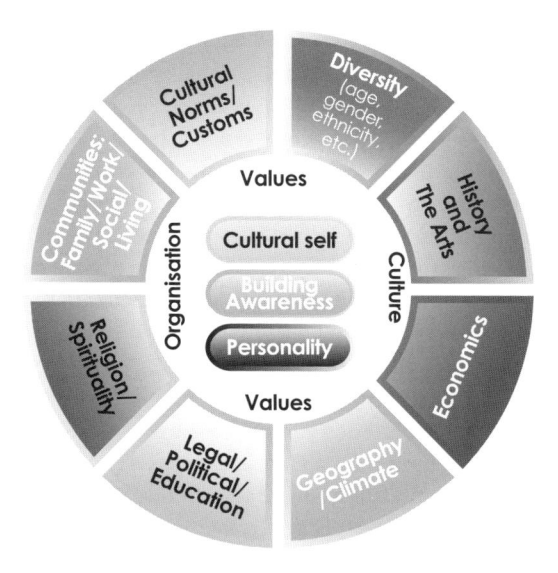

Figure 18.1 The Cross-Cultural Kaleidoscope™: a systems approach
Source: 10 Consulting Ltd © 2016.

the self in the context of the organisation culture. A comparison of the person's values with that of the organisation culture provides for depth of exploration, with values also being the link between the inner and the outer worlds (Hall, 1994). The tool has been found to deliver a greater depth of understanding quickly, and even more so when working with teams. This is because each person has a chance to explore their own values and beliefs and to be heard by their fellow teammates. Each of the team member's perspectives become included. This speeds up the 'forming' part of new team formation and therefore delivers team results more quickly.

Conclusion

In most developed countries, the law protects people against discrimination at work in the areas of dismissal, employment terms and conditions, pay and benefits, promotion and transfer opportunities, training, recruitment and redundancy.

Yet, around the world, minorities still continue to feel undervalued and oppressed. Despite progress in areas such as gender-neutral and anti-racist policies, promotions often appear to go to the majority 'in-group' and women are still under-represented and often receive lower pay for the same work.

Diversity is a complex issue and the notion of 'managing it' is fraught with the potential for pitfalls. While there are positive economic and social effects, these may not become realised. This is partly because the people responsible for their implementation are doing so from their own lens or perspective, or that of the organisation or national culture. This is characterised by a natural inclination to unconscious bias and judgment; which becomes increasingly complex the more one is exposed to different organisation cultures, life experiences, cultures and mindsets across our lifespan.

There is almost certainly no one-size-fits-all approach to diversity management; just a myriad of considerations to contemplate and the custom and practice of the organisation in which a person operates, and the legal framework at large. This chapter has explored four perspectives and suggests that an integration approach is the one that best leverages the potential for creativity and innovation within a diverse context.

These perspectives and my conclusions are based on my personal and professional experience. My son, now 22, is very much a product of a bi-cultural family and based on his experience has a strong belief in the unity perspective. It could also be that the millennials are characterised by changes in society that reflect more egalitarian values. I have experienced marketing initiatives that have reflected the matching perspective, whereby a thrust into a local market has meant that people from the target country have been hired, such as local hires in Indonesia or India. I have also worked for organisations that have created the conditions for the learning perspective such as in agile workgroups that are set up to develop a certain product, solution or approach and then disbanded once the combination of diverse mindsets has delivered the innovation expected. Coaching may also be utilised as an intervention in learning organisations where it is acknowledged that learning may be achieved by embracing difference.

I have not seen so many examples of an integration perspective, but have heard many organisations talk about leveraging the creativity and innovation in multi-cultural teams. To date, in my opinion there has not been too much discourse about how to do this. Taking a systems approach may well be the first step towards an integration perspective.

At the very least, individual practitioners and leaders can be operating from increased self-awareness of their own biases along with a conscious effort not to impose their own 'map of the world' onto others. This may require 'unlearning' in order to avoid repeating unhelpful patterns.

Finally, we must remember our cultural influences impact our values and beliefs and consequently our behaviours and working practices. This is extremely important for global organisations, because different cultures value different approaches to diversity, which can create confusion, misunderstandings, mismatched expectations and conflict. Nevertheless, companies with extensive diversity are more likely to embrace the innovative ideas and creativity to deliver new products, services and solutions (Plaister-Ten, 2017).

> **Questions and actions for personal development**
>
> 1. Reflect on your own unconscious biases towards diversity issues. What are the key ones and how might you unlearn them?
> 2. Which of the four perspectives are most evident in your organisation?
> 3. Are any issues regarding gender, race, ethnicity, disability, age, sexual orientation left unaddressed?
> 4. What do you think the remedies are to the issues identified in point 2 above?
>
> What ACTIONS are you going to take to overcome your personal unconscious biases and to improve the diversity issues in your organisation?

References

AAUW (2010). *Why so Few? Women in Science, Technology, Engineering and Mathematics.* AAUW (American Association of University Women). www.aauw.org/files/2013/02/Why-So-Few-Women-in-Science-Technology-Engineering-and-Mathematics.pdf [accessed on: 18/07/2017].

British Council (2013). *Culture At Work: The Value of Intercultural Skills in the Workplace.* British Council. www.britishcouncil.org/culture-at-work-research_march_2013.pdf [accessed on: 18/07/2017].

Davies Review (2015). *Women on Boards, Improving the Gender Balance on British Boards.* www.gov.uk/government/uploads/system/uploads/attachment_data/file/482059/BIS-15-585-women-on-boards-davies-review-5-year-summary-october-2015.pdf [accessed on: 18/07/2017].

Hall, B. P. (1994). *Values Shift; a Guide to Personal and Organizational Transformation.* Wipf and Stock Publishers.

International Business Times (2015). *Hate Crimes against British Muslims Soar by 300% in One Week.* www.ibtimes.co.uk/paris-attacks-hate-crimes-against-british-muslims-soar-by-300-one-week-1530048 [accessed on: 18/07/2017].

Plaister-Ten, J. (2016). *The Cross-Cultural Kaleidoscope: A Systems Approach to Coaching Amongst Different Cultural Influences.* Karnac.

Plaister-Ten, J. (2017). *Leading Across Cultures: Developing Leaders for Global Organisations.* Routledge. http://bit.ly/2mbDuYm [accessed on: 18/07/2017].

Rosado, C. (2006). *What Do We Mean By "Managing Diversity"?* Rosado Consulting for Change in Human Systems. www.edchange.org/multicultural/papers/rosado_managing_diversity.pdf [accessed on: 18/07/2017].

Tajfel, H. and Turner, J. C. (2004). An Integrative Theory of Intergroup Conflict. In Hatch, M. J. and Schultz, M. (eds) *Organizational Identity.* New York: Oxford University Press.

Thomas, D.A. (2001). The Truth about Mentoring Minorities – Race Matters. *Harvard Business Review*, pp. 98–107.

The Independent (2016). *Hate Crimes Rise by 42% in England and Wales Since Brexit Result*. www.independent.co.uk/news/uk/crime/brexit-hate-crime-racism-stats-spike-police-england-wales-eu-referendum-a7126706.html [accessed on: 18/07/2017].

United Nations (2015). *World's Women*. https://unstats.un.org/unsd/gender/chapter4/chapter4.html [accessed on: 18/07/2017].

19 The inner development of a Transpersonal Leader

Sue Coyne

Accepting yourself as you are whilst at the same time seeing yourself as a work in progress.

Overview

Leadership is a journey that takes us through a series of stages of development, each of which we need to master before progressing onto the next one. As such, developing as a Transpersonal Leader pre-supposes that we have mastered being a Robust Emotionally Aware Leader. Reaching the Transpersonal stage is an achievement in itself as thus far it has only been attained by a small minority of senior leaders – around 5 per cent according to Joiner and Josephs (2007).

The diagram in Figure 19.1 shows how inner development underpins the characteristics of Transpersonal Leadership.

The most important elements of our inner development include:

- becoming mindful through developing our awareness and increasing our level of consciousness

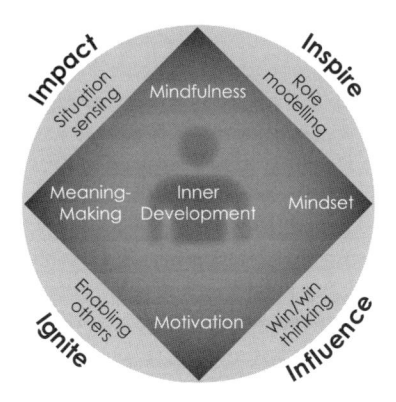

Figure 19.1 Inner development for Transpersonal Leaders
Source: Sue Coyne © 2017.

- establishing the right mindset
- tapping into our motivation
- improving our meaning-making through using reflection to understand what is happening through and around us.

This inner work enables the development of key transpersonal characteristics such as:

- inspiring others through being a role model
- thinking win/win so that we positively influence all stakeholders
- enabling others to thrive and grow so that they are ignited to fully contribute
- maximising our impact through an ability to sense what is required in different situations and contexts.

Transpersonal Leadership is about continuing to build our levels of awareness and consciousness to choose how we are being in the moment. This enables us to make the fullest contribution possible and so bring about the difference we are here to make.

Inner development: personal leadership

Mindfulness

The advanced leadership skills that are part and parcel of developing as a Transpersonal Leader are underpinned by one or more forms of attentional practice. This could comprise mindfulness, meditation or certain martial arts such as Tai Chi and Chi Gung.

Why is this so important? Most of the time we use the default network in our brains to take in the huge volume of information we receive from the outside world, filter it through our memories and interpret it. It is called the default network because it operates when we are at rest and not focused on a specific task. In this mode we tend to be past referenced and thought based.

We also have associative and synchronous networks, which utilise several different areas of the brain to take in information from all of our senses in real time (see Chapter 14). In this mode we are closer to the reality of what is happening in the moment and able to respond more flexibly as events unfold.

Leaders who have an attentional practice are able to switch between these two brain networks at will. They also develop the ability to be the observer of their own thoughts, feelings and sensations, access a state of flow and be fully present and tuned in to what is happening in the moment (Rock, 2009).

A study among leaders who trained in mindfulness (Reitz & Chaskalson, 2016) found that they became "Less reactive and more responsive" and it helped them to develop the skills that led to improvements in "the important leadership capacities of resilience, collaboration and leading in complex conditions".

So a key platform that supports our development as a Transpersonal Leader is having a regular on-going attentional practice. This has benefits in all areas of our lives.

Getting started

If you would like to start meditating you can use an app such as Headspace (www.headspace.com) to support you. Several clients who believed they would find it difficult to meditate have developed a successful personal practice using it.

Mindset

> *Mindset is: the neural blueprint that creates our view of the world and our way of being in the world.*
> —Coyne & Gairdner, 2016

A pre-requisite for developing as a Transpersonal Leader is to have a growth mindset as opposed to a fixed mindset. A growth mindset means accepting yourself as you are while at the same time seeing yourself as a work in progress, someone with further potential as you continue on your leadership journey (Dweck, 2006).

There are different layers of mindset. Starting with the most *unconscious* at the top of the list to the most *conscious* at the bottom we have:

- Identity: who am I?
- Purpose: why am I here?
- Values
- Attitudes and beliefs
- Talent/gifts
- Intention
- Behaviour, Skills, Capabilities
- Experiences

As you are transitioning into each new stage on your leadership journey it is wise to seek help to support you in moving beyond what is limiting you. Hence, it is unlikely that you will have reached the transpersonal level of leadership without having had some input from a coach, counsellor or therapist.

As a result of such support, the chances are you will be able to:

- interrupt the automatic stress response (fight/flight/freeze)
- identify limiting beliefs, e.g. *I am not loveable, I am not good enough, I don't have enough* and re-wire your brain with more empowering beliefs that are aligned with the outcomes you want
- recognise feelings, sensations and emotions as they arise and use them as information
- accept your inner diversity and integrate aspects of yourself that you previously didn't want to own so that you don't project them onto others.

All of this inner work means that you are able to bring more of yourself into your leadership role and lead from a place of wholeness and trust in your ability to do the right thing.

Getting started

Develop answers to the following questions, preferably with the help of a coach:

- Who am I as a leader? (Who you are is central to how you lead.)
- What is the difference I want to make through my leadership?
- How can I use my gifts and talents to make a difference?
- What are my core values?
- How congruent are my day-to-day behaviours and actions with my core values?

Motivation

> *Motivation is at the heart of leadership and engagement.*
> —Sale, 2016

As we develop as a leader our motivation shifts from being motivated by our own achievements, through enabling others to deliver what is required of them by the organisation, to collaborating with others to make an even greater difference.

As a Transpersonal Leader, an important aspect of enabling others to deliver what is required of them is engagement. There is a lot of focus on engagement as it is seen as one of the best predictors of the future performance of an organisation. Despite this, survey after survey reports that around three quarters of employees are either not engaged or actively disengaged (Sale, 2016).

What has motivation got to do with engagement? According to James Sale in *Mapping Motivation*, motivation comprises 70 per cent of the engagement mix. Engaging your people starts with making sure that *you* are energised, motivated and engaged.

So what is motivation? It is our inner drive and can be experienced as positive energy and enthusiasm. Motivators are deep needs within you and are also closely linked to your values. When you live your values and ensure your motivators are being met you feel happy and satisfied.

The nine motivators identified by James Sale (and reprinted by permission) are shown in Figure 19.2.

The benefits of feeling motivated are:

- high levels of energy and enthusiasm, which feels good
- the energy to cope with difficulties, problems and situations and continue to thrive
- enhanced self-esteem and confidence because you feel good about yourself
- engagement.

So how do we go about motivating ourselves?

Seventy per cent of our motivation comes from our beliefs. This links back to the section above on mindset. The ability to re-wire our brains (see Chapters 4 and 14) and install positive beliefs aligned with our motivators is a crucial skill for Transpersonal Leaders (Coyne, 2016b).

Why does motivating our people matter? Because it is core to our effectiveness as a Transpersonal Leader. This involves understanding their motivators and making sure we have ways of enabling those around us to satisfy their own motivations.

Motivated people are happier, put in more discretionary effort and are also more likely to stay with the organisation (see Chapter 10). This is one of the ways you can add value to your organisation because motivated people mean better performance, productivity and profitability.

Getting started

Identify your own key motivators. If you need support with this you can work with your own coach or contact me (scoyne@leadershapegobal.com) to arrange a Motivational Maps assessment to discover your key motivators.

Relationship Motivators

- **The Defender** — Seeks security, predictability, stability
- **The Friend** — Seeks belonging, friendship, fulfilling relationships
- **The Star** — Seeks recognition, respect, social esteem

Achievement Motivators

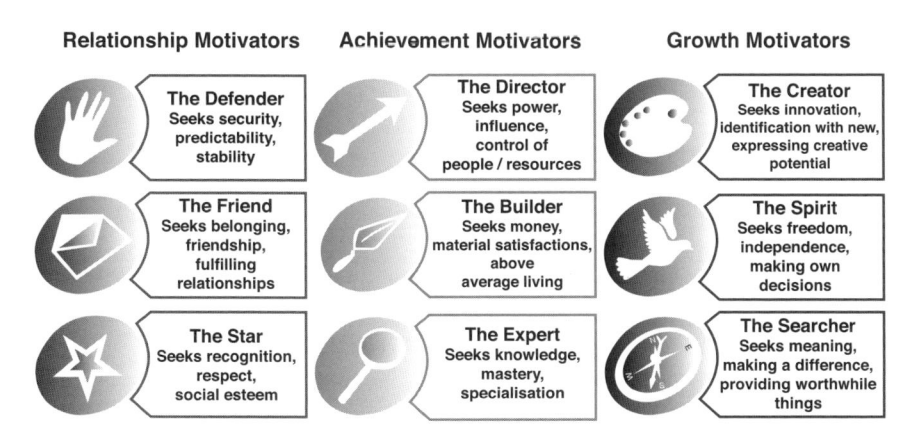

- **The Director** — Seeks power, influence, control of people / resources
- **The Builder** — Seeks money, material satisfactions, above average living
- **The Expert** — Seeks knowledge, mastery, specialisation

Growth Motivators

- **The Creator** — Seeks innovation, identification with new, expressing creative potential
- **The Spirit** — Seeks freedom, independence, making own decisions
- **The Searcher** — Seeks meaning, making a difference, providing worthwhile things

Figure 19.2 Nine motivators

Source: ©James Sale, reprinted with permission.

216 *Sue Coyne*

Meaning-making

> *The most deeply motivated people hitch their desires to a cause bigger then themselves.*
> —Pink, 2010

As we mentioned in the section on mindset, having a purpose is a key aspect of Transpersonal Leadership. Identifying your **purpose** gives you a strong "why" and gives meaning to your work and life. Find more discussion about "purpose" in Chapters 17 and 20.

It is not easy to uncover your purpose and you may need to seek the support of a coach. I recall how emotional I felt when I discovered my life purpose as a result of several coaching sessions in 2004. It completely changed my life, as it became the filter through which I viewed everything. So before agreeing to or taking on anything I would think of my purpose, which is *"to allow myself and others to experience our magnificence and that of the world we live in"* and ask *"is this aligned with my purpose?"*

From my experience, when you align your work with your purpose you experience vitality, unleash your creativity, feel passionate and spend more time in flow. What is more, when you are on purpose it is difficult for others to knock you off balance.

But also how aligned is your individual purpose to that of your organisation?

> *When the individual and organisational purpose enter into resonance and reinforce each other, extraordinary things can happen.*
> —Laloux, 2014

Another aspect of meaning-making is developing a reflective practice.

There are two types of reflective practice (Schon, 1983):

1. Reflection-in-action – the ability to reflect on a situation while performing it.
2. Reflection-on-action – the ability to look back and critically analyse a situation, with a view to doing things differently next time.

Reflective practice gives you the ability to make meaning from different situations and so become a responsive leader rather than a reactive one. It is the secret weapon in the Transpersonal Leader's tool kit. Also see the section in Chapter 5 on learning though reflection.

With reflective practice, the challenges you face are the next piece of curriculum on your leadership journey. There are many approaches to reflection-in action but the simplest I have come across is one based on Otto Scharmer's Theory U (Scharmer, 2009), developed by Giles Hutchins and Elaine Patterson called the Flow Process of Retreat, Reflect and Return, shown in Figure 19.2 with permission from Elaine Patterson (Patterson, 2017a & b).

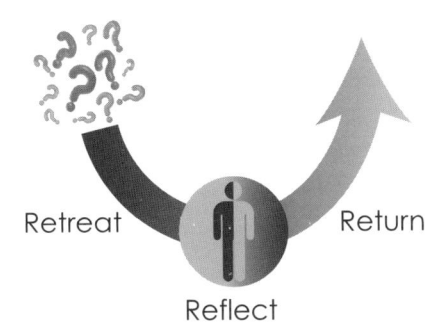

Figure 19.3 Reflection in action

This involves:

1. Retreat: pausing to interrupt your automatic, reactive ways of thinking and behaving
2. Reflect: taking the time to explore the possibilities and what wants to happen instead
3. Return: gathering new insights, which inform the actions you choose to take

For reflection-on-action see Chapter 11 for details how to create a reflection note.

Your efforts in taking the time to develop this skill will be repaid by:

- improved self-awareness
- greater creativity
- deeper sense of purpose
- new insights
- wiser decisions
- more effective relationships
- more time and energy.

Reflective practice is one of the easiest things to drop when the pressure is on, yet this is exactly when you will most benefit from it. Time spent on reflective practice will ensure that you consistently focus on doing the right thing and are able to maintain a transpersonal approach to leadership no matter what the situation.

Getting started

Start using the Retreat, Reflect, Return process and keep a learning journal so that you can review its impact.

External capabilities of Transpersonal Leaders: leading others

The inner work on mindfulness, mindset, motivation and meaning making is the foundation for the four external capabilities of Transpersonal Leaders shown in Figure 19.1 as listed below and thereafter described in more detail.

- Inspire through "role modelling"
- Influence through "win/win thinking"
- Ignite through "enabling others"
- Impact through "situation sensing"

Inspire through "role modelling"

> No matter what role you play at work or at home, you influence people around you – you teach and lead by example – because people notice what you do. As a leader you inspire by example. Albert Schweitzer said 'In influencing other people, example is not the main thing; it is the only thing.' You embody the qualities you would like to see in others. You focus on what's right, not on who's right. You shift the focus from what's in it for me to what serves the highest good of all concerned.
>
> —Millman, 2011

Leaders create the climate because 70 per cent of what happens in organisations comes from people imitating the leaders (Marlier & Parker, 2009). Please refer to Chapter 10 for more details about climate and the impact leaders have on it.

This ability to imitate is enabled by our mirror neurons, the part of our brain circuitry that accelerates our ability to learn and tune into the emotions of others. What this means is that our behaviour and our emotions are contagious (Nabben 2014).

Role modelling starts with you being aware of and able to manage your behaviour and emotional state. That is why the inner work already described is so important. Through working on your mindset you are clear about your values and how to live them day to day; you have a positive set of beliefs that produce effective behaviours, you are aware of your own emotional landscape and can shift your emotional state as required.

As a Transpersonal Leader you are able to create and maintain a safe environment in which people feel trusted and appreciated. In this sort of environment you are a role model of authenticity and so let others know that it is safe to be authentic. You show through your behaviours that it is ok to be vulnerable and admit when you don't know or that you have made a mistake. This gives permission to others to do the same. In this sort of climate people are willing to experiment, try out new things, make suggestions for improvement and embrace change. It makes possible the levels of agility and innovation that are necessary for sustainable success in the twenty-first century.

Change is a constant and as a Transpersonal Leader you lead from the front so that even when change brings up fear, you embrace it and lead yourself through it in order to catalyse it in others. You model agility by using self-directed neuroplasticity to re-wire your brain in line with the requirements of the change you are leading (Coyne, 2016a).

Other qualities that you model as a Transpersonal Leader are open mindedness, tolerance, courage, wisdom, abundance, transparency, candour, resilience, consistency and integrity.

As a result you inspire others by being a role model of what it takes to be happy, healthy and a sustainably high performer. In this way you create an environment in which you and your people can thrive.

Influence through "win/win thinking"

> *I believe the win-win mentality is fundamental not just to business but to all of life's relationships. It's the ticket to entry into a human being's heart. Without a win-win mentality there is no trust, no confidence, no moving forward together.*
>
> —Covey, 2011

Effective stakeholder engagement is founded on a win/win mentality, which means that success is mutual and relationships are long term. As a Transpersonal Leader this is exactly the sort of influence you want to have on your stakeholders. Win/win is about being collaborative rather than competitive, focusing on the success of others and not just your own, and about building community and relationships rather than just executing the task.

The characteristics of a win/win mentality are:

- Integrity: sticking with your true feelings, values, and commitments
- Maturity: expressing your ideas and feelings with a balance of courage and consideration for the ideas and feelings of others
- Confidence: in yourself and others and your collective ability to find a better way
- Abundance mentality: believing there is plenty for everyone
- Both/and thinking: not thinking in terms of either I am right or I am wrong but how can we take both of our views as being valid and build on them to come up with something even better.

There are four key steps to adopting a win/win approach:

1. a mutual willingness to accept that together it is possible to come up with something better than you could have done as individuals; then being willing to accept an idea that is better than your original one without getting defensive
2. agree a set of criteria that define what success would look like in this situation
3. brainstorm possible solutions to meet the criteria making sure that no limitations are applied

4. keep working at this until you come up with a synergistic solution that generates excitement.

The late Stephen R. Covey was convinced that win/win thinking is the key to solving many of the world's problems. It is certainly central to Transpersonal Leadership.

Ignite through "enabling others"

> As a leader you empower others. You become a bridge over which others may cross.
> —Millman, 2011

If you want to ignite your people you need to understand their motivations. It is easy to assume that their motivations are similar to yours or even similar to each other's but this may well not be the case. Understanding individual motivations enables you to tailor how you reward and recognise people, ensure you are playing to their strengths and tapping into what drives them; all of which ignites their passion, commitment and enjoyment of their work, which, in the end, leads to greater productivity.

Then, just as you created meaning for yourself by discovering your own purpose you do the same for your people by enabling them to find theirs.

When you align the purpose "of your people to the broader mission of the organisation, tremendous energy and engagement are released" (Cashman, 2008).

Also, what ignites people is to have a leader who believes in their potential. Whenever we ask workshop participants to think of a great leader who made a difference to their lives they usually come up with someone who believed in them more than they did in themselves. This enables them to do things they never dreamt they were capable of.

Seeing your people growing and developing enhances your motivation and so it becomes a virtuous cycle through which you all realise your potential and enable the organisation to do so too.

Impact through "situation sensing"

> We are all natural sensors. With self-management everyone can be a sensor and initiate changes – just as in a living organism every cell senses its environment and can alert the organism to needed change. Sensing happens everywhere, all the time, but in traditional organisations, the information often gets filtered out.
> —Laloux, 2014

Organisations are living systems and living systems evolve naturally. Transpersonal Leaders sense energetic shifts and tune into the wider system to see patterns and identify what wants to emerge. How do they do this? Attentional practice and reflective practice underpin this ability. Situation sensing requires you to be slowed down, centred and present in the moment so that you are self-aware and in full consciousness of what is going on around you. This approach enables you to break out of the pattern of needing to control or fix things and helps you to feel comfortable with ambiguity, not knowing and uncertainty. Situation sensing gives you the ability to interrupt your reactive behaviours, create a 6–10 second choice space in which to choose how to respond, bringing with it an agility that ensures your intention and impact are aligned (Rock & Page, 2009).

In conclusion, becoming mindful, installing the right mindset, understanding your motivators and making meaning through reflection brings a level of personal mastery that will enable you to walk alongside the small minority of Transpersonal Leaders. This will bring with it the ability to inspire, influence and ignite the passion of your stakeholders for maximum impact.

Questions and actions for personal development

Here are a few questions you might want to think about. Spending some time answering them will support your inner development.

1. What sort of attentional practice do you have or would be appropriate for you? How can you get started if you haven't already done so?
2. What is your purpose and the difference you want to make through your leadership?
3. Have you got a set of transpersonal beliefs that underpin your leadership? If not a coach can help you with this.
4. What are your key motivators and how do you ensure they are satisfied?
5. Do you have a reflective practice? If not how can you get started on this?
6. How would you rate yourself out of 10 (where 10 is the highest score) for the following:
    a. inspiring through role modelling
    b. influencing through win/win thinking
    c. igniting others through enabling them
    d. impact through situation sensing.
7. What, if anything, are the steps required to get each to a higher level?
8. What is the first step you are committing to take to build the transpersonal characteristics covered in this chapter?

References

Cashman, K. (2008). *Leadership From The Inside Out.* Berrett-Koehler Publishers Inc.
Covey, S. (2011). *The 3rd Alternative.* Simon & Schuster.
Coyne, S. (2016a). *Stop Doing, Start Leading: How to Shift from Doing the Work Yourself to Becoming a Great Leader.* 10-10-10 Publishing.
Coyne, S. (2016b). *Sustainable Leadership; Rewire Your Brain for Sustainable Success.* Routledge. http://bit.ly/2gRmvZ1 [accessed on: 18/07/2017].
Coyne, S. and Gairdner, J. (2016). Mindset, Flow and Genius. In Downey, M. (2016) *Enabling Genius,* LID Publishing Ltd.
Dweck, C. (2006). *Mindset, How You Can Fulfil Your Potential.* Random House.
Joiner, B. and Josephs, S. (2007). *Leadership Agility.* Jossey-Bass.
Laloux, F. (2014). *Reinventing Organisations.* Nelson Parker.
Marlier, D. and Parker, C. (2009). *Engaging Leadership.* Palgrave Macmillan.
Millman, D. (2011). *The Four Purposes of Life.* New World Library.
Nabben, J. (2014). *Influence: What It Really Means and How to Make It Work for You.* Pearson Education Ltd.
Patterson, E. (2017a). Waking up to the Power of Reflection to Unlock Transformation in People, Teams and Organisations. In Alvinius, A. (Ed.) *Contemporary Leadership Challenges – Chapter 1.* www.intechopen.com [accessed on: 18/07/2017].
Patterson, E. (2017b). Reflection is an Oasis for Busy People in Busy Times. *Coaching Perspectives* January 2017, Issue 12 (The Association for Coaching Global Magazine).
Pink, D. (2010). *Drive: The Surprising Truth About What Motivates Us.* Canongate Books Ltd
Reitz, M. and Chaskalson, M. (2016). How to Bring Mindfulness to Your Company's Leadership. *Harvard Business Review.*
Rock, D. (2009). *Your Brain at Work.* Harper Collins..
Rock, D. and Page, L. (2009). *Coaching with the Brain in Mind.* John Wiley and Sons Inc.
Sale, J. (2016). *Mapping Motivation.* Gower Publishing Ltd.
Scharmer, O. (2009). *Theory U: Leading From The Future As It Emerges.* Berrett-Koehler Publishers Inc.
Schon, D. (1983). *The Reflective Practitioner.* Basic Books Inc.

20 Choice and for the greater good

John Knights

It is our choices that make us who we truly are.

Overview

At the end of the day it is all about choice and then acting upon the choices we make; but it would seem there are different kinds of choice. There are those we make non-consciously and are liable to bias and prejudice, those we make consciously for our own benefit and those we make for the greater good. While humans cannot claim to be alone among all species in making choices (Santos & Rosati, 2015), one of the key characteristics that make us human is that we can think about alternate future scenarios and make deliberate choices accordingly (Suddendorf, 2014) – though even those "deliberate" choices may be plagued by unconscious bias and prejudice.

As we have seen in the various chapters of Part 2 of this book, there are many things that influence our choices. We can improve our decision-making and judgement, manage our egos, develop our purpose and bring our values to full consciousness. But at the end of the day only we, ourselves, can make that choice.

The important thing as Transpersonal Leaders is that we make the right choices for the greater good. To make the right choices it is important to reflect on everything we have discussed in this book. We need to understand our own purpose, our spiritual belief system (as explained in Chapter 12) and how that manifests itself into ethical behaviour.

To help us achieve this, we can learn how to create our own touchstone that we can use every time we make a choice. It contains the key Transpersonal Qualities and our own core values.

If we can actually become a Transpersonal Leader, we will leave the world and the people we touch in a better place for the future.

Choices maketh the woman

It is our choices that make us who we truly are. Every time there is a decision to be made we have a choice and that choice will depend on our judgement of a particular set of circumstances or facts. We discussed decision-making and judgement in some detail in Chapter 16 where we focused primarily on "how" decisions are made. Choices are more concerned with the "why". I chose to use "woman" instead of "man" in the subtitle above!

There are many ways of defining the kind of decisions we have to make and they are grouped in different ways by various experts:

- Command, Delegated, Avoided and No-Brainer decisions (Tracy, 2007)
- Command, Consultative, Consensus, Convenience (Rivers, 2014)
- Intuitive, Technical, Deliberative, Bureaucratic (Van Gelder, 2010)
- Command, Consult, Vote, Consensus (Meier, 2017)
- Strategic, Tactical, Operational (Business Case Studies, 2017)

There are many more. The point is that we have a choice in every decision and every kind of decision we make. We have a choice on how we go about making the decision (see Chapter 16), whether to make a choice or not, and whether to leave the decision to someone else.

However, as Transpersonal Leaders the important thing to consider is whether we are making the right choice from a radical, authentic, ethical, caring, sustainable, emotionally intelligent and performance-enhancing point of view and in the interests of the organisation and its stakeholders. This is in addition to the more obvious threshold choice as to whether the logic or rationale is correct or, the more limiting choice of a leader, as to whether it is in our own self-interest. The "right choice" will also include choosing to allow those who are impacted by any decision, to be involved in the decision wherever possible (see Chapter 10).

Often choices are made non-consciously based on our habits, bias and prejudices. As explained throughout Part 2 of this book, we need to be at full consciousness to truly operate as Transpersonal Leaders.

Our suggestion is to create a personal touchstone that we refer to every time we have to make a choice. This touchstone should include our personal core values (see Chapter 17) and whether we are honouring our Transpersonal Qualities. After a while it will become second nature and sub-conscious, and we will only need to use it explicitly by bringing it to full consciousness when we have a difficult choice to make. Figure 20.1 provides an example of a touchstone. The Transpersonal Qualities are standard, coming from our definition of Transpersonal Leadership (Chapter 1) and which can perhaps be more easily remembered using the CREASEP anagram.

Transpersonal Qualities (CREASEP)

Caring: primarily showing kindness and concern for others, often for others who need support, but also a care for the things that will create a better world. However, similarly to not confusing empathy with sympathy (see Chapter 7), the essence of caring is not about being "nice". Sometimes caring

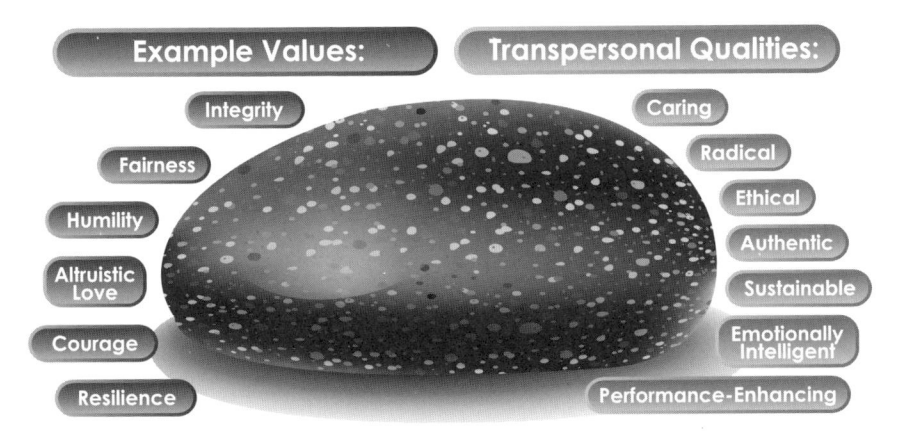

Figure 20.1 Example touchstone

Example Values: Integrity, Fairness, Humility, Altruistic Love, Courage, Resilience

Transpersonal Qualities: Caring, Radical, Ethical, Authentic, Sustainable, Emotionally Intelligent, Performance-Enhancing

can mean having tough conversations and challenging people but in a way that is for the other's benefit. It is important in such a situation that the other person knows we care in order to minimise negative emotions and distress, but our motive should be about concern for another not because we want to be liked.

In general, we have too little care in our organisations and because of that we are often brainwashed into thinking there is no place in our organisations for caring. I remember talking to a senior executive of one of our clients who had recently joined having come from a government department. He explained that the reason he left the department was because he was criticised every time he was kind to someone. Actually, "caring" is the main creator of productivity through people being willing to put in extra discretionary effort for people or things they care about. Our default "alpha male" organisation cultures also tend to consider toughness as desirable and caring as a weak attribute. When working recently on organising a conference on leadership, I was advised not to put "caring" in the title as it might turn business leaders off from attending. As Transpersonal Leaders we must work to overcome this default.

Radical: a move away from tradition and the expected through innovation or progress. This is not about "throwing out the baby with the bath water" but challenging the status quo and questioning the value and validity of how we do things. As far as leadership is concerned, and as described in Chapter 12,

> We need to have the courage, fearlessness, conviction and ideas to move to a less materially oriented approach, realise we might need an alternative to continuous growth and create a happier, fairer society. There may also be times when we need disruptive thinking for survival.

Ethical: not only integrity but a social conscience and a willingness to follow the rules – or get them changed if that is what is needed (from Chapter 12). As leaders we have a responsibility to create ethical cultures in organisations. See Routledge's White Paper on ethical leadership (Knights, 2016).

Authentic: act as you truly are. As explained in Chapter 12,

> *we must be honest with ourselves and others. Excellent leadership is not a game, it is not something we can pretend to do and get right. The human being is very good at seeing through the falseness of others, although often not in a conscious way. "Authentic" also implies that the leader is the same person (though may behave appropriately differently) in all circumstances – their values are operating at full consciousness and they don't leave them at the door to the office when they come back from a quality weekend with the partner and/or children during which they have been a model family member.*
>
> (Knights, 2011)

Sustainable: enduring into the future while upholding and defending. It is not about maintaining the status quo but rather providing the foundations, systems and design to enable continuation and improvement into the foreseeable future. Sustainability does not only require a vision, a plan and actions but also an interrelationship between the people, the other stakeholders and the purpose of the organisation. As we move forward we need to rethink the current mindset of continually increasing turnover or profits, which will not be sustainable in all cases. Regardless, we need to find new measures of sustainability but we must also be practical in the real world.

Emotional intelligence: is being aware of and managing our own emotions and the emotions of others (see Chapter 7 for full details).

Performance-enhancing: last but by no means least, this is a critical quality for any leader and any organisation. In a transpersonal sense, long- versus short-term performance is often an important choice. Many companies, for example, remain or revert to a private status so that they are no longer under pressure from stock markets for short-term performance. What is important is to build leadership capability that reflects sustainable and enhancing performance. It is also important to define what performance means in the context of our own purpose and that of our organisation and its stakeholders. Pure financial performance goals will only be of benefit to shareholders and perhaps employees (more usually the senior executives) rather than the full range of stakeholders.

An example of demonstrating Transpersonal Qualities

A small successful company in the environmental technology field with global class technology was at a crossroads. The company was established 25 years ago but because of the financial crisis, changing environmental laws and a change in management due to illness, it had only been successful in the last couple of years. However, the company had an excellent culture with the people feeling both valued and that they had an opportunity to develop. The founding and long standing shareholders were all reaching retirement age, there was no second generation both suitable and interested to take over the shareholding or manage the business, and the current management could not raise the finance to buy the company at a price the shareholders considered reasonable. Also, a few of the shareholders needed to sell to top-up their retirement needs. So the company had to be sold.

However, the shareholders insisted they sell to a company that would want to maintain and grow the business rather than sell at the highest price to a competitor who just wanted the technical drawings and customer list and who would make most of the staff redundant. Finally, this UK company found a Chinese buyer who was excited about growing the business in Europe, Middle East and Africa while obtaining the technology much needed in China itself, thus maintaining the integrity and purpose of the shareholders who established the company.

Example values

In the example list in Figure 20.1 I have included my personal core values that I find are particularly relevant to me for making choices. It includes those from "who I am" and "what I want to do with who I am" as discussed in detail in Chapter 17. To choose your own set of "Choice Core Values" you need to really decide who you are and how each one links to one or more Transpersonal Qualities. Then you can choose from the lists in Chapter 17 – or take other values of your own, but making sure they meet the criteria of a value as explained in the same chapter.

As a guide to helping you to develop your own list of Choice Core Values, let me explain how I chose mine. Looking at my list in of values in Figure 20.1, Integrity is very important because it fundamentally allows me to be Authentic. Fairness, a value that is deeply part of me (some would say because I am a Libran!) is connected to the transpersonal quality of being Ethical. Humility, a value I have learned as I have matured, enables me to be more Caring and aid Sustainability. Altruistic Love, a value that has grown as part of my coaching practice and as I learned to understand people better, is related to Caring. Courage, something I continue to aspire to, is required to be Radical and Authentic. I find it a particularly important value when one needs to say or do something that might not be popular, despite the fear of how people might react or the consequences. Finally, Resilience – just never giving in and being strong enough to keep it up – is really required to enable Sustainability. Some of these values are more natural to me than others – it is the ones you have to work at that provide some of our continuous development as we shall discuss in Chapter 21.

Of course I, like all of us, make mistakes and don't always get things right, but my touchstone has become very valuable in my efforts to operate as a Transpersonal Leader.

For the greater good

As a Transpersonal Leader, our ultimate goal must be to work for the greater good, however we define it personally. Before thinking about "what" we do for the greater good, the bigger questions are "why" and "how".

The "why" can be categorised by our desire to serve others – our stakeholders, from the people we work with through to our planet Earth and the universe (see Chapter 15) – and contribute positively to the world we live in.

The "how" is being our own person, developing our own unique balance of leadership styles, and being aware of both our strengths and limitations. As the classical Greek philosopher Socrates said, "Divine wisdom is knowing everything. Human wisdom is knowing your limitations".

It is the key Transpersonal Qualities and our Choice Core Values that enable us to succeed with the "what", which is to achieve our purpose, whatever that might be (as discussed in Chapters 17 and 19). If you are still having difficulties identifying or developing your purpose think about whether your desire to work for the greater good relates to any of these areas in a passionate way: environment, service to others, joy, poverty, discrimination, abuse, health/healing, safety, security, education/developing others, quality of life.

If not, work on finding something you are passionate about that is not of direct benefit to you.

When you consider what your purpose is, check it against these four questions:

1. Does it provide a broader reason for your actions than the action itself?
2. Is its direction totally consistent with your values?
3. Is it strategic about your life and what is to be achieved for the greater good?
4. Is it consistent with your life goals?

When we can answer an unequivocal "yes" to all these questions, then we may well have our purpose. However, it may still not be the eventual or final purpose, as that can change. We should nevertheless always have our current purpose in our full consciousness and under review.

As Bill George, the iconic leader of Medtronics and author of the seminal book *Authentic Leadership* stated, "if not me, then who? If not now, then when?" He suggested that the truly authentic leader is motivated by their mission, not their money; taps into their values, not their ego; and connects with others through their heart, not their ego (George, 2003).

It is important that we must be aware of the possible consequences of our actions. We must always think, both about who will benefit from our actions and who could be harmed and how.

Figure 20.2 Transpersonal touchstone

Questions and actions for personal development

Working on the questions and exercises below will aid you in making the right choices and working towards the great good.

1. What is the value of a Core Values Touchstone?
2. What are the Transpersonal Qualities we include in our Core Values Touchstone that most resonate with you?
3. What are the personal core values you would include in your touchstone? Use Figure 20.2 to build your own touchstone.
4. How do the core values you have chosen connect to each of the Transpersonal Qualities?
5. You have been asked to describe your purpose in Chapters 17 and 19. Check your purpose against the criteria in this chapter. Does your purpose remain the same or would you like to amend it? If so, what is your revised purpose?

What are the specific actions you are going to take as a result of this chapter?

References

Business Case Studies. (2017). *Decision Making Techniques: A CIMS Case Study*. Business Case Studies, http://businesscasestudies.co.uk/cima/decision-making-techniques/types-of-decisions.html [accessed April 2017].

George, W. (2003). *Authentic Leadership: Rediscovering the Secrets to Creating Lasting Value*. Jossey-Bass.

Knights, J. (2011). *The Invisible Elephant and the Pyramid Treasure.* Tomorrow's Company. www.leadershape.biz/invisible-elephant [accessed on: 18/07/2017].

Knights, J. (2016). *Ethical Leadership: Becoming an Ethical Leader.* Routledge. http://bit.ly/1Uh6vHL [accessed on: 18/07/2017].

Maier, J. (2017). *4 Decision Making Methods.* Source of Insight. http://sourcesofinsight.com/4-decision-making-methods/ [accessed April 2017].

Rivers, D. (2014). *4 Types of Decision Making For Team Leaders.* LinkedIn Blog. www.linkedin.com/pulse/20140917050211-118756103-4-types-of-decision-making-for-team-leaders [accessed April 2017].

Santos, L. and Rosati, A. (2015). The Evolutionary Roots to Human Decision Making. *Annual Review of Psychology* 66: 13.1–13.27.

Suddendorf, T. (2014). What Makes US Human? *Huffington Post – The Blog*, 8 Feb. www.huffingtonpost.com/thomas-suddendorf/what-makes-us-human_b_4414357.html [accessed on: 18/07/2017].

Tracy, B. (2007). *Time Power: A Proven System for Getting More Done in Less Time Than You Ever Thought Possible.* Brian Tracy International.

Van Gelder, T. (2010). *Decisions in Organisations – 4 Kinds.* Tim van Gelder. https://timvangelder.com/2010/11/03/decisions-in-organisations-four-kinds/ [accessed April 2017].

21 Continuous personal development

John Knights

We can always contribute either something more or something better.

Overview

As Winston Churchill famously remarked in the British House of Commons after the Allies won their first major battle of the Second World War in November, 1942, "Now this is not the end. It is not even the beginning of the end. But it is, perhaps, the end of the beginning" (British Pathé, 2014). So it is with our Transpersonal Leadership journey. We are reaching the end of sharing with you the many steps to becoming a Transpersonal Leader. Although we might claim it as the current manual and treatise on Transpersonal Leadership, we know that this body of work developed over 20 years is just the beginning. Knowledge around neuroscience will explode over the coming decades and the application of that information will inform how best we can develop as Transpersonal Leaders. In addition, although we know that a healthy body has many general advantages for becoming a successful and excellent leader, we are not at the stage where we can propose a specific route for how to bring together a healthy body and mind.

As individuals who have persevered to read this book and complete the many exercises and actions, you are also at the end of the beginning, as am I.

The vital and difficult part of being a Transpersonal Leader still lies ahead: continuing to increase our awareness, changing our unwanted habits, bringing our minds to full consciousness and making full use of our ethics and values in whatever we do. No mean task, and as a human, impossible to perfect; there will always be another layer to uncover, another hurdle to overcome, and a new setback to redress. As we said at the beginning of this book it is a lifelong journey, with only a direction and no final destination.

> *We must become the change we want to see.*
> —Mahatma Gandhi, leader of the Indian independence movement in British-ruled India [1869–1948]

By now, you are fully aware that continuous personal development requires us to persistently work on increasing awareness and bringing the non-conscious

232 John Knights

to full consciousness. For each step we need to identify and then focus on the next granular item of improvement with regular short bursts of practice in the work place. This will enable our neural pathways to rewire and then for the connections to strengthen so our new ways develop into a habit and eventually become subconscious.

To aid you, we provide in this chapter four models to help you check where you are on your own journey. These are:

1. six levels of awareness and consciousness
2. core transpersonal practices, based on the laws of nature
3. the stages of human development
4. the evolution of intelligences.

The journey never ends – and it is not easy

Neither the experience to date of becoming a Transpersonal Leader, nor our continued development going forward is a simple linear experience. It is iterative, circular and holistic. Our awareness and consciousness will continue to increase at different levels. Behaviours will continue to develop and improve with effort, determination, focus, practice and time, which in turn will positively impact our attitudes, mindsets and thus values at full consciousness (see Figure 21.1).

Developing into a Transpersonal Leader of the highest level requires continued focused development, which will be hard work. But as leaders you will already have shown you are determined, hardworking and committed in what you do, so if you make the "choice" that you want to develop into a Transpersonal Leader, you can and will do it!

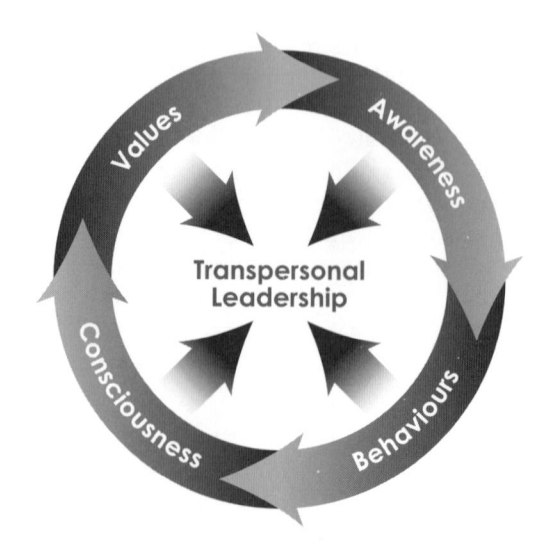

Figure 21.1 The transpersonal cycle

As explained in Chapter 6, one of the main obstacles to achieving this development is FEAR, which reminds us of the importance of emotions. Fear acts as an important inhibitor about what we might have to let go of, who we might become and most importantly, the judgement and criticism of others (Rossiter, 2006).

As leaders we often "know" more than we "do". We are much better at advising others how to improve while our own imperfections remain out of sight in our non-consciousness. As I wrote in *The Invisible Elephant and the Pyramid Treasure* (Knights, 2011), we have many invisible elephants. It is important not to be self-satisfied or think we are that little bit better than others. We must keep in mind that as humans we are equal to all other humans (Knights, 2016). We may be different, we may even be more knowledgeable than others, but better – NO!

As Jim Collins noted in *Good to Great,* "humility and intense will are the two most important characteristics of the leader in the 21st century" (Collins, 2001).

We can always contribute either something more or something better, even if we are at the top of our game and the pinnacle of our organisation. But to achieve that, we always need to learn something new and realise we are not perfect. We will at least occasionally be hijacked by our emotions and we will be unable to always have our whole being in full consciousness, so it will happen that our touchstone is compromised.

Finally, there are always new unknowns due to changes in our environment and personal context. We are always being met with new challenges.

Regardless, the voyage of development described in this book hopefully provides the knowledge, practice and experience, and with it the confidence, to continue on the path to serve our stakeholders, and through them, ourselves.

Checking where you are on your journey

The rest of this chapter explains the four models to guide you on your journey, to help you identify where you are and what you might need to do next. Once you have identified your next action, find the right chapter in the book and refresh. Often, the many references will offer detailed investigation and learning in even greater depth than we are able to provide in a single book.

The endeavour for awareness and full consciousness

In some ways, developing awareness of self and others and then bringing our non-conscious processes to full consciousness is the most challenging aspect towards our development as a Transpersonal Leader. Everyone will experience this in their own unique way. For me, a person who was trained as an engineer, and very goal and task focused, it has sometimes been a struggle to learn to reflect and then understand why I reacted or performed in a certain way. Although still on the journey, I now have a much more holistic and emergent view of life, which better enables me to support and enable others towards long-term performance. I know if I had possessed this extra awareness during my days as a corporate leader, I would have increased my effectiveness.

We have developed six levels of awareness and consciousness (see Table 21.1) built on earlier work on the connection between spiritual intelligence and leadership (Wigglesworth, 2006). This is a simple scale by which we can measure our progress and better understand where we as leaders might need to develop next.

Table 21.1 The six levels of awareness and full consciousness

1. Have a logical/analytical understanding of what Awareness is
2. An understanding of my own self-awareness, especially what triggers things to go wrong
3. Through being actively empathetic I let people know I understand how they are feeling and the cause of their perspective
4. I listen to my conscience, values and ethics, and separate it from what I want to do for myself
5. I listen and take note of my inner self through bringing personal conscience, virtues and self-determination values to full consciousness
6. No longer a struggle between my ego (what I want for myself) and the greater good

It is possible that we may feel we sometimes act as if we are at one level and sometimes at another depending on the context. We may even feel we are operating at two levels at the same time and they may not be adjacent. For example, I have known leaders who operate at levels 2 and 4 but struggle at level 3. Once we have identified the level(s) we operate at we can think about which level we aspire to and the actions we need to take to get there.

Transpersonal practices as a complex adaptive system

Armed with the values of social conscience and self-development, together with their emotional intelligence and their intellect, Transpersonal Leaders need to bring all these together as transpersonal practices. These practices must be for the benefit of all stakeholders and … for the greater good.

We can learn how to define these transpersonal practices from nature itself. The whole of nature depends on relationships, patterns, iterations and emergence. It requires a system to manage everything in the universe: the weather, immune systems, social systems, ecosystems, and more specifically, termite mounds, a murmuration of starlings, Darwin's model of genetic mutation, the design of the shell of a snail … and consciousness itself.

This approach, known as **Complex Adaptive Systems (CASs)** is a relatively new field that has gained ground since the 1980s, originated at the Santa Fe Institute in New Mexico when a group of scientists came together to discuss the central problems and approaches in areas such as biology, chemistry, computer science, economics and physics (Miller & Page, 2007). In January 2000, Stephen Hawking stated, "Complexity is the science of the twenty-first century" (Hawking, 2000). Even though this field is still in its formative stages the study and understanding of complex non-linear systems has become highly influential over the last 30 years (Holland, 2014).

Most of the systems we design, like an automobile, or a marketing campaign do not learn and do not evolve. Unfortunately, that is how most of our "corporate" systems thinking works and why they are rarely successful with major transformations. Artificial Intelligence is making strides with learning and evolving but as yet is only based on the inherent design and inputs. As Dame Ellen MacArthur[1] explains, we need to move from a linear economy where everything is used once and disposed of to a circular one where everything is reused, restored or regenerated and sustained (MacArthur, 2015).

CASs, on the other hand, do learn and do adapt, and often in unpredictable ways. As Transpersonal Leaders we must operate within a CAS environment and indeed operate in this way ourselves. So a CAS is a good model to check for our own continued development. Danah Zohar, a quantum physicist who is also a thought leader in management and spiritual intelligence, attempted to link CASs to the principles of leadership transformation in her book, *Spiritual Capital* (Zohar & Marshall, 2004) and her most recent book, *The Quantum Leader* (Zohar, 2016).

According to Colella (2001) and Project Guts (2017), CASs:

- are made up of many individual parts or agents
- follow simple rules
- provide no leader to coordinate the action of others
- generate emergent patterns through the interaction of agents
- react and adapt if the elements of the system change.

Based on the general characteristics of Complex Adaptive Systems, we have developed a set of key transpersonal practices shown and described in Table 21.2.

Table 21.2 Eleven transpersonal practices of a CAS

Practice		Description
1.	Everyone's a leader	Unlike predictable hierarchical systems, CASs have no central control mechanism. For a Transpersonal Leader this means delegating and decentralising whenever we can. To achieve this, we need to maximise everyone's potential through development and practice.

(continued)

Table 21.2 Eleven transpersonal practices of a CAS *(continued)*

Practice		Description
2.	Value-led sustainability	Providing consistency by acting from principle, based on core values and being transparent in doing so. Actions should be based on what is best for the long term, sacrificing short-term gain where appropriate.
3.	Emergent thinking	The complex world we live in does not give us the comfort of making detailed plans that we expect to remain the same. We can set direction but need to continually adjust depending on how things develop. We must be much more open minded and intently curious.
4.	Holistic approach	We must take the broadest view. Be aware of patterns, relationships and connections. We must be fully conscious so that we can make full use of all our decision-making processes. We must also feel we belong to the system we are involved with.
5.	Self-awareness and Self-management	To be aware of our emotions and to be able to manage them effectively for ourselves and the greater good.
6.	Balancing feedback vs. independence	A CAS survives because it responds to the feedback system within. So must Transpersonal Leaders encourage and value feedback. The balance between accepting and responding to feedback versus standing up for your beliefs and convictions is critical.
7.	Adaptive	We must be sensitive to external change by learning, and where necessary recreating ourselves and our organisations to respond. With people we must have empathy and compassion to understand and respond.
8.	Managing chaos and random probability	Small changes (random chance or intended) can have huge consequences. Only a CAS can bring order to such a system. For a Transpersonal Leader it means the positive use of adversity – learn from mistakes, see problems as opportunities and being resilient.
9.	Norming diversity	In a CAS, each part plays a full role. We must value all other people, cultures and situations in celebration of their difference, not despite them.
10.	Vocation	Within nature, humans are probably alone in *wanting* to serve something greater than oneself. It comes from deep within to want to serve others or the universe. For some, this can happen from early adulthood but for most this comes later in life in wishing to give something back in gratitude for what one has received.

Practice		Description
11.	Enjoyment	One of the key criteria of a sustainable performance-enhancing culture is enjoyment (see Chapter 10). We can't be happy all the time as we react to everything that happens in our lives but as Transpersonal Leaders we should make every effort to bring joy to the lives of others.

The stages of human development

There is no doubt that our development as a Transpersonal Leader is connected to our development as a human being. Many experts have developed models to show the development of the human being. The most famous is Maslow's Hierarchy of Needs (Maslow, 1943), from which many other models have been based. We have found one of the most useful models for Transpersonal Leaders is "The Five Stages of the Evolving Self" developed by Robert Kegan (Kegan, 1982; Garvey Berger, 2006). This model was used as a reference when first constructing the development of a Transpersonal Leader.

The first two stages of development are related primarily to that of the child and adolescent so we will focus on the three adult stages:

3. The Socialised (or Traditional) Mind: This is usually a younger adult who will have based their view of the world on role models and on the opinions and views of others rather than their own. They have an unformed ego. Most people never reach beyond this stage. Their behaviour is likely to be seen by being a team player, a faithful follower, aligning with others, seeking direction and/or being reliant on others. However, they will also have the ability of abstract thinking and self-reflection. Their thinking is bounded by the views of others.
4. The Self-Authoring (or Modern) Mind: This is usually thought of as the "normalised" adult state but research has shown that not many adults actually reach this stage. These individuals have formed their own view of the world partly based on learning from experience (many do not learn from experience!). At this stage it is difficult to get such individuals to change their view. They have formed their ego. The characteristics these individuals are most likely to demonstrate are those of being agenda-driven, learning to lead, having their own compass and framework, being independent and problem solving. Their thinking is bounded by their own views.
5. The Self-Transforming (or Post Modern) Mind: This is a stage only a very few adults reach, according to research. They have learned the limits of their own inner systems and indeed of having an inner system or specific worldview at all. They have a reformed ego. They reach out for similarities with others rather than differences. These individuals no longer see the world as black and white, rather seeing the world in shades of grey. They

Survival → Sustainability and enlightenment

Individual → Global organisation

Intelligence	'What I'	Accounts for	Instinctive driver	Evolutionary benefit	Associated neurology	Resistance to disruption	Context
Physical	Do	Basic nutrition	Survival	• Increasing probability of catching food	Reflex	★★★★★	Individual
Rational	Think	Competence	Curiosity and inquiry	• What's good to eat, how to catch it/grow it • Development of tools	Serial hard-wired Little scope for adaptation	★★★★	Individual
Emotional	Feel	Relationships	Communication and knowledge transfer	• Accelerated knowledge transfer to benefit above and increase survival in young • To coordinate the hunt	Associative neural network adaptable with effort through awareness	★★★	Group
Spiritual 1	Am	Meaning	Identification/ achievement of common goals	• The development of altruism for genetic survival • Determination of tribal rules	Intra brain resonance (synchronous neural oscillations)	★★	Team
Spiritual 2	Will do	Purpose	Collaboration / "for the greater good"/ beyond the ego	• Successful outcomes of inter-tribal rivalry • For the benefit of all stakeholders	Highly adaptable through full consciousness	★	All Stakeholders

Figure 21.2 Hierarchy of intelligencies

lead in order to learn. These individuals can hold contradictions, work with ambiguity, find solutions from adversity and move from the linear to the holistic.

This is the development path for humans in general. Most of us are not at any one pure stage but travelling from one to another at our own pace and very much in between stages. There are many more people between stages 3 and 4 than there are between 4 and 5, and even fewer have reached stage 5. However, usually this process depends on one's own personality, one's intellect, but most of all on serendipity: on who our parents are, who we meet along the way and what experiences we have. It is fairly random. The whole point of the Transpersonal journey is to proactively help people towards attaining stage 5 and beyond (Hill & Katz, 2017) proactively rather than by luck.

This model can not only be used to ascertain your own positioning but is a model that can be very valuable in ascertaining the stage of development of others. This will enable you to be best placed to identify their development needs and how that might best be achieved.

The hierarchy of intelligences

We discussed the history of intelligences and the linking of the three core intelligences (rational, emotional and spiritual) in Chapter 13. There is also an evolutionary aspect to the development of these core intelligences predated by a primitive physical intelligence that lies in the ancient reptilian part of the brain (the brainstem and the cerebellum).

The chart shown in Figure 21.2 provides a map of the hierarchy of intelligences and their various characteristics along various parameters. The further you go down the chart, the closer you come to being a Transpersonal Leader. You may find it useful to keep this chart in mind as your continue to develop by identifying which level you are at and what you need to do to get to the next level.

And remember – do enjoy the ride!

Note

1 Dame Ellen MacArthur made yachting history in 2005, when she became the fastest solo sailor to circumnavigate the globe.

References

British Pathé (2014). *Mr Churchill on Victory*. Available on YouTube. www.youtube.com/watch?v=Mkvf1-ROsY8 [accessed on: 18/07/2017].

Colella, V., Klopfer, E. and Resnick, M. (2001). *Adventures in Modeling: Exploring Complex, Dynamic Systems with StarLogo*. Teachers College Press.

Collins, J. (2001). *Good to Great: Why Some Companies Make the Leap… And Others Don't*. Harper Business.

Garvey Berger, J. (2006). *Key Concepts for Understanding the Work of Robert Kegan*. Kenning Associates.

Hawking, S. (2000). Unified Theory Is Getting Closer, Hawking Predicts. Interview in *San Jose Mercury News* (23 Jan).

Hill, A. and Katz, H. (2018). *Adult Development: Its Role In The Leadership Journey*. Routledge. www.routledge.com/posts/12783

Holland, J. (2014). *Complexity: A Very Short Introduction*. University Oxford Press.

Kegan, R. (1982). *The Evolving Self*. Harvard University Press.

Knights, J. (2011). *The Invisible Elephant and the Pyramid Treasure*. Tomorrow's Company. www.leadershape.biz/invisible-elephant [accessed on: 18/07/2017].

Knights, J. (2016). *Ethical Leadership: Becoming an Ethical Leader*. Routledge. http://bit.ly/1Uh6vHL [accessed on: 18/07/2017].

Maslow, A. (1943). A Theory of Human Motivation. *Psychological Review* 50(4): 370–396.

McArthur, Dame E. (2015). *The Surprising Thing I Learned Sailing Solo Around the World*. TED Talks. www.youtube.com/watch?v=ooIxHVXgLbc&feature=youtu.be [accessed on: 18/07/2017].

Miller, J. and Page, S. (2007). *Complex Adaptive Systems: An Introduction to Computational Models of Social Life*. Princeton University Press.

Project Guts. (2017). *What is a Complex Adaptive System?* Project Guts. http://projectguts.org/files/What_is_a_CAS_0.pdf [accessed April 2017].

Rossiter, A. (2006). *Developing Spiritual Intelligence – The Power of You*. O Books.

Wigglesworth, C. (2006). Why Spiritual Intelligence Is Essential to Mature Leadership. *Integral Leadership Review* VI(3). http://integralleadershipreview.com/5502-feature-article-why-spiritual-intelligence-is-essential-to-mature-leadership/ [accessed May 2017].

Zohar, D. (2016). *The Quantum Leader*. Prometheus Books.

Zohar, D. and Marshall, I. (2004) *Spiritual Capital: Wealth We Can Live By*. Bloomsbury.

Part 3
Implementation of Transpersonal Leadership development

22 Modern learning principles and methodologies

Danielle Grant

Blended learning is a powerful, combined way of learning.

Overview

Most of today's leaders were brought up with rote learning and 'experts' lecturing them at university and beyond. They are often likely to print out articles to read, or use published books in preference to reading e-books or important information solely on screen. While repetition is a way to remember things, this is not enough to ensure long-term embedding and use of what is then just information. For real learning that promotes change, a sense of the overall picture, an emotional connection and personal meaning has to be integrally linked to the subject matter. In the absence of these factors, the ability to adapt any learning to a new context or circumstances is severely limited. The fundamental issue is the brain resists being told. Almost everyone will have experienced a time when they have had a sense of 'discovery' in learning and recognise that it creates excitement and energy. While the brain is only about 3 per cent of the body's mass, it uses over 20 per cent of its energy requirement. No wonder learning is tiring!

As explained in Chapter 4, when the brain learns something new or improves a skill, it uses neuro-plasticity to physically create new or richer neural networks. Logically, it follows therefore that the more stimulus associated with learning, the greater the likelihood of richer neural networks being established that means real learning being embedded and applied over the long term.

Younger leaders are online 'natives'; this means their learning is more often electronically accessed, their personal relationships are fostered online and remotely. Their leisure activities frequently involve elaborate onscreen interactions such as games and competitions. While visual stimulus is always more powerful than other types, including auditory, today's emerging leaders have a fundamental expectation that visual and online learning is indispensable and they want to create their own meaning through doing so. The principles that have emerged from neuroscience since 2000 have given us new guidelines for the design of embedded learning programmes for leadership. This includes how and where learning is provided, how learners are engaged, the length and frequency of learning interventions and what conditions optimise the learning experience. This approach has become known as '**blended learning**'.

Programme inspiration

A key event, in 2008, provided the insight that resulted in my research to create brain-friendly blended leadership learning. I was leading a programme for a group of younger leaders in a digital creative agency. There were unexpected difficulties in getting them engaged in the learning. They were distracted and focused on simply critiquing things such as the design of the slide presentation and the handouts as their creative thinking was at odds with word-heavy slides. They also came unprepared for the concepts being introduced with very little sense of how these related to them and their work context. We were keen to create conditions for people to have insights, and thus be engaged and energised, but the traditional, primarily 'talk and chalk' methodology in use was not achieving these objectives and was not congruent with enabling insights. Feeling the lack of engagement, I went away and created puzzles, interactive games, reflective exercises and stripped wordy slides down to a few images and key words. The change in the group interactions and energy at the subsequent sessions was dramatically improved and satisfaction scores soared. My Master's degree research that subsequently followed enabled me to codify and crystallise these embryonic and intuitive ideas with the latest neuroscientific approaches to learning for adults.

Principles of blended learning

Blended learning is a powerful, combined way of learning, combining group workshops, individual learning and workplace practice and reflection. It is especially effective for leadership learning built on emotional intelligence, as the elements work together to enable and reinforce embedded change. We know from our experience and evidence that this works.

Example

One of the best examples of an emotional intelligence-based leadership programme is the **Weatherhead School of Management** *programme, which had a strong blended learning approach. The long-term results showed that:*

> *five to seven years after program completion, changes in EI were found to be sustained at 50% improvement. In comparison, typical management training programs have been found to yield only 10% improvement three to eighteen months after training.*
> *(Goleman et al., 2002)*

Using Leadershape's blended learning process jigsaw in Figure 22.1 as an example framework, the start point for blended learning is priming the learner with self-directed online learning (ALIVE© Prep[1]) that is both fun and begins the process of linking learning to the individual's work context. A crucial aim of a blended approach is to provide a range of opportunities that relate the

Figure 22.1 Blended learning processes

learning to real life. This could be in the form of interactive work in masterclasses (workshops), reflective exercises drawing on real world experiences, or opportunities to apply the new learning in the workplace, alongside other forms of learning. It is only when the new ideas and concepts are given a practical application that learning really becomes embedded. This is especially true for leadership programmes because they succeed or not based on the degree to which participants practise new behaviours in a real workplace situation. It is this putting ideas into practice that makes the learning most relevant and meaningful. Embedding learning is supported by encouraging the development of a habit of critical reflection in learners and some form of support through social learning. Developing a reflective habit provides a life-long benefit, as experience shows us that most leaders do not spend time in reflection and thereby miss out on learning opportunities (see Chapter 11 for further details).

These blended learning principles work in alignment with the EI learning principles recommended by Cherniss and Goleman (1998) as well as with Ripples Theory (Race, 2001) where the learner's interest, desire and need sit at the core of learning 'rippling' outwards (see Figure 22.2.). This includes reflection as a component of making sense of the 'doing', along with seeking and accepting feedback as an integral part of the whole process.

So, taking each element of the blended learning jigsaw (Figure 22.1) in turn, we can develop an understanding of how to create leadership learning programmes that can deliver long-term change.

Pre-masterclass online prep

This starting point for an effective blended learning approach is the pre-masterclass (or pre-workshop) preparation (identified as ALIVE© Prep in Figure 22.1). This is accessed through an interactive online portal with a personal link provided

Figure 22.2 Ripples on a pond: factors that underpin successful learning

Source: © Race 2012, reproduced with permission.

to each learner up to 4 weeks ahead of the planned workshop/masterclass activities. The material provides a content primer so all learners come into a workshop session with at least a baseline of understanding of the topic being covered. The prep supports the process of wanting, needing, doing and making sense, as within the online work each person is provided with a wide range of ways to find meaning and connection with the learning. Sparking the interest of learners ahead of a workshop allows more engaging and experiential group activities to be done in the workshop, rather than basic information transfer. Within the Online Learning System, the core principles needed to generate a baseline around the subject can be provided in an interactive format, incorporating, reading, quizzes, video, audio and importantly, reflective questions. This enables the learner to start to link the subject matter to their daily workplace experience.

The design of the prep takes into account some very important learning principles that recent advances in neuroscience have provided.

The first element to consider is to have a high level of visual stimulus. Even when people feel they have an auditory or kinaesthetic preference, research shows that recall is improved when a visual cue is added. We know from research data that the combination of audio *with* visual stimulus, promotes higher recall after 14 days (50 per cent) vs. audio only (20 per cent) or visual only (30 per cent) (Medina, 2008). This provides a good rationale for the inclusion of multimedia input (video/audio) and more storytelling activities. Medina (2008) says in Brain Rules 4 (P74, Kindle Edition): 'Attention: Emotional arousal helps the brain learn. Audiences check out after 10 minutes, but you can keep grabbing them back by telling narratives or creating events rich in emotion.' In the online prep we provide this ongoing stimulus with regular video/audio clips, often using stories in the form of well-known movie clips to illustrate a point and then asking learners to relate these to their own experiences and workplace observations. The other element of visual stimulus in addition to video is the use of clear images, diagrams and graphics; avoiding clutter and wordiness and, where appropriate, using imagery that generates an emotional response, whether a smile or a frown.

The online prep approach is also designed to begin to create conditions for the individual to have insights. Insights are indispensable to deep, embedded learning and long-term change. An insight must be a personal experience (Rock & Schwartz, 2006) *felt* at first hand to give that rush of energy that stimulates ownership by the individual experiencing it. This enables the learner to overcome the brain's default resistance to change that is due to the effort and energy needed to create learning and change in the brain (see Chapter 16 for more details on insights).

Surface learning tends to be experienced as an uphill struggle, characterised by fighting against boredom and depressive feelings. Deep learning is experienced as exciting and a gratifying challenge (more often, at least!)
—Atherton, 2011

That rush of energy and excitement does not come about by merely listening to another's experience. Insights may be inspired by something outside oneself, whether an event, situation or person, but they happen inside the individual; it is the feeling of having an 'aha' moment (Sadler-Smith, 2010). To create the conditions for insight and change we need to offer the learner impactful and emotional stimulus, affecting multiple senses. This rich stimulus ideally needs to be combined with practical exercises and activities so as to promote the transfer of necessary information while also enabling the conditions where insights can occur.

Neuroscientific research into how the brain learns best gives us some further ideas around how to best create long-term retention and embedding of learning. First, we need to gain the learners' focus and attention and tap into their motivation to learn, so they see 'what's in it for me'. Seeing a benefit helps generate ownership of learning. As we have seen, the emotional connection both through stories and feedback is a vital ingredient; then allowing enough time between learning sessions for practice and consolidation to allow new neural networks to become established strengthens the embedding. The other idea to connect here is the need to focus on one topic or idea and not to attempt to multitask. The importance of this is to activate the hippocampus (the part of the brain associated with memory – see Chapter 4) as these factors are shown to increase recall. We manage focus and spacing in the pre-workshop online prep by providing single topic, short segments (ca. 20-minutes each). This includes reflective exercises that participants access and spread out over 3–4 weeks ahead of a workshop or reflective ALIVE© Call (see below for further details). These principles are highlighted in the AGES theory (Davachi et al., 2010).

Summary of key principles of leadership learning design

1. Prioritise visual stimulus
2. Provide a range of ways for learners to engage and follow curiosity and interest
3. Address the principles of how the brain learns best, as explained by the AGES model – Attention, Generation, Emotion, Spacing (Davachi et al., 2010) – social learning is a key part of this
4. Create an environment where insights can happen
5. Encourage reflection
6. Nurture ownership of learning
7. Enable learning to be applied in the workplace.

(Grant, 2013a)

The blended learning approach ensures that the whole programme addresses all these principles in a way that reinforces each element in as many of the learning activities as possible.

Masterclasses (workshops)

The second stage in the jigsaw is the masterclass. Given the prior priming of the online prep ahead of the workshops, the structure and purpose of the face-to-face event shifts strongly from 'sage on the stage' input and knowledge transfer, to focusing on the application of knowledge in the participants' workplace. This is achieved through a focus on deepening reflection, extending insights (and thus ownership), creating emotional connection and gaining feedback.

Maintaining the principles outlined of having one clear focus and spacing between learning events can be done by covering fewer topics in a session, as well as moving to shorter workshop time spans (e.g. half day vs. multi-day) and by planning appropriate gaps between learning events, so that the brain does not become overloaded. Addressing these needs thereby allows new neural pathways to be better consolidated. We tend to leave a few weeks between workshops to allow participants time to practice, reflect and so consolidate learning.

To explain more about the importance of providing a single focus for learners, this can be summarised by the phrase 'multitasking is a myth'. There is useful research (Medina, 2008) that the brain can only truly focus effectively on one task at a time. That is, people who feel they can multitask actually switch from task to task rapidly, losing focus for at least a few moments each time they do so.

Masterclass design principles

To make a masterclass really work, we need to address the same design principles as in the online prep, creating emotionally and visually rich stimulus materials, ensuring relevance to the individual and their workplace. As we already know, vision trumps all other senses. Research shows that 'If information is presented orally, people remember about 10%, tested 72 hours after exposure. That figure goes up to 65% if you add a picture' (Medina, 2008: 234). I have found that when an evocative visual is offered to learners, their body language indicates higher interest and engagement and they often spontaneously discuss the visual after the learning event. One example is the image of a modern man looking into the mirror and seeing the reflection of a stone-age man as originally shown in Chapter 4 and replicated in Figure 22.3.

It is relatively easy to ensure that visual inputs in the form of slides are evocative, simple and not too wordy. Using video and multimedia in a workshop can make a strong contribution to the event. It is a good idea to sometimes repeat a key video from the online prep, or choose another that provides a new way of looking at a topic. But be sparing with multiple clips as the time needed for watching videos may encroach on other planned interactions. Also, do make sure you check out all the necessary links on site, in advance!

As well as video, we strongly advocate the use of oral storytelling as a way to maintain emotional connections. Narrative taps into the age-old human storytelling tradition, improving understanding. Stories create visual images in the mind and so they provide a more vivid memory to recall. An impactful way to make this work is for the facilitator to bring their own examples and 'war stories' to illustrate key points and to ask participants to volunteer theirs.

Since this behavioural learning is best achieved through active learning, it is paramount that a real experience of trying out the new learning is provided. In a workshop, this may be through a simulation exercise or at least a participative discussion; using a real workplace example is much more effective than practising with a made up scenario. Committing to an action post-workshop, back in the real world, is the most valuable way to take learning forward. We know from both experience and research that retention after 14 days rises from 70 per cent

Figure 22.3 Stone Age man in mirror

Figure 22.4 An engaging exercise using real workplace content

for an exercise to 90 per cent for a real life experience. The principle of this is that the more hooks to memory that are provided, the richer the encoding and therefore the greater the retention (Medina, 2008). This is a key consideration in creating exercises or discussions.

Using a variety of different approaches rather than focusing purely on intellectual discussion is of far greater value. Useful ways to achieve this include providing puzzles or getting people drawing, engaging both creative and logical processes in the brain and contributing to the learning being 'sticky' (see Figures 22.4 and 22.5).

Jack Kytle explains eloquently about engaging the whole person, 'brain-mind-body'. As he says,

> *The human animal learns best, it seems when many body systems beyond the merely cognitive are involved in doing the work of learning…*
>
> *Physical, emotional, cognitive and spiritual anchors – all are needed if we expect new learning to endure and to integrate new knowledge into existing knowledge and behaviour.*
>
> (Kytle, 2004: 182)

Figure 22.5 A social and creative exercise

Optimising pace and content

In workshops we use exercises where participants bring real examples from work into group discussions or capture their reflections so as to help them identify and commit to an action that will take an insight back into their workplace, for practice and further reflection. Participants experience the emotional impact of sharing and reflecting on individual real life experiences with others, perhaps with the addition of some emotionally engaging video clips. Learning in a social setting also supports the enjoyment element. It is an important responsibility for the facilitator to establish a lively, supportive and enjoyable environment in the group. This enjoyment promotes the body to increase production of oxytocin and other positive brain chemicals that create bonding, creativity and clarity of thought.

In our face-to-face workshops we try to provide the group with some autonomy in the form of choices of ways to take a topic forwards (e.g. some groups dislike exercises they see as artificial role-play and prefer drawings and games or discussion about real situations).

> In one instance, the facilitator had relied very heavily on group discussions and the group requested an exercise where they broke into smaller sets and 'drew' a picture of how a situation/learning appeared to them. This yielded deeper insight and understanding than discussion alone.

Serving learners

It is crucial for the facilitator to focus on the facilitation. The most positive learning outcomes take place when the facilitation is firm and focused on enabling an insightful learning process, as opposed to a didactic one. A strong foundation for a successful programme is to have a real understanding of the context and the culture of the organisation to meet its needs flexibly. Using the wrong phraseology or omitting to relate learning points back to the real life organisational context risks reducing engagement in the learning. In order to ensure this cross fertilisation between online prep, group learning and workplace activity, the facilitator needs to be well aligned with the culture and context of the organisation they are working with, so as to transfer information, while enabling the conditions where insights can occur. The best way of ensuring this is to carry out a diagnostic exercise before the programme begins whereby the facilitator meets each participant (plus the programme champion if they are not one of the delegates) to ascertain their perception about themselves, their colleagues and the organisation.

There is therefore a strong message that the facilitator has to be 'in-service' of their learners, while at the same time being comfortable delivering in their own style. A facilitator should avoid appearing to be driven by a desire to act as the 'expert' or to spend a disproportionate amount of time establishing personal credibility rather than serving the learning needs of the participants.

Remote delivery masterclasses

The emotional and social aspects of learning with others are, as we have discussed, indispensable in devising a blended learning approach. When face-to-face masterclasses are not possible or need to be limited for logistical or budgetary purposes, we provide the experience 'virtually' through an effective remote delivery process. This takes the group through the learning objectives from the online prep via a set of pre-prepared reflective questions posed by the facilitator, drawing on the group's experience of the prep to deepen and extend their understanding. We also sometimes get group members working together in smaller break out groups on a mini experiential project between group calls, to feed into the next masterclass.

We evaluated different remote platforms and developed the ALIVE© teleconference process. We elected to use a telephone bridge line wherever feasible, to avoid VoIP bandwidth issues and, since we are aiming for a strong social connection and a single focus in the group, we do not use webinars for this purpose, as they are more suited to a larger group and less interactive. For our purposes, the webinar distractions of voting, commenting, having email 'pop up' etc. disturb the single thread of focused discussion we are after. These masterclass conference calls are a simple, strongly moderated telephone based, reflective, remote workshop format. For this to succeed, it is key to effectively enable a sense that the participants co-own the experience and engage emotionally. We ensure that the aims, ground rules and agenda are fully understood in advance. Most importantly, we foster the emotional connection by starting a remote delivery session with each participant volunteering a brief anecdote or personal story relevant to the call topic. We recommend a maximum of nine participants in each remote masterclass to enable a reasonable minimal active participation by each person. If the overall number of participants in the programme is greater than this number, as is often the case, then it can be split into smaller groups for the remote interventions.

Remote calls

We also use our teleconferencing process as a way to support masterclasses. These are the next step in the jigsaw and are referred to as ALIVE© calls in Figure 22.1. These remote calls are valuable adjuncts to support and embed learning. They are usually scheduled in between workshop/masterclasses to maintain momentum and deepen the cohort's learning and engagement. Probably the most important element of an effective support-focused call is to have individuals reflecting in the group about tasks and actions they committed to practicing at work, from both the online prep and prior workshops. The facilitator has a key role in drawing together threads of experience, offering deeper and challenging perspectives and thereby extending the learning.

Leading enjoyable and engaging remote calls and masterclasses demands energy and humour from the facilitator, keeping people on their toes, so that participants never feel they can anticipate when they will next be called on to contribute to the discussion, thereby keeping them alert and focused throughout. These sessions act to strengthen the emotional connection and feedback in the group and act as 'glue' between or, where applicable, in lieu of face-to-face workshops.

> **Blended (remote) learning case study**
>
> This was a remotely delivered, 12-hour ALIVE© programme, using ALIVE© Prep, masterclasses and calls to develop leadership skills within a team ethos for geographically dispersed managers working for a 'supported living' charity. Feedback from this cost-effective intervention reported significant change in meeting their objectives, including:
>
> - increased understanding of how to lead (as opposed to day-to-day management)
> - recognition of natural leadership styles and comfort about using a wider spectrum of leadership behaviours
> - more awareness and better ability to manage emotions and responses
> - changes regarding the ability to give and receive feedback.
>
> This is an impressive result for such a short programme – and there are indications that this is embedded learning, which will continue to strengthen with time.
>
> Senior manager comment: Managers are discussing situations, approaches and responses differently – they actively seek feedback and try new things as a result – capabilities and confidence are growing. Exactly what we hoped!

The diagram in Figure 22.6 is derived from participant feedback from our blended learning programmes over the past 5 years.

Work-based learning

The overarching principle that binds the learning experiences together is that of real learning being primarily work-based. This is something that has not changed in millennia of human experience.

> *One must learn by doing the thing; though you think you know it, you have no certainty until you try.*
> —Sophocles, 495–406 BC

The blended learning approach ensures that insights generate energy and commitment to experiment with the new ideas in the workplace and to share these experiences with others in the cohort. The process is to reflect, and then receive validation, feedback and emotional support to refine practice and then try again. It becomes an iterative process that increases competence and confidence. It is easy to see how this contributes to strengthening neural connections thereby creating positive new ways of behaving that become natural and, eventually, effortless.

This process travels from *learning about*, through *learning to do*, all the way to *learning to be,* so as to develop a new way of being. If one likens it to learning a language, we can superficially *learn about* (say) Mandarin and we can begin to

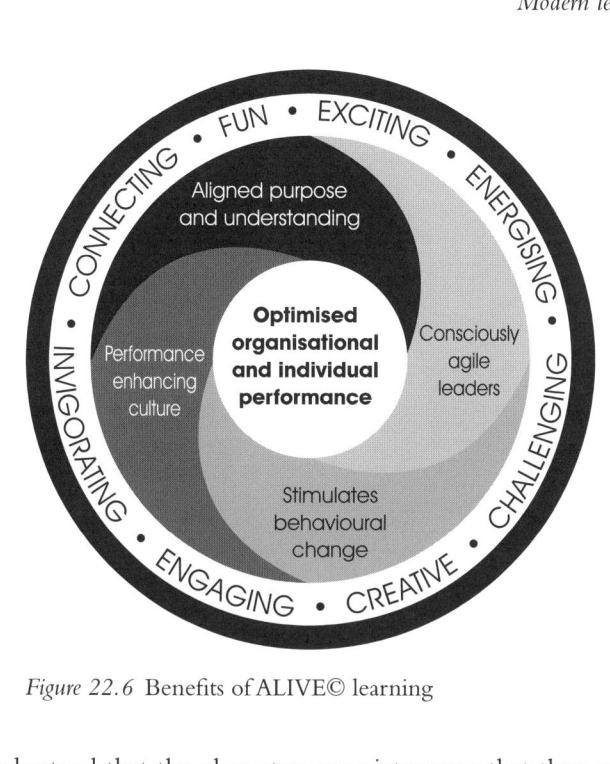

Figure 22.6 Benefits of ALIVE© learning

understand that the characters are pictograms that they are written vertically rather than horizontally. The next level is to *learn to do*; so we can learn to write the pictograms and read them and speak (hopefully with an accent that is not too abysmal!), however there is a whole world beyond 'do' in *learning to 'be'* in a way that is Chinese, that would involve new behaviours and habits being integrated into our own way of being.

Participants seem to need quite considerable support and encouragement to apply their learning in the workplace so that the real embedding and long-term change can occur. We always set the expectation that participants will update their cohorts on their activity, experiences and learning at the start of each masterclass/workshop whether remote or face-to-face. However, since the number of masterclasses/ workshops in a programme is always limited, this requirement for support and encouragement needs other means of implementation. This challenges us to provide a mechanism or stimulus after the workshops, not only to energise the participants, but also help cement the learning.

We've found a simple email prompt or extra, short support-focused conference call or some form of mutual support from the facilitator and/or cohort members can be enough. One successful way this can be addressed is by creating a social media group for the cohort, using a platform such as 'WhatsApp' to share on-going experiences in real time. This sort of informal communication provides emotional support and feedback as well as encouraging practical trial by trying-out the activity using the workplace as a 'live laboratory' (Grant, 2013b), and feeding back on progress.

Figure 22.7 Levels of leadership

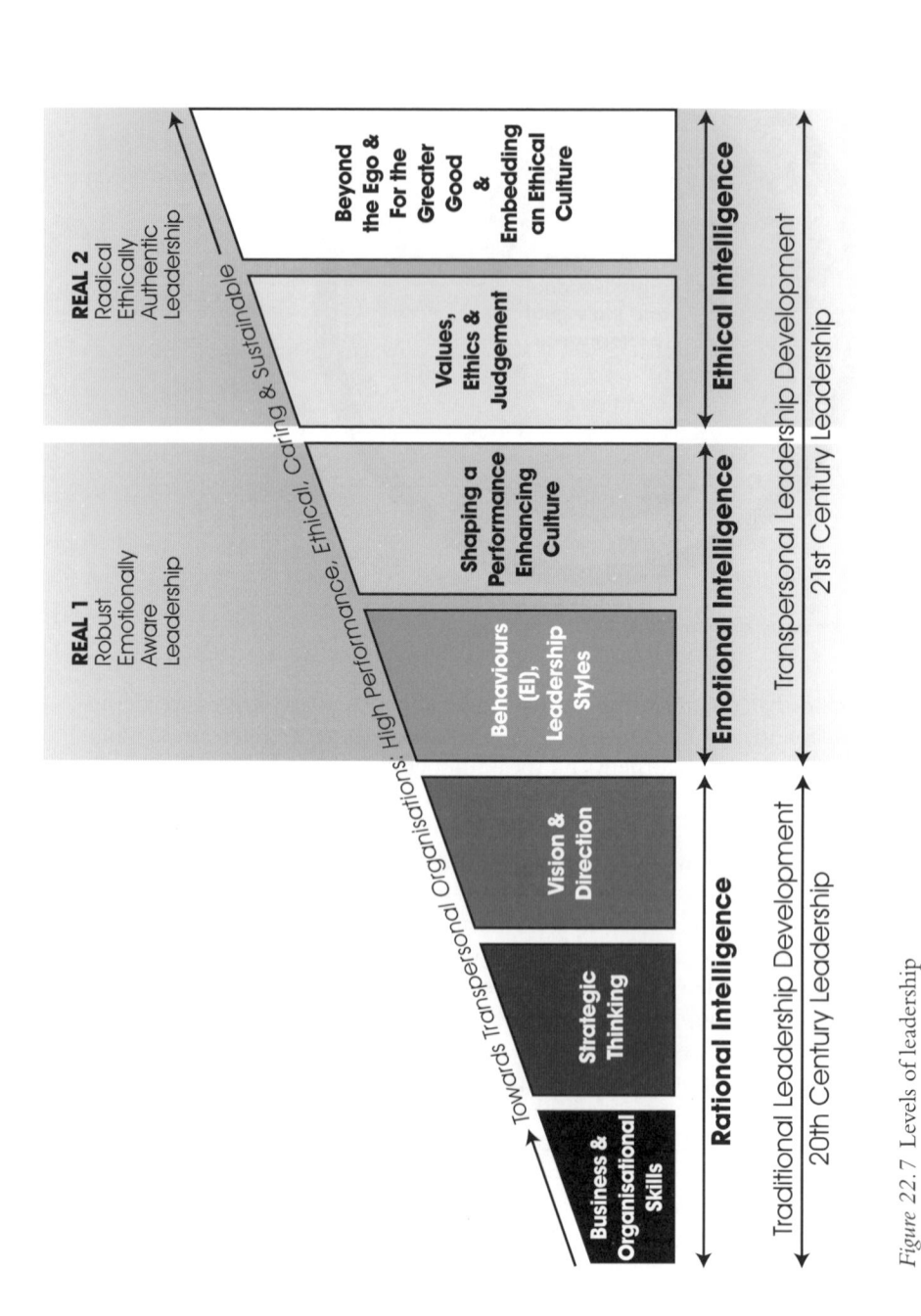

Source: © LeaderShape 2015.

Case study

A financial regulatory authority with a highly qualified senior team commissioned a 12-month leadership programme in 2014. It covered the key range of important leadership issues as described in Chapter 3 (Figure 3.1) and reproduced here as Figure 22.7 (i.e.: Strategy, EI and Leadership styles with a focus on the Coaching style, Creating a performance enhancing culture, Values, Judgement and Ethics). The programme was designed in alignment with the brain-friendly principles described in this chapter and consisted of:

1. ALIVE© online prep, which was completed prior to workshop activities
2. face-to-face experiential workshops, incorporating social, interactive and varied exercises and activities
3. reflective ALIVE© call, designed as action learning conference calls, to deepen and extend reflection on the actions tried out as a result of the online and workshop learning.

The hard test of the long-term sustainable success of this programme could not be known immediately after the completion of the programme, so an evaluation 12 months after completion was undertaken, which demonstrated the lasting impact of a brain-friendly, well executed programme design.

Key findings: *12 months after the end of the programme*		
Payback example 1	**Payback example 2**	**Payback example 3**
'In my area, working on the basis of 30 per cent uplift in performance of 39 senior officers on a minimum salary of £75k. Thirty-nine people are now delivering the work of 51 so the cost saving of a more productive team over employing more senior officers to deliver the same output is £900k pa, a greater than a 5 × return on investment per year for the whole programme.'	'In terms of performance of general casework: customer satisfaction, case resolution and case progression are all the highest they have ever been. A direct causal link with the programme is difficult to establish but the way we tackled it (reducing general casework queue) was influenced by what we learned on the programme.'	'There has been a trial of the new operating structure blueprint; I managed the trial area initially of 100 but now 300 people. Merging judgment and operational side into one role – this should bring a total 40 per cent saving across the organisation. The programme highly influenced my thinking of how I managed it.'

Individual benefits	Organisational benefits
1. **Built EI, empathy, understanding of different leadership styles and when to use them** 2. **Increased delegation through use of Coaching style** 3. **Developed leadership maturity, self-confidence and a support network** 4. **Access to a catalogue of development tools**	1. Established a networked leadership resource 2. Gone some way to developing a learning organisation 3. Improved performance in areas of participants' influence 4. Several new accounts amounting to significant return on investment

Feedback on ALIVE© Prep

'Most important part was reflective – thinking of own behaviour linked to the theory that had been outlined – online prep exercises provide good opportunity for this.'

'ALIVE© Prep was enjoyable, engaging, light, fun, accessible and wasn't what was expected (expected it to be serious and more learned). It's right to whet taste buds and expectations. Can't be authentic about giving people ownership if you hand it all to them on the day.'

'Online material most enjoyable and thought about everything – helped to understand the models being used and scope and coverage – scene setter – left feeling secure in the ground so more able and open to learn at a deeper level and to insights.'

Positive feedback on exercises and workshops (social and emotional learning)

'Group work (workshop and ALIVE© call) built on expectations from the ALIVE© prep through creating a frame or platform and expectation of fun and curiosity etc. ... shared experience and personal interest.'

'Drawing session where we worked in small groups and created a visual representation of what it was all about.'

'Group exercises that get me thinking for myself tend to make me take learning further.'

'The discussion towards end of day ... was potentially transformational, depending on the extent to which it is taken forward.'

'In terms of the workshop, a safe space to express those insights and I took that because I have been testing that space out.'

'Connecting to what's really important in a process that was inclusive and non-threatening.'

> **Questions and actions for personal development**
>
> Here are a few questions you might want to think about. Spending some time answering them will enable you to consider how you structure learning in your organisation so it is brain-friendly and promotes long-term change.
>
> 1. What is blended learning?
> 2. Why is it useful for leadership learning?
> 3. What is the importance of using a variety of stimuli?
> 4. Why is visual stimulus so important?
> 5. What is the contribution of prep activities ahead of workshops?
> 6. How can you promote/provide emotional and social learning?
> 7. Why is using new learning in the workplace so important?
> 8. What is the role of reflection?
> 9. What is the value of having well-spaced, shorter learning experiences?
> 10. What is one exercise you have experienced and could include in a workshop that would be likely to generate insights?
>
> ACTION: What are the first three actions you can take to change your approach to learning experiences, when would you like to achieve them by and how will you evaluate the impact?

Note

1 LeaderShape's ALIVE© process is an acronym for "**A**ccelerated **L**earning **I**n a **V**irtual **E**nvironment".

References

Atherton, J. (2011). *Learning and Teaching; Deep and Surface Learning.* www.learningandteaching.info/learning/deepsurf.htm [accessed on: 02/04/2017].

Cherniss, C. and Goleman, D. (1998, October 7). *Bringing Emotional Intelligence to the Workplace.* www.eiconsortium.org [accessed on: 09/09/2014].

Davachi, L., Kiefer, T., Rock, D. and Rock, L. (2010). *Learning that Lasts through AGES.* www.ahri.com.au/__data/assets/pdf_file/0016/16144/Learning-that-lasts-through-AGES.pdf [accessed March 2017].

Goleman, D. Boyatzis, R. and McKee, A. (2002). *Primal Leadership: Realising the Power of Emotional Intelligence.* Harvard Business School Press.

Grant, D. (2013a). *Master's Submission to University of Chester.* Unpublished work.

Grant, D. (2013b). Chapter 7 in *Leadership Assessment for Talent Development.* (Tony Wall & John Knights Eds). Kogan Page.

Kytle, J. (2004). *To Want to Learn: Insights and Provocations For Engaged Learning.* Palgrave Macmillan.

Medina, J. (2008). *Brain Rules: 12 Principles for Surviving and Thriving at Work, Home and School.* Pear Press.

Race, P. (2001). *Using Feedback to Help Students Learn.* The Higher Education Academy.

Rock, D. and Schwartz, J. (2006). *The Neuroscience of Leadership* Summer 2006 43. www.strategy-business.com/article/06207?gko=6da0a [accessed January 2017].

Sadler-Smith, E. (2010). *The Intuitive Mind: Profiting from the Power of your Sixth Sense.* Wiley.

23 Infusing ethics in leadership learning and development

Tony Wall

13 June 2016 at 3.47pm:
Because human nature is basically compassionate, I believe it is possible that decades from now we will see an era of peace – but we must work together as global citizens of a shared planet.
—His Holiness, The 14th Dalai Lama, the Spiritual Leader of Tibet

15 January 2017 at 11.00am:
For many years our country has been divided, angry and untrusting. Many say it will never change, the hatred is too deep. IT WILL CHANGE!
—Donald Trump, the then soon-to-be President of the US

Overview

Whether or not ethics is explicitly covered in leadership learning and development activity, every intervention has the potential to reinforce or disrupt ethical values, standards and behaviours. How it is organised, how it is delivered, what it covers, what it excludes and who is involved all contribute to the learning of being an ethical leader. This chapter considers subtle but key considerations in designing leadership learning and development towards ethics. It also highlights cutting-edge research and practice of how to re-orient the content, delivery, assessment and evaluation, towards infusing greater connectedness and collectiveness in leadership learning and development.

Weaving 'beyond the ego' into the fabric of (organisational) life

We have known for some time how cultures perpetuate and sustain themselves; the subtle, taken for granted ways of working have a major role in maintaining the status quo in organisational life (Nonet et al., 2016; Giorgi et al., 2015). For example, it is not necessarily the content of the two quotes at the start of this chapter which are at odds; indeed, some might read a *similarity* in the message of the two comments. Rather, the subtlety is really in where the messages place our *attention* – the first places our attention on *togetherness and sharing*, whereas

Infusing ethics in leadership 261

the second places it on *division and hatred* (Wall & Perrin, 2015; Wall, 2016a, 2016b, 2016c, also see Chapters 15 and 20).

We now have considerable evidence that indicates self-serving behaviours can be developed in leadership learning and development activity (e.g. Miller & Xu, 2016; Wall & Knights, 2013; Wall & Jarvis, 2015; Akrivou & Bradbury-Huang, 2015; Wall et al., 2016). This has grown to the extent that the United Nations created the *Principles of Responsible Management Education* (PRME) initiative with over 600 business schools in over 85 countries, to promote a more ethical and responsible direction in the learning and development activity of leaders and managers.

Indeed, in witnessing what might be considered a global ripple of irresponsible and unethical leadership practices across the globe, the PRME recently released a statement to re-assert its position. The email, entitled 'PRME Statement in Defense of Universal Values and Principles as Preconditions for Responsible Management Education', stated:

> *Our global community has thrived on the commitment and the ideas brought by people from around the world ... we are speaking up to defend universal values and principles of... equality, non-discrimination, freedom, and diversity. We are convinced that these values and principles are one of our greatest strengths. Therefore, we are deeply concerned about growing protectionism, nationalism and populism on the global stage.*
> (Main Wilson & Haertle, 2017)

When we live and work 'beyond the ego' (see Chapters 1 and 15), we are establishing and living cultural values and perspectives that orient our attention to wider collective benefit – beyond immediate, individual gain, towards collective gain (including current and future customers) (see Chapters 15 and 20). One way for organisations to generate meaningful conversations about what this collective gain may look like is by becoming familiar with the United Nations' *sustainable development goals* (SDGs). The 17 SDGs are listed in Table 23.1.

We know that attempting to embed all of these goals into all leadership learning and development activity is problematic – there are inherent tensions and dichotomies among the goals, which can halt rather than mobilise action and commitment (Longo et al., 2017; Wall et al., 2017a). Instead, the 17 goals can be seen as a way to cast a wider net to what we decide to focus our *attention* on, when it comes to our collective responsibility in an organisation. Within the context of a more ethical culture, these sorts of discussions become more possible and the business benefits of acting responsibly more explicit (see Chapter 15 and 20).

One approach of considering how to infuse ethics and responsibility within leadership learning and development practices is to consider where the subtle practices orient the *attention* of leaders. We can then make decisions about what might be possible and appropriate in the context of particular leadership learning and development activities (alongside the context of contemporary learning methods – see Chapter 22). In taking this approach, it is possible to identify the

Table 23.1 The United Nations' sustainable development goals

1. End poverty in all its forms, everywhere
2. End hunger, achieve food security and improved nutrition
3. Ensure healthy lives and promote well-being for all, at all ages
4. Ensure equitable education and promote lifelong learning opportunities for all
5. Achieve gender equality and empower all women and girls
6. Ensure availability and sustainable management of water and sanitation for all
7. Ensure access to affordable, reliable, sustainable and modern energy for all
8. Promote sustained and inclusive employment, and decent work for all
9. Build resilient infrastructure and foster innovation
10. Reduce inequality within and among countries
11. Make cities and human settlements inclusive, safe, resilient and sustainable
12. Ensure responsible and sustainable production and consumption
13. Take urgent action to combat climate change and its impacts
14. Conserve the oceans, seas and marine resources
15. Protect and promote sustainable use of terrestrial ecosystems (including biodiversity)
16. Promote peaceful and inclusive societies and accountable institutions
17. Strengthen the means of implementation through global partnerships

(Based on United Nations, 2017)

extent to which the *attention* of leaders is directed towards individualistic, self-gain responses within a short-term mindset, or signs of collective, connected and longer term mindsets. Each of these are now discussed.

Individual – me, myself, and I (now)

It can be difficult and even personally challenging to *notice* some of the subtleties of how short-term, individual gain is embedded in organisational life – especially when the local culture does not explicitly prize ethics and responsibility. For example, some psychometric assessments may well be reliable in identifying particular personality traits, and they can be productive as a way to measure the possible effects of an intervention. In both cases, however, *attention* can be placed on the individual, rather than the broader effects on the team, organisation or its communities.

Such practices can therefore be part of the fabric that supports individuals to excel at the cost of other aspects or measures of organisational performance and social gains (e.g. Miller & Xu, 2016). Evidence tells us this can happen in the context of evaluating leadership interventions (even across cultural boundaries), thereby *signalling* the cultural importance of short-term, monetary and/or individual gain (see Wall et al., 2017c). These signals act as cultural co-ordinates on how to act in work (Wall, 2016a; Wall, 2016c).

The specific behaviours of those delivering the leadership learning and development activities can also contribute to the promotion of short-term thinking and individual gain in subtle ways. For example, when facilitators, trainers or coaches guide or direct conversations or ask questions, they are all subtly modelling where to place *attention*, or validating which areas of attention are legitimate. So when a coach encourages a leader to identify a well-formed goal, are they encouraging 'manageable' goals (which are *short term*), from the leader's *individual* position/perspective, and with a single, *monetary* focus in terms of measurability? In this way, they may well be an unexpected accomplice (Wall et al., 2017a).

A summary of other examples is provided in Table 23.2, and is followed by a case study of how a professional services and leadership development team had initiated a re-orientation away from an individualistic towards the sustainable development goals.

Table 23.2 Possible principles towards shorter-term individual gain

Context	• Purposes, which primarily aim to resolve immediate changes and gains, typically from a monetary perspective (e.g. 'fixing' management issues through coaching).
	• Making the learning and development opportunities (potentially unconsciously) accessible to an elite or a specific group in the organisation (e.g. white men).
Content	• Content that positions leadership as a discreet activity independent from wider impacts on people and planet (e.g. leadership as transactions, delegation, or as task management).
Methods	• Methods that primarily support individual leaders making sense of situations alone, from their own, current perspective (e.g. predominantly individual study).
Delivery	• Delivery that is predominantly (potentially unconsciously) designed to benefit an established elite or group (e.g. block delivery can make it difficult for people with caring responsibilities to arrange cover while maintaining the well-being of carer and/or family).
	• Deliverers who model (potentially unconsciously) the views above, and/or take a deficit or remedial approach to differences in backgrounds and circumstances (e.g. assuming particular forms of leadership style are superior to others).
Assessment	• Assessments that primarily focus on individual changes and gains (e.g. the use of psychometrics with individually focused coaching).
Evaluation	• Evaluation that typically evaluates against a narrow set of outcomes, including individual and immediate gain.

> ### Case study – professional services and leadership development team re-orienting towards sustainable development goals
>
> An international professional services firm that focuses on the development of high-level senior leaders had integrated ethics as a key theme through its training and coaching activities. Indeed, it had ethical approval processes related to every work-based project it supported.
>
> However, over time, it also recognised that it had a narrow conception of what it meant to be a responsible and ethical leader. The basic assumption was that being such a leader meant taking into account wider impacts beyond economic gain.
>
> Led by a facilitator, it decided to utilise the UN's sustainable development goals as a framework for:
>
> 1. mapping what it currently considers when referring to ethics, responsibility and sustainability
> 2. having conversations about what it can possibly integrate in the immediate term
> 3. having conversations about what the firm might be able to integrate in the longer term.
>
> The first of these activities identified that it covered half of the goals to a degree, and the second of these led to clarifying another group of goals that could easily be integrated into the training and development activity. The final activity is leading to wider, but more fundamental conversations among the team about what their organisation should focus on. This indicates a real engagement with responsibility at the highest levels.

Connected and collective – *I am because we are* (beyond now)

An alternative set of mindsets and values can be described as connected and collective, beyond the now. It is characteristic of a number of ancient philosophies including Ubuntuism (an African philosophy of life) and Confucianism (an Oriental philosophy) (Wall & Jarvis, 2015; Wall, 2016a; Wall, 2016b; Wall, 2016c; Wall, 2017), which prioritise the interconnectedness of self with other (things). This is a shift from '*I* think therefore *I* am' to 'I am *because we* are'.

The subtleties of this shift are found in all of the same dimensions discussed in Table 23.2, but with a broader, collective net. For example, it means re-orienting assessments towards collective interpretations of leadership behaviours, as a proxy for how the wider world is receiving the behaviours (or how those behaviours are impacting the wider world). In the context of evaluation, multi-stakeholder measures and participatory approaches also provide a wider scope,

Infusing ethics in leadership 265

but also a more holistic approach to making judgements about performance (Wall et al., 2017b).

Similarly, from this more transpersonal mindset, the idea of *reciprocal* approaches to learning and development assumes that each individual brings a rich set of learning assets from which each leader can grow with and from (Wall & Tran, 2015; Wall, 2017). This means making sense of the opinions of individual leaders from their own heritage (or the background and experiences of the person), valuing it, and validating it from that perspective – yet at the same time offering alternative perspectives that might 'add to the repertoire' of leadership behaviours across contexts (Wall & Tran, 2016).

This can be a deeply challenging approach for facilitators, trainers or coaches who may have a preferred or prefixed set of behaviours (Wall et al., 2016), as it involves them also becoming a fellow traveller in their leadership learning journey. This is akin to forms of coaching that are more open-ended, and non-directional. It requires transpersonal facilitators.

A summary of other examples is provided in Table 23.3, and is followed by a case study of how a training and development organisation re-orientated towards a more holistic perspective.

Table 23.3 Possible principles towards connectedness, collectiveness and beyond 'the now'

Context	• Purposes, which consider longer term changes and gains, typically engaging with different perspectives of what 'gain' means. • Making the learning and development opportunities accessible to aspiring leaders in the organisation, with value placed on equality and diversity.
Content	• Content that positions leadership as interrelated with people and planet (e.g. transpersonal ideas or complex adaptive systems).
Methods	• Methods that involve leaders making sense of situations from/with diverse perspectives (e.g. discussion exercises, multiple stakeholder activities).
Delivery	• Delivery designed to be inclusive to all (e.g. the deliverers take into account the diversity of backgrounds and circumstances of the participants in the learning and development activity). • Deliverers typically treat diversity in backgrounds and circumstances as learning assets for learning contexts (e.g. enabling differences in experiences to be displayed, valued, and validated from different participants).
Assessment	• Assessments primarily focused on group, team or wider changes and gains, from different perspectives (e.g. multiple stakeholder diagnostics, balanced scorecard approaches, corporate social responsibility diagnostics).
Evaluation	• Evaluation that typically makes judgements against a range of collective and longer term outcomes (or indicators of these outcomes) (e.g. social return on investment methodologies).

Case study – organisation taking a collective leadership position

The board of a national organisation decided to re-orient itself in how it delivered training to its client base. Originally, it understood itself as providing training and events for a certain professional grouping, that is, human resource professionals at all levels.

As part of a re-visioning programme for the organisation, a facilitator led a number of simple questions around purpose. One of the questions was 'what would we like to give to the world?', which is infused with a transpersonal perspective.

This led to a wide variety of perspectives, but to three main strands of purpose:

- We are here to give gifts to the world.
- We are here to bring connectivity.
- We are here to create surprises.

As a significant re-orientation from events to gifts, connectivity and surprises, it acknowledged a different level of interrelatedness to the world around the organisation, including its customers. This led to a reconceptualisation of each 'interaction' as offering these elements, such as:

- time to connect with the people in the 'interaction', and get to know each person in the group
- a clear and explicit gift, such as resources to embed well-being in the organisation
- an element of surprise, as a way to inspire new, collective action.

Examples of the new 'interactions' being developed include:

- a 'derive' (i.e. a mindful walk) next to a river – a space for leaders to organise their thoughts with others in a natural environment
- a storytelling event in a building of faith (e.g. a cathedral) – a space for leaders to contemplate their wider life purpose in a building of spiritual (but not necessarily religious) thought
- roundtable discussion groups about well-being with other leaders – a space for like-minded leaders to share and get feedback on their own practices with others, plus build their own connectedness to others.

Conclusion

If we commit to infusing ethics into leadership learning and development, it means we need to weave the notion of 'beyond the ego' into the cultural subtleties of leadership interventions such as training, action learning, peer group learning, coaching and mentoring. It means taking a close look at where these interventions place our attention – the shorter term, self-gain, or the longer-term collective gain. The consequences of such an approach will often need transformational change, as suggested in the two quotes at the start of this chapter.

The journey to get there is one which requires a transpersonal journey for those involved, and will involve making challenging decisions about where the collective gain is targeted. The United Nations' sustainable development goals are a useful place to start from dialogue, but it is important that the wider leadership collective owns the direction. To emphasise a sentiment of The Dalai Lama, 'human nature is basically compassionate', so it is likely that some of these goals are already present in your leadership learning and development – so the call to action is how else can we orient ourselves towards longer term, collective gain. Or, more broadly, how else can we live a transpersonal life, for the benefit of others?

Questions and Actions for Personal Development

Here are a few questions you might want to think about. Spending some time answering them will enable your personal development and may make other chapters in the book more meaningful.

1. Which of the sustainable development goals (listed in Table 23.1) is your team already engaged in? Which might be a next step for your team or organisation?
2. Looking at the principles of promoting short-term individual gain (Tables 23.2), which areas can you identify in your own context? What might be the effects in your context?
3. Looking at the principles of promoting longer-term collective gain (Table 23.3), which areas can you identify in your own context? What might be the effects in your context?
4. Looking at your answers above, which areas might generate value or benefits for you, your team, your organisation or other important stakeholders?
5. How might you initiate or further develop conversations about some of the areas you might like to develop?

ACTION: What will you commit to doing to initiate or further develop the infusion of ethics and responsibility into your leadership learning and development activity? What are the steps, and the timeframes for each of those steps?

References

Akrivou, K. and Bradbury-Huang, H. (2015). Educating Integrated Catalysts: Transforming Business Schools Toward Ethics and Sustainability. *Academy of Management Learning and Education*, 14 (2), pages 222–240.

Giorgi, S., Lockwood, C. and Glynn, M.A. (2015). The Many Faces of Culture: Making Sense of 30 Years of Research on Culture in Organization Studies. *Academy of Management Annals*, 9 (1), pages 1–54.

His Holiness, the 14th Dalai Lama, the Spiritual Leader of Tibet (2016). The Dalai Lama: Why I'm Hopeful about the World's Future. *The Washington Post*, Opinions, 13 June 2016.

Longo, C., Shankar, A. and Nuttall, P. (2017). 'It's Not Easy Living a Sustainable Lifestyle': How Greater Knowledge Leads to Dilemmas, Tensions and Paralysis. *Journal of Business Ethics*. ISSN 0167-4544, E-ISSN 1573-0697.

Main Wilson, A. and Haertle, J. (2017). *PRME Statement in Defense of Universal Values and Principles as Preconditions for Responsible Management Education*. Email communication.

Miller, D. and Xu, X. (2016). A Fleeting Glory: Self-Serving Behavior Among Celebrated MBA CEOs. *Journal of Management Inquiry*, 25 (3), pages 286–300.

Nonet, G., Kassel, K. and Meijs, L.J. (2016). Understanding Responsible Management: Emerging Themes and Variations from European Business School Programs. *Journal of Business Ethics*, 139 (4), pages 717–736.

Trump, D. (2017). https://twitter.com/realDonaldTrump/status/820707210565132288 [accessed on 08/12/2017].

United Nations (2017). *The Sustainable Development Goals*. http://www.un.org/sustainabledevelopment/sustainable-development-goals/ [accessed on: 29/03/2017].

Wall, T. (2016a). Author Response – Provocative Education: From Buddhism for Busy People® to Dismal Land®. *Studies in Philosophy and Education*, 36 (6), pages 649–653.

Wall, T. (2016b). Reviving the Ubuntu Spirit in Landscapes of Practice: Evidence from Deep within The Forest. *Journal of Work Applied Management*, 8 (1), pages 95–98.

Wall, T. (2016c). Žižekian Ideas in Critical Reflection: The Tricks and Traps of Mobilising Radical Management Insight. *Journal of Work Applied Management*, 8 (1), pages 5–16.

Wall, T. (2017). Reciprocal Pedagogies – Flexible Learning Exemplar. In Devitt-Jones, S. (Ed.) *Flexible Learning Practice Guide*. HEA/QAA.

Wall, T. and Jarvis, M. (2015). *Business Schools as Educational Provocateurs of Productivity Via Interrelated Landscapes Of Practice*. London, Chartered Association of Business Schools.

Wall, T. and Knights, J. (2013). *Leadership Assessment for Talent Development*. Kogan Page.

Wall, T. and Perrin, D. (2015). *Slavoj Žižek: Žižekian Gaze at Education*. Springer.

Wall, T. and Tran, L. (2015). Learning to Be an International Work-Based Learner. In Helyer, R. (Ed.) *Work Based Learning Student Handbook*, second edition, pages 205–226. Palgrave.

Wall, T. and Tran, L. (2016). A Transcultural Dance: Enriching Work-Based Learning Facilitation. In Helyer, R. (Ed.) *Facilitating Work-Based Learning: A Handbook for Tutors*, pages 227–246. Palgrave.

Wall, T., Tran, L. and Soejatminah, S. (2017a). Inequalities and Agencies in Workplace Learning Experiences: International Student Perspectives. *Vocations and Learning*, 10 (2), pages 141–156.

Wall, T., Iordanou, I., Hawley, R. and Csigás, Z. (2016). *Research Policy and Practice Provocations: Bridging the Gap: Towards Research that Sparks and Connects*. Brussels, the European Mentoring and Coaching Council.

Wall, T., Jamieson, M., Csigás, Z., and Kiss, O. (2017b). *Research Policy and Practice Provocations: Coaching Evaluation in Diverse Landscapes of Practice – Towards Enriching Toolkits and Professional Judgement*. Brussels, the European Mentoring and Coaching Council, 35 pages.

Wall, T., Hindley, A., Hunt, T., Peach, J., Preston, M., Hartley, C. and Fairbank, A. (2017c). Work-Based Learning as a Catalyst for Sustainability: A Review and Prospects. *Higher Education, Skills and Work-Based Learning*, 7 (2), pages 211–224.

Index

NB numbers in bold refer to tables; numbers in italics refer to figures

8ICOL® 139–41, 142–51, *144, 148*, 186; brief history 144–5; linking core intelligences 145–7; model 147–50; overview 143–4; questions/actions for CPD 150
"30 per cent club" 202
360° assessment tool 5–8, 125, 127, 129, 145

AAUW 202
"ABO" commitment 122
accepting psychological theories 36
achievement 86, 112, *113*, 114, 117
acting on choices 223
action learning 5–7
action plan 127–30; establishing 127–9; implementing 129–30
activation 61
activism 53–4
adding ethics into development 260–67; *see also* infusing ethics
advanced journey 133–240; beyond ego 163–73; choice and for the greater good 223–30; continuous personal development 231–40; Eight Integrated Competencies of Leadership 143–51; improving judgement 174–85; inner development of Transpersonal Leader 211–22; introduction 135–42; managing diversity 200–210; neuroscience of consciousness 152–62; values of leadership 186–99
Affiliative style of leadership 83, 87, 91, 109–10, 117
AGES theory 248
"aha" moment 116, 126, 175, 247
AI *see* artificial intelligence

Alexander, Graham 98–9
ALIVE© 248, 253, 255, 257, 258
ALIVE© Prep 245–8, 257–8
ALIVE© programme 244–58
Alkire, Michael 157
Allen Institute for Brain Science 157–8
altruistic love 190–1, 227; personal reflection on 190–1
amazing human brains 37–8
amygdala 41–3
andragogy 3–4
anti-social attitudes 167
applying consciousness to leadership 152–62; *see also* neuroscience of consciousness
Aristotle 56
arousal 61
artificial intelligence 156, 235
As-usual Leadership 16–18
asking right questions 101–2
aspects of emotion 60–1
associative connections 40
Atherton, J. 247
Attitude Bell Curve 121
attitudes 49
Authentic Leadership 228
authenticity 226–7; *see also* transpersonal qualities
avoidance of opinion 102
awareness vs. consciousness 135–42
Ayurveda 158

bad leadership **32**
Bakshi, Pavan 71, 178
basic emotions 59
basics of consciousness 153–4

BE REAL 2; *see also* Radical, Ethically Authentic Leaders
behavioural change 117–19, *118–19*
behavioural economics 179
being a bat 154–5
being radical 225–6; *see also* transpersonal qualities
beliefs 187
benefits of ALIVE© learning *255*
Bennis, Warren 3
beyond ego 163–73; definition 164–5; managing our ego 166–7; moving beyond ego 165–6; overview 163–4; questions/actions for CPD 172; self vs. organisation 167–70; working for all stakeholders 170–2
binding problem 156, 158
black and minority ethnics 202
blended learning 244–58, *245*; example 244–5; leadership learning design 248; masterclasses 248; masterclass design principles 248–51; optimising pace 251–2; pre-masterclass online prep 245–8; remote delivery masterclasses 252–4; serving learners 252; work-based learning 254–8
"blind spots" 74
Block, Ned 154–5
BMEs *see* black and minority ethnics
body language 61, 101, 249
Boston Research Group 74
brain adjustment in modern world 38–9
Brain Boxx 55
brain cells 39–40
brain efficiency 43–4
brain interactions 42–3, *43*; *see also* emotional highway
Brain Rules 4 246
brainstorming 219
Brexit 202
BRG *see* Boston Research Group
Brief History of Transpersonal Psychology 1
bringing about Ideal culture 120–2; contracting expectations 120–1; implementing change 121–2, *121*

call to action 143–4
capability levels 27–30, *28*
caring 224–5, 227; *see also* transpersonal qualities
case studies: blended learning 254; Chatham House Rules 171; collective leadership approach 266; consultancy partnership 168–9; culture survey 116–17; *Ethical Leadership* White Paper 147; European charity 108–9; financial regulatory authority 257–8; global toy retailing 89–90; international recruitment 88; leadership development goals 264; public sector service organisation 169–70; Ridgeway Partnership 29–30; stakeholder priority 171
CASs *see* complex adaptive systems
chakra system 158
challenge vs. nurture 103–4
Chalmers, David 153
change catalyst 71, 73–5
characteristics of good/bad leaders **32**
Chatham House Rules 171
chemical "bursts" 62–3
Cherniss, C. 245
Chi Gung 212
choice 223–30; choices maketh the woman 223–7; for the greater good 228–9; overview 223; questions/actions for CPD 229
choice core values 227–8
choice of EI models 67–8
choices maketh the woman 223–7; demonstrating transpersonal qualities 226–7; greater good 228–9; transpersonal qualities 224–6; values 227
Churchill, Winston 231
clarifying decision-making 174–85; *see also* improving judgement
clarity 107
claustrum 157–8, *157*
climate 106–8
Coaching style of leadership 82, 87–8, 94–105, 109–10, 117, 127–9, 257–8; challenge vs. nurture 104; definitions 94–6; developing proficiency 98–102; natural 1:1 style 102–3; overview 94; questions/actions for CPD 105; when to use 96–8
Colella, V. 235
collective gain 264–6
Collins, Jim 3, 233
CoME *see* Contract of Mutual Expectations
Commanding style of leadership 84, 86, 87, 110–11, 117
commitment 107
committing to infusing ethics 267

common strengths 71–4; employee self-control 72; optimism 72; organisational awareness 72; service orientation 72
compassion 267
complete 8ICOL® model 147–50; four intelligence competencies 149–50; intellect/logic 148–9; personal conscience/self-determination 150; personality/preferences 149
complex adaptive systems 234–7; transpersonal practices of **236–7**
components to proficiency in Coaching style 98–102; asking right questions 101–2; effective listening 101; having no opinion 102; one-to-one communication process 100; simple process 98–100; use of silence 102
confirmation of leadership styles 94
conflict management 71, 73
Confucianism 264
Confucius 48, 188
connecting neuroscience to consciousness 155–7; neural connections 155–6; technical details 156–8
connections in the brain 39–40
conscientiousness 189
conscious decision-making processes 174–83, *175*; rational/logical 174, 178–9
consciousness 152–62; see also neuroscience of consciousness
content optimisation 251–2
context of diversity 200–2; gender diversity 201–2; racial/ethnic diversity 202
continued existence of emotions 61–2
continuous personal development 11, 141, 150, 194, 231–41; checking where you are 233–9; never ending journey 232–3; overview 231–2
continuum *95*
Contract of Mutual Expectations 120, 122
contracting expectations 120–1
core values 195; touchstone 229
corporate social responsibility 172, 183
counselling/mentoring/coaching continuum *95*
"courageous integrity" 195
Covey, Stephen 3, 220

CPD *see* continuous personal development
CREASAP 224–6; *see also* transpersonal qualities
creation of performance-enhancing culture 106–24; bringing Ideal culture to fruition 120–2; climate vs. culture 107–8; culture parameters 112–17; definitions 106–7; importance of climate 108–9; linking leadership with performance 109–11; overview 105; performance-enhancing culture model 117–19; questions/actions for CPD 123
credibility 169
Crick, Francis 155, 157
criteria for ethical behaviour **195**
Cross-Cultural Kaleidoscope™ 206–7, *207*
CSR *see* corporate social responsibility
culture 106–24, **113**
culture model for Transactional Leadership 110–11, *110*
curiosity 52

Dalai Lama 10, 260, 267
Dalí, Salvador 150
Darwin, Charles 180
Davies Review 200, 202
dealing with emotions 58–65; *see also* understanding emotions
decision-making processes 167–83, *175*
default position 36–46
definitions: "ABO" commitment 122; awareness 135; climate 106–7; coaching 94–6; Coaching style of leadership *96*; consciousness 135, 153–5; culture 107; diversity 200–1; ego 163–5; emotional intelligence 67, **70–1**; emotions 58–61; "good" leadership 31–3; leadership 22–3; managing diversity 201; self-awareness 48; spiritual intelligence 139, 160; Transpersonal Leadership 1–2, *2*; values 186
Democratic style of leadership 84, 87–91, 109–10, 117
demonstrating transpersonal qualities 226–7
detail of personal conscience 187–91; altruistic love 190–1; beliefs 187; ethics/morals 187–8; forgiveness 190; patience 189–90; values/virtues 188–9

developing others 71, 73, 75
Developing Spiritual Intelligence 60
developing successful leadership 1–11; aim of book 3–4; definition of Transpersonal Leadership 2; developing Transpersonal journey 5–11; example 4; readership of book 5; using the book 5
development of EI models 67–8
development needs 71–4; change catalyst 73; conflict management 73; developing others 73; empathy 73; initiative 74; inspirational leadership 74
development priority analysis 72
development stages 211–104
development strengths 71–4
development of Transpersonal Leadership 241–70; *see also* implementation of Transpersonal Leadership development
difference between climate and culture 107–8
different leadership styles 80–91
DISC 51
discrimination 20, 207–8
Disney 8
disrupting ethical values 260
diversity 200–10; conclusion 207–8; context 201–2; overview 200–1; perspectives on managing diversity 202–7; questions/actions for CPD 209
DNA evidence 37
dopamine 159
drive 60–1
Drucker, Peter 3, 106, 192

Eagleman, David 153
echolocation 154
effective listening 101
effective use of decision-making processes 183
ego 164–5
ego management 166–7
ego self-image 165–6, *165*
Ego-based Leadership 16–17
EI *see* emotional intelligence
Eight Integrated Competencies of Leadership 143–51; *see also* 8ICOL®
Ekman, P. 59
emergence of emotions 58–61; "real anger" 60
emotional highway 41–3, *41–2*, 61–2

emotional intelligence 66–79, *69*, 226; capabilities **70–1**, 74–5, *75*; impact on rational intelligence *18*; self-assessment **77–8**; *see also* transpersonal qualities
emotional self-awareness 15–16, 68–70, 75, 89–90, 141
emotional self-control 71–2, 75
emotions 36–46
empathy 71, 73, 88, 258
enabling others 220
endeavour for awareness 233–4
establishing action plan 127–9
Ethicability 182
ethical behaviour 195–6, 226; criteria for **195**; *see also* transpersonal qualities
Ethical Leadership White Paper 22–3, 59, 115, 145–7, 181, 187–8; case studies from 147; quoting 146
ethical philosophy 175, 181–3; identification of 182
ethics in leadership learning 187–8, 260–7; *see also* infusing ethics
ethnic diversity 201–2
example of how brain works 43
example of leadership 43
example of "real anger" 60, 63
excellence 188
experiencing 135–7, 152
experiencing the moment 153–5; basics 153–4; Thomas Nagel 154–5
explaining actions 98
expression 61
external capabilities 218–21; enabling others 220; role modelling 218–19; situation sensing 220–1; win/win thinking 219–20
extremism 3
extroversion 49–51, 61

facial expressions 59–60, *59*
fairness 189, 227
fear 233
feeling 50
fight/flight response 214
five stages of evolving self 235
flexibility 107
Flow Process of Retreat, Reflect and Return *215*, 216–17
forgiveness 190; personal reflection on 190
Fortune 100 7
foundation of journey 15–22; step-by-step process 16–20

274 *Index*

four EI competencies 68–71, *69*, 149–50
four parameters of culture 112–17, *112*
Freud, Sigmund 164–5; psychoanalytic personality theory 164–5
Fry, L. W. 139
FTSE 350 202
full consciousness 135–42, 233–4, *234*
functions of consciousness 49

Gandhi, Mahatma 187, 231
Gardner, Howard 144
gender difference 74–6
gender diversity 201–2
George, Bill 3, 228
globalisation 3
Goleman, Daniel 3, 67, 106, 108, 115, 245
Goleman/Boyatzis model 67–8, 80–1, 144
"good" leadership 31–3, **32**; characteristics of **32**
Good to Great 233
granular behaviours 117–18, *118*, 125–6, 232
Gray, C. 146, 155
greater good 223–30; *see also* choice
Greenleaf, Robert 3
Griffith, Richard 139, 144, 160
Grof, Stanislav 1
GROW model *see* "ToGrow" model
growth in self-awareness 47
"gut feeling" 49, 159, 174, 176; *see also* intuition
gut neurons 158–9

hallucinations 156
Handy, Charles 112
Harris, L. 112, 115, 117
Harrison, Roger 112–13, 115
Hawking, Stephen 235
Headspace 213
heart neurons 158–60
Hegel, Georg Wilhelm Friedrich 156
Hewlett Packard 76
hierarchy of intelligences 145–50, *145*, *238*, 239; EI competencies 149–50; intellect/logic 148–9; personal conscience/self-determination 150; personality/preferences 149
Hierarchy of Needs 237
hippocampus 42–4, 247
history of intelligences 144–5
Hogan Personality Index 51

honesty 188
Honey and Mumford Learning Styles Questionnaire 52, 54
How to Develop Ethical Leaders 141
how to manage emotions 62–4; "anger" example 63
how we learn 51–5; learning styles 53–4
HSBC Bank 195
human senses 55–6
humility 188–9, 227
Hutchins, Gary 216
Hwang, H. S. 59–60

id 164–5
Ideal culture *114*, 120–2
identifying ethical philosophy 182
identifying motivators 215, *215*
identifying strengths 125–31
ignite through enabling others 220
impact of emotions 58
impact through situation sensing 220–1
implementation of Transpersonal Leadership development 241–70; infusing ethics 260–67; modern learning principles 243–59
implementing action plan 129–30; Reflection Note 129–30
implementing change 121–2, *121*
importance of climate 108–9
importance of nonconsciousness processes 175–8
improving development areas 125–31
improving judgement 174–85; five decision-making processes 178–83; importance of nonconscious processes 175–8; overview 174–5; questions/actions for CPD 184; using decision-making processes effectively 183
improving performance *119*
increasing self-awareness 47–57; *see also* self-awareness
individual gain 262–4; principles towards **263**
influence through win/win thinking 219–20
infusing ethics 260–7; conclusion 267; connected/collective 264–6; "me, myself, I" 262–4; overview 260; questions/actions for CPD 267; weaving "beyond ego" into fabric of life 260–2
ingroups 206–7
initiative 74, 86

inner development of Transpersonal Leader 211–22, *211*; external capabilities 218–21; overview 211–12; personal leadership 212–17; questions/actions for CPD 221
insight 175, 180
insights 44
inspirational leadership 33–4, 71, 74
inspire through role modelling 218–19
instinct 174–5, 180
integration perspective on diversity 205–7; advantages of 205; disadvantages of 206
integrity 188, 227
intellect 148–9
intelligence quotient 40, 67–8, 148
interactions of amygdala *42*
intermediate journey 13–132; Coaching style of leadership 94–105; creating performance-enhancing culture 106–24; dealing with emotions 58–65; identifying strengths 125–31; increasing self-awareness 47–57; introduction 15–21; neuroscience of leadership 36–46; power of emotional intelligence 66–79; understanding leadership 22–35; using different leadership styles 80–91
International Women's Day 202
introversion 49–51, 61
intuition 49–50, 174, 176–7, 179
Invisible Elephant and the Pyramid Treasure, The 177, 233
IQ *see* intelligence quotient

Johnson & Johnson 117
Joiner, B. 211
Josephs, S. 211
JTI *see* Jungian Type Index
Jung, Carl 49–51; theory of psychological types 49, 51
Jungian Type Index 49

Kahneman, Daniel 179
Kant, Immanuel 156
Kegan, Robert 237
kinds of neuron *39*
King, Martin Luther 195
Klein, Gary 181
Koch, Christof 157–8
Kolb, D. 52, 54–5
Koubeissi, M. 158
Kytle, Jack 250

Laloux, F. 220
leader capability levels 27–30, *28*
LeaderShape Global 1–2, 5–9, 22, 81, 87, 126–7, 139, 145, 177–8
Leadership Assessment for Talent Development 71
leadership impacts *111*
Leadership in India White Paper 71
leadership styles 80–91, **81**, *115*; in action 86–91; overview 80; questions/actions for CPD 92–3; six styles 80–6, **81**
leadership vs. management 23–7, **24**
Leading Across Cultures White Paper 59, 115
leading others 218–21
learning cycle *53*
learning methodologies 243–59; *see also* modern learning principles
learning perspective on diversity 204–5; advantages of 204–5; disadvantages of 205
learning styles 53–4, *53*; activist 53–4; pragmatist 54; preferences **54**; reflector 53–4; theorist 53–4
left hemisphere of brain *157*
LEIPA® 68, 71, 76, 126–7, 145, 149–50
"letter of the law" 183
levels of awareness 233–5, **234**
levels of intelligence *2*
levels of leader capability 27–30, *28*
levels of leadership *256*
limitations of nonconsciousness processes 175–8
linking core intelligences 145–7
linking leadership and performance 109–11; transactional leadership 110–11; transformational leadership 109–10
Litwin, Richard 106–7
Llinás, Rodolfo 156–7
locating self-awareness in leadership 48
LOCS Culture Shaper tool 112–14
logic 148–9
logical decision-making process 174, 177–9
"love" hormone 159
love *see* altruistic love

MacArthur, Ellen 235
McClelland, David 106–7
magneto-encephalograph 155
mainstreaming of EI 66

maintaining standards 107
making change happen *see* implementing change
management questionnaire 24–7, **25–6**
managing diversity 200–210; *see also* diversity
managing the ego 163–4, 165–7; power 167; prestige 167; recognition 167; reward 167
managing emotions 66–79; *see also* power of emotional intelligence; understanding emotions
Manwaring, Tony 177–8
Mapping Motivation 214
Marshall, Ian 10
Mashour, George 157
Maslow, Abraham 237
masterclass design principles 248–51
masterclasses 248
matching perspective on diversity 203–4; advantages of 204; disadvantages of 204
Matsumoto, D. 59–60
maximising development 125–7
Mayer, J. D. 67
meaning-making 216–17; getting started 217
Medina, J. 246
meditation *see* mindfulness
Medtronics 228
MEG *see* magneto-encephalograph
mentoring 95
Mezirow, Jack 51
Milk Train Doesn't Stop Here Anymore, The 153
Millennials 3, 189
Millman, D. 218, 220
mindfulness 212–13; getting started 213
mindset 213–14; getting started 214
misunderstanding leadership 22
model for performance-enhancing culture 117–19
modern learning principles 243–59; overview 243–4; principles of blended learning 244–58; questions/actions for CPD 259
modern world brain adjustment 38–9
morals 187–8
motivation 58–61, 214–15; getting started 215
Motivational Maps assessment 215
moving beyond ego 165–6
MRI scanning 67

multitasking 248
Myers Briggs Type Indicator 49–51

Nadkarni, Anant 177
Nagel, Thomas 154–5
naivety 178
narrative 249
natural 1:1 style 102–3
near death experiences 160
negative traits *113*
Nehru, Nikhil 178
neural connections 39–40, 44, 155–6, *156*
neural wiring 38, 51
neuro-plasticity 38, 40, 243
neurons 39–40, *39*, 58, 156–9
neuroscience of consciousness 152–62; connecting neuroscience to consciousness 155–8; definition 153–5; neurons in heart and gut 158–60; overview 152–3; questions/actions for CPD 160; spiritual intelligence 160
neuroscience of leadership 36–46; brain adjustment 38–9; how brain works 39–44; meaning for leadership 44–5; overview 36; questions/actions for CPD 45; Stone Age brain 37–8; value of neuroscience 37
never-ending journey 232–3
New England Skeptical Society 159
nineteen EI capabilities 68–71, *69*
non-rational functions 49; intuition 49; sensation 49
non-sub-conscious decision-making processes 174–83, *175*; ethical philosophy 175, 181–3; insight 175, 180–1; instinct 174, 180; intuition 174, 179; Professor Sadler-Smith 179–80
non-verbal communication 61–2, *62*
Novella, Steven 159
nurture 104

Obama, Barack 109
observation 135–6
Ogbonna, E. 112, 115, 117
one-to-one communication process 100
1:1 style *102*, 103–4, *104*
Online Learning System 246
optimising pace 251–2
optimism 56, 71–2
oral storytelling 249, 266

organisational awareness 71–2
organisational ego 170–2
organisational life 260–2
other areas of self-awareness 56
outgroups 202
oxytocin 159

Pace-Setting style of leadership 85, 87–8, 110–11
parameters of culture 112–17, *112*, **113**
patience 189–90; personal reflection on 189–90
Patterson, Elaine 216
performance enhancement 226; *see also* transpersonal qualities
performance-enhancing culture 106–24
personal conscience 143, 150, 186–99; *see also* values of leadership
personal leadership 212–17; meaning-making 216–17; mindfulness 212–13; mindset 213–15; motivation 214–15
personal preferences 143–4
personal reflection on patience 188–90
personality preferences 49–51, 149; example 51
perspective 61
perspectives on managing diversity 202–7; integration perspective 205–7; learning perspective 204–5; matching perspective 203–4; unity perspective 203
personal identity 164–5
PFC *see* prefrontal cortex
phobias 40
Pink, D. 216
Plato 155
positive feedback 258
positive traits *113*
post-materialism 160
post-modern mind 237
power 112, *113*, 114, 166–7
power of emotional intelligence 66–79; choice of EI models 67–8; common strengths/development needs 71–4; definition 67; four EI competencies 68–71; gender difference 74–6; nineteen EI capabilities 68–71; overview 66; questions/actions for CPD 77
"power and love" 195
pragmatism 54
preferred leadership style 80
preferred learning style **54**

prefrontal cortex 41–3, *157*
prestige 166–7
Primal Leadership 7
Prime Meridian 178
principled conscience 182–3
principles of blended learning 244–58
principles of connectedness **264**
principles of leadership learning design 248
Principles of Responsible Management Education initiative 261
principles towards individual gain **263**
PRME *see Principles of Responsible Management Education* initiative
productivity 87–8
proficiency in Coaching style 98–102; explaining process 98; six-step process 98–102
programme inspiration 244
Project Guts 235
provision of information 44–5
psychoanalytic personal theory 164–5
purpose 192, 216; personal reflection on 192
Pythagoras 61

Quantum Leader 235

racial diversity 201–2
Radical, Ethically Authentic Leaders 135–6, 141–2, 183
rational decision-making process 41–2, 174, 178–9
Rational, Ego-based, As-usual Leaders 8, 16–18
rational functions 50; feeling 50; thinking 50
rational intelligence 148–9; impact of emotional intelligence on *18*
REAL-1 *see* Rational, Ego-based, As-usual Leaders
REAL-2 *see* Robust, Emotionally Aware Leaders
REAL-3 *see* Radical, Ethically Authentic Leaders
recognition 166–7
reflection 53–4, 216–17, *217*
Reflection Note 52, 129–30; key learning points 130; SMART goals 130; thinking, feeling, behaving 130; what happened 130
Reflective Practice 126, 129, 216
relationship management 19, 68, 149–50

remote delivery masterclasses 252–4, *255*; benefits of 255
resilience 52, 193–4, 227
responsibility 107
responsiveness 61
rewards 107, 166
Ridgeway Partnership 29–30; mission 29; vision 29–30
"right choice" 224
Ripples Theory 245–6, *246*
Robust, Emotionally Aware Leaders 15–16, 20, 125–7, *126*, 135–6, 183, 211–12
role modelling 218–19
Rosado, C. 201
Rossiter, Altazar 60
rote learning 243–4
routes of decision-making *176*
rule compliance 182–3

Sadler-Smith, E. 179
Sale, James 214–15
Salovey, P. 67
Scharmer, Otto 216
Schon, Donald 129
Schopenhauer, Arthur 156
science behind Jung's theory 49
SDGs *see* sustainable development goals
self vs. organisation 167–70
self-absorption 163
self-assessment of values *197*
self-authoring mind 237
self-awareness 18–19, 47–57, 86, 149–50; definition 48; how we learn 51–5; in leadership 48; other areas of 56; our five senses 55–6; overview 47; personality preferences 48–51; questions/actions for CPD 57
self-confidence 68, 75, 165–6
self-consciousness 155
self-control 41
self-determination 143, 150, 186–99, **191**; purpose 192; values of 192–4; *see also* values of leadership
self-directed learning 3–4
self-image 165–6, *165*, 166
self-management 19, 68, 149–50
Senge, Peter 3
sensation 49
serendipity 239
serial connections 40
serotonin 159
service orientation 71–2, 75

serving learners 252
"seventh emotion" 59–60
SI *see* spiritual intelligence
silence 102
Silicon Valley 188
Singer, W. 146, 155
situation sensing 220–21
six leadership styles 80–6, **81**; Affiliative 83; Coaching style 82; Commanding style 86; Democratic style 84; Pace-Setting style 85; Visionary style 81; *see also* leadership styles
six-step process to proficiency 98–102; asking right questions 101–2; effective listening 101; one-to-one communication 100; opinion avoidance 102; simple process 98–100; use of silence 102
16PF 51
sixth sense 56
slow thinking 179
SMART action plan 100, 128–31, *131*
SNOs *see* synchronous neural oscillations
social awareness 19, 149–50
social conscience 182–3
social intelligence 67
socialised mind 237
sociopathy 167, 183
Socrates 228
Sophocles 254
sound logic 174–5
spectrum of 1:1 styles *103*
Spiritual Capital 235
spiritual intelligence 8–10, 138–41, 146, 153, 160–3
Spiritual Intelligence 10
spiritual intelligence 8–10, 38–40, 138–9, *138*, 146, 152–62
stages of human development 235–9
stakeholder set 170–2
standards 107
starting meditation 213
Steare, Roger 182
step-by-step journey to Transpersonal Leadership 16–20; As-usual leader 17–18; Ego-based leader 17; Rational leader 16–17
"sticky" learning 250
Stinger, Richard 106–7
Stone Age brain 33, 37–8, 43, 76, 176, *249*
strengths vs. development areas 71–4, *72*, 125–31; identifying development

needs 127–9; implementing action plan 129–30; learning review 127; most common 71–4; overview 125–7
structure 112, *113*, 114, 117
styles of leadership in action 84–9
superego 164–5
support 112, *113*, 114, 117
sustainability 227; *see also* transpersonal qualities
sustainable development goals 261–2, **262**, 264, 267
synchronous neural oscillations 40–1, 155–6
systems approach to diversity *206*

Tai Chi 212
"talk and chalk" approach 37, 244
Tata Group 172
thalamus 41–3, 58, *157*, 158
theorism 53–4
theory of psychological types 49, 51
Theory U 216
thinking 50
Thinking, Fast and Slow 179
Thomas, David 20, 202
tick-box compliancy 201
togetherness 260–1
"ToGrow" model 98–100, *99*, 104
Tolstoy, Leo 1
Tomorrow's Company 177–8
tools for transpersonal leadership 152–3
touchstones 166, 195, 223–4, *225*, 227; transpersonal *228*
Transactional Leadership 110–11, *110*
Transformational Leadership 109–10, *110*
transparency 71–2, 75
transpersonal cycle *232*
Transpersonal Leadership development journey to excellence *9*, 15–21, *16*, *136*, *138*
transpersonal practices 233–9, **236**
transpersonal psychology 1
transpersonal qualities 224–6; authentic 226; caring 224–5; emotional intelligence 226; ethical 226; performance-enhancing 226; radical 225; sustainable 226
transpersonal resilience 193–4, *194*
transpersonal touchstone *229*
Trump, Donald 109, 260

trust 24, 33, 63, 67, 85–6, 109, 137, 174–8
trustworthiness 188

Ubuntuism 264
ultimate leadership competence 191–4; developing core values 195; purpose 192; values 192–4
UN *see* United Nations
unconscious bias 174
understanding emotions 58–65; how to manage emotions 62–4; overview 58; questions/actions for CPD 64; what are emotions? 58–61; why emotions still exist 61–2
understanding leadership 22–35; definitions 22–3; inspirational leadership 33–4; leadership vs. management 23–7; levels of capability 27–30; overview 22; questions/actions for CPD 34; vision to performance 30–1; what is "good" leadership? 31–3
understanding the TL journey 137–8
understanding your mindset 214
United Nations 201–2, 261–2, **262**, 264, 267; SDGs 261–2, **262**, 264, 267
unity perspective on diversity 203; advantages of 203; disadvantages of 203
unlearning 206
unleashing talent 201
use of silence 102
using decision-making processes effectively 183
using different leadership styles 80–91
using reflection 217

valence 61
values of leadership 186–99; details of personal conscience 187–91; developing core values 195; ethical behaviour 195–6; overview 186; questions/actions for CPD 196; self-assessment *197*; self-determination 191–4
values of neuroscience in leadership 37
values self-assessment *196*
values of self-determination 192–4; aspiration 193; continuous personal development 194; courage 193; drive 193; motivation 192–3; resilience 193–4
Van Gogh, Vincent 58

virtues 186–90; conscientiousness 189; forgiveness 190; humility 188–9; patience 189; *see also* values of leadership
vision to performance 30–1, *31*
Visionary style of leadership 81, 87, 109–10, 117
VUCA world 17

Weatherhead School of Management 244–5
Welch, Jack 125
Weldon, William 117
what "ego" is 164–5
what "good" leadership is 31–3
WhatsApp 255
when to use Coaching style 96–8
where you are on the journey 233–9; complex adaptive system 234–5; endeavour for awareness 233–4; hierarchy of intelligences 239; stages of human development 235–9

Whitmore, John 94–5, 98–9
why emotions still exist 61–2
Wigglesworth, Cindy 8–9, 139
Williams, Tennessee 153
win/win thinking 97, 219–20
Women, Naturally Better Leaders White Paper 74–5
Woodrow Wilson, Thomas 191
work-based learning 3–4, 254–8
working for all stakeholders 163–73
workings of brain 39–44; brain cells/connections 39–40; brain efficiency 44; emotional highway 41–3; simple leadership example 43; Stone Age example 43
World's Women 201–2

Young, Greg 22–3, 33

Z Generation 3
Zebrowitz, L. 59
Zohar, Danah 10, 144, 160, 235

LeaderShape Global
Shaping Transpersonal Leaders

LeaderShape Global is a UK headquartered organisation with a global culture that operates without borders. It exists to develop people around the world who can lead beyond their ego to be radical, ethical and authentic, i.e. Transpersonal Leaders. It provides work-based learning through a faculty of senior executives who are accredited coaches and experienced facilitators, blended with online content and web-based tools.

> Join the Transpersonal Leadership – Leading beyond the Ego LinkedIn Group at www.linkedin.com/groups/8257117
>
> Download the FREE **LeaderShaper** © App and improve your ability to lead! Visit leadershapeglobal.com/leadershaper for more information.

If you would like to discover how LeaderShape Global can work with you or partner with you anywhere in the world, or you would like direct contact with any of the authors or editors of *Leading Beyond the Ego*, please email us at info@leadershapeglobal.com and your enquiry will be forwarded to the appropriate person.

Develop as a leader with the *Transpersonal Leadership White Paper* series

Featuring cutting edge leadership topics and written by members of the LeaderShape team, these free White Papers have been download tens of thousands of times worldwide. To find out more and download your free copies, visit: www.bit.ly/2tkz5Wy

Routledge
Taylor & Francis Group